EPIC AND EMPIRE IN NINETEENTH-CENTURY BRITAIN

In the nineteenth century, epic poetry in the Homeric style was widely seen as an ancient and anachronistic genre, yet Victorian authors worked to re-create it for the modern world. Simon Dentith explores the relationship between epic and the evolution of Britain's national identity in the nineteenth century up to the apparent demise of all notions of heroic warfare in the catastrophe of the First World War. Paradoxically, writers found equivalents of the societies which produced Homeric or Northern epics not in Europe, but on the margins of empire and among its subject peoples. Dentith considers the implication of the status of epic for a range of nineteenth-century writers, including Walter Scott, Matthew Arnold, Elizabeth Barrett Browning, William Morris and Rudyard Kipling. He also considers the relationship between epic poetry and the novel and discusses late nineteenth-century adventure novels, concluding with a brief survey of epic in the twentieth century.

SIMON DENTITH is a Professor of English at the University of Gloucestershire.

CAMBRIDGE STUDIES IN NINETEENTH-CENTURY LITERATURE AND CULTURE

General Editor
Gillian Beer, *University of Cambridge*

Editorial Board
Isobel Armstrong, *Birkbeck College, London*
Kate Flint, *Rutgers University*
Catherine Gallagher, *University of California, Berkeley*
D. A. Miller, *Columbia University*
J. Hillis Miller, *University of California, Irvine*
Daniel Pick, *Queen Mary, University of London*
Mark Poovey, *New York University*
Sally Shuttleworth, *University of Sheffield*
Herbert Tucker, *University of Virginia*

Nineteenth-century British literature and culture have been rich fields for inter-disciplinary studies. Since the turn of the twentieth century, scholars and critics have tracked the intersections and tensions between Victorian literature and the visual arts, politics, social organization, economic life, technical innovations, scientific thought – in short, culture in its broadest sense. In recent years, theoretical challenges and historiographical shifts have unsettled the assumptions of previous scholarly synthesis and called into question the terms of older debates. Whereas the tendency in much past literary critical interpretation was to use the metaphor of culture as 'background', feminist, Foucauldian, and other analyses have employed more dynamic models that raise questions of power and of circulation. Such developments have reanimated the field.

This series aims to accommodate and promote the most interesting work being undertaken on the frontiers of the field of nineteenth-century literary studies: work which intersects fruitfully with other fields of study such as history, or literary theory, or the history of science. Comparative as well as interdisciplinary approaches are welcomed.

A complete list of titles published will be found at the end of the book.

EPIC AND EMPIRE IN NINETEENTH-CENTURY BRITAIN

SIMON DENTITH

University of Gloucestershire

UNIVERSITY PRESS

CAMBRIDGE UNIVERSITY PRESS
Cambridge, New York, Melbourne, Madrid, Cape Town, Singapore, São Paulo

Cambridge University Press
The Edinburgh Building, Cambridge CB2 2RU, UK

Published in the United States of America by Cambridge University Press, New York

www.cambridge.org
Information on this title: www.cambridge.org/9780521862653

First published 2006

Printed in the United Kingdom at the University Press, Cambridge

A catalogue record for this publication is available from the British Library

Library of Congress Cataloguing in Publication data
Dentith, Simon.
Epic and empire in nineteenth-century Britain / Simon Dentith.
p. cm. – (Cambridge studies in nineteenth-century literature and culture; 52)
Includes bibliographical references and index.
ISBN-13: 978-0-521-86265-3
ISBN-10: 0-521-86265-5
1. English literature – 19th century – History and criticism.
2. Epic literature – History and criticism. 3. Literature and history – Great Britain – History.
4. National characteristics, British, in literature. I. Title. II Series.

PR451.D46 2006
821'.103208–dc22

2005037571

ISBN-13 978-0-521-86265-3 hardback
ISBN-10 0-521-86265-5 hardback

Contents

v

Acknowledgements

I wish to thank my colleagues at the University of Gloucestershire, who enabled me to complete this book. Above all I thank my friend and colleague Peter Widdowson, who has been endlessly encouraging and supportive and who heroically undertook to read the whole typescript; the book has immeasurably profited from his incomparable editorial eye, in addition to all his other help. Bill Myers read very substantial portions of the book at crucial stages in its writing; I am deeply grateful to him for his helpful advice and encouragement. Roger Ebbatson also generously undertook to read and advise on chapters of the book, and I thank him for his kindness and encouragement.

I am also grateful to the many colleagues in different universities who have heard and commented on sections of this book in earlier manifestations: Geoff Ward and Marion Wynne-Davis at the University of Dundee, Gavin Budge at the University of Central England, Pam Morris, Glenda Norquay, Elspeth Graham and Tim Ashplant at Liverpool John Moores University, Ian Baker and Robert Miles at Sheffield Hallam University, Richard Pearson at University College Worcester, Marion Thain at the Midlands Victorian Seminar, and Stan Smith, John Lucas and Sharon Ouditt at Nottingham Trent University. My thanks to all of them. For the love and support of my family during the writing of this book thanks are inadequate, but thanks are all I have.

'Epic' by Patrick Kavaragh is reprinted from *Collected Poems*, edited by Antoinette Quinn (Allen Lane, 2004), by kind permission of the Trustees of the Estate of the late Katherine B. Kavanagh, through the Jonathan Williams Literary Agency.

Introduction

> Is Achilles possible with powder and lead? Or the *Iliad* with the printing press, not to mention the printing machine? Do not the song and the saga and the muse necessarily come to an end with the printer's bar, hence do not the necessary conditions for epic poetry vanish?[1]

Marx's question, posed for himself in his notebooks in 1857, trenchantly formulates a characteristic nineteenth-century idea, though this brief quotation gives it an especially technological emphasis. What are the historical conditions which underlie the production of epic poetry, and do the wholly different social circumstances of modernity prevent the writing of further poetry in the same heroic mode? Marx was not alone in assuming the radical historical otherness of the social world from which epic emerged; he was the heir, indeed, of a considerable intellectual tradition, with its roots in the Enlightenment, for which the essential antiquity of primary epics such as Homer's was a central contention.[2] In this tradition, epic becomes the foremost evidence of the historical alterity of the barbaric world; by the same token, it becomes a principal indicator of our own modernity. The implications of this fundamental insight are pursued in what follows.

This book addresses, then, one particular understanding of epic in the nineteenth century, briefly summed up under the phrase 'epic primitivism'. It pursues the consequences of this idea for the meaning of a national poetry in Britain, for the translation of epic, for the possibility of writing a national epic and for the conception of empire and its subject peoples. A principal argument will be that ideas of modernity current in the nineteenth century, though established in the eighteenth, are predicated upon an engagement with the sense of historical distance carried by primary epics, especially those of Homer. This primitivist understanding of epic entailed consequences not only for poetry but also for the

I

novel, and indeed more widely for ethnology and the relations between the imperial centre and its colonised margins. The book will therefore discuss a series of attempts to write epic poetry; styles of translation; the difficult question of the relation of epic to the novel; and the close cousin of epic, at least as understood in the light of epic primitivism, the national ballad tradition.

This is certainly not the only study that might be written of epic in the nineteenth century, which is a larger topic than might at first appear to readers who are scratching their heads as they struggle to think beyond Tennyson's *Idylls of the King*, whose epic credentials are anyway doubtful, or perhaps, in quite a different register, Barrett Browning's *Aurora Leigh*. A very different book needs to be written about Milton's epic inheritance for Romantic poetry and subsequently; readers will find no discussion here of Wordsworth or Blake. Equally, there is no attempt here to provide a survey of all epics written in the nineteenth century, many of which persisted in a broadly neoclassical idiom. Innumerable epics or shorter poems written in the high heroic style were composed after 1800, often on topics connected with Britain's military or naval history; these will only appear in what follows when they relate to its central themes.[3] Many such poems were once popular, but their appeal was effectively killed by the social and military history of the twentieth century; they survived only in dusty anthologies in school stock-cupboards into the 1950s and 1960s. It is sufficient now to recall that 'war poetry' means for most people the 'anti-war' poetry of the First World War. That whole, earlier, tradition of poetry, now effectively lost, needs neither revival nor further debunking; I attempt neither, though the connection of epic to empire entails at least some discussion of the anthology of heroic national poetry established in the nineteenth century.

What the book *does* attempt is both a history and a map; indeed, this is an area in which history and geography are inseparable: as we shall see, a map of the world according to epic is at once a history of certain of its peoples. It also attempts a conceptual map; I try to trace out a problematic, an interrelated set of ideas bequeathed to the nineteenth century by the eighteenth, whose consequences are worked out with varying differing emphases by the writers discussed hereafter. These include Walter Scott, whose importance in transforming ideas about epic and ballad can scarcely be overestimated; Matthew Arnold and Thomas Carlyle, for both of whom the question of epic was central to their thinking about national history; the historian George Grote; the lesser-known writers William Maginn and F. W. Newman, translators of Homer; Tennyson and William

Morris, whose *Sigurd the Volsung* is the most sustained attempt at *quasi* primary epic in the nineteenth century; George Eliot and Elizabeth Barrett Browning, who both sought, in different ways, to transform the generic inheritance of epic to contemporary and female ends; Rudyard Kipling, who wrote a demotic and popular version of the epic of empire; and those writers of imperial adventure stories at the end of the century, Rider Haggard, Robert Louis Stevenson and Joseph Conrad, for whom epic was the appropriate way of understanding the historical experience of the subject peoples of the empire.

The theme which links these apparently diverse writers together is a consciousness of the antiquity of epic as a genre. To use a phrase of F. W. Newman's, Homer is 'essentially archaic' – Newman coined the phrase in 1856, contemporaneously with Marx's notebook entry on the *Iliad*. It is not merely that Homer is an old writer in relation to the moment in history which we have now reached, but that he belongs to a phase of human history which we have now definitively surpassed. The same could be said of all the writers of primary epics that were either known about or rediscovered in the eighteenth or nineteenth centuries. This consciousness of the archaism of epic entails a concomitant consciousness of the modernity of the present era of human affairs; indeed, I assert that an engagement with epic is at the heart of those theories of human progress which take hold in the eighteenth century and continue, in however modified a way, into the nineteenth. Why stop there? However discredited the notion of 'progress' may be, politically as the central notion of 'progressive' politics, or philosophically as the supreme example of a grand narrative which we must now forgo, some such notion must remain in our accounts of human history: the passage from hunter-gathering to globalised late capitalism may not represent any moral progress, but it is certainly a narrative of a succession of extraordinary social transformations, and the dynamics of this progression require explanation. I emphasise this simply to underscore the fact that these apparently faded debates about epic and modernity, which introduce the book and which underlie the writing I discuss, should not be approached as dead letters; there is no readily available contemporary perspective in the light of which these old conundrums can be straightforwardly resolved. Homer remains 'essentially archaic'; we too are the heirs of those Enlightenment philosophers, historians and critics who established that; and the nature of our engagement with his epic writings, and those of others, remains a matter of emotionally and intellectually complex negotiation. I do not write in the spirit of someone who, by virtue of his lucky posteriority, has solved the problems that the book lays out.

The study follows a broadly chronological path through the nineteenth century; it starts with a brief account of eighteenth-century theories of epic primitivism and their relationship to notions of modernity, and then follows through the implications or entailments of those notions at various points in the intellectual and artistic history of the succeeding hundred years. However, there is no sense here that this is a continuously developing or unfolding narrative; on the contrary, what is traced are various reworkings of a problematic, in different contexts and in relation to differing problems, so that an interconnected set of ideas and aesthetic challenges are worked through to sometimes congruent and sometimes opposed or contradictory conclusions. The first half of the book is broadly concerned with poetry: not just with epic poetry, but also with the closely connected history of the ballad. In the second half I pursue the same questions into the history of the novel; I take this to be the characteristic modern form for the nineteenth century, which seeks to assimilate in various ways all the forms and modes of writing which precede it. My discussion of the novel necessarily involves an account of those twentieth-century critics for whom the relationship of epic to novel is crucial: Georg Lukács, Mikhail Bakhtin and Franco Moretti. The assimilative capacity of the novel – its power to absorb and subordinate experience understood in epic terms – provides the central question which I address to the novels discussed. Given the nature of epic primitivism, this means that the discussion of the novels will be framed by the question of the representation of barbarous or heroic peoples, or more precisely the appropriate mode or genre in which this representation might be conducted. We begin, however, with the relationship of epic and modernity as it was conceived by the Enlightenment thinkers of the eighteenth century.

EPIC AND MODERNITY

How ought historicist criticism to be conceived? That is to say, what do we take to be the characteristic procedures of an approach to literature which seeks to understand it in its historical context – 'context' here understood to mean not the mere simultaneity of historical events, but the manners, *geist* or social system which that literature is both produced by and illuminates? When did such procedures come to be adopted? The answer to this last question is undoubtedly that the first extensive effort at historicist criticism occurred in relation to the poetry of Homer in the eighteenth century. But the answer to the previous question about the characteristic procedures of historicist criticism is not so straightforward. It seems right to assume that historicising criticism should start with the history and then proceed to the literature: to the extent that 'history' is the larger category, it must necessarily precede, both logically and in actuality, any literary product that is thought to emanate from it. But that is not the case with eighteenth-century historical understanding of Homer. On the contrary, the literature precedes the history, which is in effect deduced from the literary text and then adduced to explain it. This extraordinary interpretative circle must be the starting-point of any account of epic and modernity.[4]

This productive circularity can be traced back to Vico at the beginning of the eighteenth century, though it was the writers of the Scottish Enlightenment who produced the most accessible and comprehensive accounts of the progress of human society through various stages, in which the reading of epic poetry provides some of the most persuasive evidence. In fact, the history of Homeric criticism in the eighteenth century has been carefully documented; this is how Kirsti Simonsuuri summarises Vico's account of Homer in the *New Science*:

This Homer was not an individual poet of genius, but could be found anywhere if circumstances sufficiently similar to the Greek heroic age occurred. A people that had created the heroic epic had by this fact also created its thought, its social institutions, its leaders and its entire history. Homer's poems were the myths of their people and their ways of understanding and reacting to the world and the age they lived in; and in a rigorous sense they were fully intelligible only to those who had created and used them. The true Homer was a conglomerate of the myths of the Greek people, an expression in language of their dreams and actions: 'Homer was an idea or a heroic character of Grecian men insofar as they told their history in song'. And Vico's more crucial discovery, implicit in this idea of Homer, was that languages and linguistic forms are the key to the minds of those who use words, and constitute the most profound evidence available of the mental, social and cultural life of human societies.[5]

Vico's *New Science* is not primarily an account of Homer; it seeks to trace the history of human societies through their various stages. But Homer is central to this argument, precisely because, as Simonsuuri indicates, he can be read to reveal the self-understanding of heroic society. Vico's claim to scientificity, however, rests not on the historical taxonomy that is implicit in the book, but on the philological method that sustains this taxonomy. Our knowledge of the heroic world that Homer gives us access to is dependent upon philological method. We can know the history thanks to appropriate attention to the text; in the light of the history we can reinterpret the text.

The knowledge that is deduced in this way creates the sense of historical specificity, both of the heroic world and of contemporary civil society. Take the case, for instance, of the characters of the Homeric heroes Agamemnon and Achilles, about whom Vico writes thus: 'This is Homer, the incomparable creator of poetic archetypes, whose greatest characters are completely unsuited to our present civilized and social nature, but are perfectly suited to the heroic nature of punctilious nobles!' (p. 357). This indeed is perhaps the central tenet in this mode of reading Homer; it is precisely the ferocity of the Homeric heroes which leads reader after reader in the eighteenth century to repudiate them as poetic models in the neoclassical manner, and to read them instead as symptoms of a previous regime of manners or stage of society. It is in this sense that epic and modernity are interdependent notions from Vico onwards: the sense of contemporary civility is produced out of a repudiation of the heroism celebrated in epic, especially the *Iliad*.

This repudiation is not a straightforward matter, however; Vico again anticipates a characteristic subsequent attitude in the ambivalence with which he regards the ferocious heroism of the characters of primary epic: 'The gruesome atrocity of Homeric battles and deaths is the source of the astonishing power of the *Iliad*' (*New Science*, p. 371). This is not a theme which Vico develops, but it will be developed at length later in the eighteenth century. From the perspective of our modernity we can repudiate the 'gruesome atrocity' of barbarous society, but respond also to its sublimity or its power: we have lost as much as we have gained, or rather, the price of our progress to civility is the loss of power and a world made more pallid. Reading epic is henceforth going to be a complicated matter; the reader will at once respond to its power, and at the same time recognise the pastness of the world which produced such men, such manners and such excitement. The progress to modernity is not unequivocally a positive one.

Vico's *New Science* provides, then – sometimes in unexpected or undeveloped ways – some of the principal terms of the problematic that I am seeking to set forth. It traces the progression of human society through various stages, and in doing so adduces epic poetry as central evidence of the heroic or barbarous stage which precedes contemporary civility. Our knowledge of that heroic stage is produced out of an engagement with epic, especially Homer; our sense of our own modernity is conceived in the same act of engagement. This experience is ambivalent and does not typically produce a simple repudiation of the heroic past. And finally, this whole historicising mode of reading can be viewed as an interpretative circle in which knowledge of history and text derive from and reinforce each other.

The *New Science* was published in 1744; twenty-five years later Adam Ferguson published *An Essay on the History of Civil Society*, in which the same tropes are rehearsed in a more systematic way. Ferguson carefully distinguishes between the early stages of society: the 'savage' precedes the 'barbarian', with the latter characterised by the presence of property but the absence of the long-settled differences of a monarchy. All these stages are radically different from contemporary civil society. Like Vico, Ferguson was not writing a book about Homer, but, in effect, a conspectus of early human history; it is nevertheless striking how central Homer also is to his arguments about the barbarous stage of mankind. Indeed, many of his accounts of this stage of civilisation are in effect deductions from the text of Homer. On this matter he is explicit:

It were absurd to quote the fable of the Iliad or the Odyssey, the legends of Hercules, Theseus or Oedipus, as authorities in matters of fact relating to the history of mankind; but they may, with great justice, be cited to ascertain what were the conceptions and sentiments of the age in which they were composed, or to characterise the genius of that people, with whose imagination they were blended, and by whom they were fondly rehearsed and admired.[6]

Homer will be the principal witness of this kind, the behaviour of his heroes being adduced as evidence of the mentality of the stage of civil society from which they came.

This is especially evident when it comes to the matter of warfare; Ferguson uses Homer to point out the differing conceptions of honour, chivalry, respect for one's enemies, and so on, which are evident in Homer's battle scenes. Thus in the following passage the method of historicist deduction is clearly visible:

If the moral or popular traditions, and the taste of fabulous legends, which are the production or entertainment of particular ages, are likewise sure indications of their notions and characters, we may presume, that the foundation of what is now held to be the law of war, and of nations, was laid in the manners of Europe, together with the sentiments which are expressed in the tales of chivalry, and of gallantry. Our system of war differs not more from that of the Greeks, than the favourite characters of our early romance differed from those of the Iliad, and of every ancient poem. The hero of the Greek fable, endued with superior force, courage and address, takes every advantage of an enemy, to kill with safety to himself; and actuated by a desire of spoil, or by a principle of revenge, is never stayed in his progress by interruptions of remorse or compassion. Homer, who, of all poets, knew best how to exhibit the emotions of a vehement affection, seldom attempts to excite commiseration. Hector falls unpitied, and his body is insulted by every Greek. (p. 200)

Our sense of distance from the manners of Homer's time, then, is traceable to the very different notions of chivalry and courtesy which have supervened between then and now, and which can in turn be traced in the romances of more modern epochs.

Ferguson provides, in short, a powerful Enlightenment account of the stages through which mankind has passed in the transition from a savage past to contemporary civility. Like Vico again, his account is by no means unambivalent; he finds much to admire in the mentality of barbarous peoples, and in his case his own Highland background lent some of these passages a particular poignancy – though, as we shall see, the association of epic with Highland society or its global equivalents will become much more than a personal matter. We can take Ferguson as providing, in an exemplary way, the general terms in which the transition from barbarity to civility was to be thought in the late eighteenth and nineteenth centuries. Central to his account was a reading of Homer: a sense of modernity is in part produced out of a sense of the anachronistic pleasures to be derived from a reading of the *Iliad*.

Ferguson was doubtless the most 'philosophical' of the 'philosophical historians' of the Scottish Enlightenment; in his work the imbrication of notions of modernity with a historicist reading of epic is especially clear. In part cognate with these overarching progressive accounts of human history, and in part independent of them, the eighteenth century also saw the development of a bardic theory with relation to Homer which both reinforces and complicates the general story told by the philosophical historians. Historicism, insofar as it understands culture as expressing in some sense the manners of the social world from which culture emerges, appears to downplay the element of individual genius which produces any cultural object; bardic theory, by contrast, emphasises the central importance of the exalted artist. These potentially contradictory theories, though they were certainly successfully combined, nevertheless provided differing emphases for the understanding of epic origins both in the eighteenth century and later.

Thomas Blackwell's *An Enquiry into the Life and Writings of Homer* (1735) provides one important source for the bardic theory of epic origins – and we can take it as the exemplary scholarly instance in the eighteenth century, though of course there was a massive poetic interest also in the figure of the bard.[7] For Blackwell, Homer was simply a bard, at once a 'stroling [sic] indigent Bard' and a member of a profession of great '*Dignity*'.[8] Bardic theory had at its heart an imaginary scene of recitation. This is how Blackwell describes the 'daily life of the AOIΔOI' (which Blackwell translates as 'Bards'):

The Manner was, when a Bard came to a House, he was first welcomed by the Master, and after he had been entertained according to the ancient Mode, that is, after he had bathed, eaten, and drank some MEΛINΔEA OINON, *heart-chearing wine*, he was called upon to entertain the Family in his turn: He then tuned his *Lyre*, and raised his *Voice*, and sung to the listening Crowd some Adventures of the *Gods*, or some Performance of *Man*. (p. 116)

This is a scene which will be constantly reimagined for the next 150 years. The extent of the dignity attached to such figures will be a matter of intense debate throughout that period; the aptness or otherwise of the implicit comparison between Homer and the myriad bard-like figures to be found in the present or in recent history will also be a matter of controversy. But the origins of epic in the recitation of some ancient bard becomes a central element in notions of the genre as 'essentially archaic', both in popular and scholarly conceptions.

The most important popular conduit for bardic ideas into the nine-teenth century, as we shall see in the following chapters, will be Walter Scott, whose *Lay of the Last Minstrel* (1805) is effectively a dramatisation of the scene of recitation imagined by Blackwell. On a more scholarly level, the Homeric controversy, which was conducted from the late eighteenth century through to the late nineteenth century (and arguably has never been resolved), took some of the elements of bardic theory and sought to argue them through in technical philological terms. That is to say, some scholars began to dissolve the *Iliad* and the *Odyssey* into pre-existing 'lays' – of presumed bardic (and hence non-literate) origin – and to use the methods of philological criticism to determine the activity of some subsequent literate editor in transforming them into connected and coherent narrative wholes. The most famous scholar in this vein was the German F. A. Wolf, whose 1795 *Prolegomena to Homer* became the most notorious item in the controversy. I discuss the Homeric (or sometimes 'Wolfian') controversy briefly in the next chapter; the point here is that some proponents of Bardic theory (such as Walter Scott) could be strongly antipathetic to Wolfian views because they appeared to downgrade the 'original genius' of Homer himself. The instability introduced into historicist accounts of epic, and the now related forms of romance, lay, and ballad, remains the same in both popular and scholarly accounts: the original genius of the bard threatens to outweigh or unbalance the original historicising impulse which consigns traditional forms to their originating social moment.

'Epic primitivism' was thus a powerful if potentially unstable con-catenation of ideas that came to be established in the late eighteenth century. I shall refer to this nexus of notions – combined in differing ways – as a 'problematic'; that is, a connected set of ideas which can be pushed to differing conclusions, but which provides the same episte-mological horizon for disparate-seeming arguments. It took as its model the poetry of Homer rather than his neoclassical imitators, and it sought the origins of epic verse in the barbaric or 'heroic' stage of society. The very sense of modernity or contemporary civility was constructed out of the contrast with the manners to be deduced from the Homeric poems. The appropriate comparison for early epic poetry was therefore not the finished poetic products of the modern world but traditional and popular poetry, traces of which were still to be found, especially in rude or undeveloped regions. The originators of this early poetry, or bards, had their historic equivalents in many societies, though their status was a matter of controversy. But the scene of bardic recitation linked together both theories of epic origins and ballad performance.

THE ENTAILMENTS OF EPIC PRIMITIVISM

The problematic of epic primitivism entailed for the nineteenth century a series of consequences not just for the understanding of epic poetry, but for its translation and composition also; these consequences extended equally to the writing of other forms of poetry, notably the ballad. Subsequent chapters of this book will explore these entailments as they work themselves through a range of nineteenth-century writing.

Epic primitivism suggested, in the first place, an equivalence between the surviving traditional balladry of the contemporary world and the ballad or popular sources of the epic in both the ancient world and other barbarous or heroic societies. This suggestion was most strongly followed through in both the poetry and the critical writings of Scott and his successors; in Britain it had particularly important consequences for the translation of Homer, for which it began to seem that some version of ballad metre might be more appropriate than the various kinds of neoclassical or educated metres available after Pope or Cowper. Elsewhere in Europe, this equivalence was to have explosive consequences in the context of the various national revivals that convulsed the Continent in the course of the nineteenth century; country after country discovered an authentic national epic in the previously overlooked or slighted ballad traditions in which their newly coined 'national stories' were told.

So, secondly, such traditional balladry became in effect the 'national song' of the peoples to whom it was attributed. This is a relatively clear process in the very differing national contexts of France, Germany, Spain, Finland or even the United States: the *Chanson de Roland*, the *Nibelungenlied*, the ballad of the *Cid*, the *Kalevala* and, in imitation, Longfellow's *Hiawatha*, were all advanced as expressions of the national spirit of varying degrees of relevance to the contemporary world. But in the British context the search for a traditional national epic was complicated by the complexity of the national question in these islands, as we shall see in a subsequent chapter on Tennyson and Morris. At all events, one tradition of criticism in the nineteenth century advanced the 'national ballad metre' as the authentic British prosody.

The belief in the essential antiquity of epic and its related traditional forms meant, furthermore, that the exercise of writing an epic in the modern world was always going to be a matter of pastiche. Since this is an important notion for what follows, it is worth briefly dwelling on 'pastiche'; it is here understood to mean the effort to imitate a manner or a style without hostile intent. It is thus to be distinguished from parody, which in most usages is presumed to have a mocking or polemical relationship to whatever is being imitated.[9] Pastiche became inevitable because the antiquity of epic, and other forms now understood as premodern, meant that the poet who wrote in these forms, or the translator of them, sought to reproduce in the modern reader the kind of effect that reading an essentially archaic poem would have: an experience which itself entailed some sense of the presumed original experience of the first listener. This is a problem that beset the writing of many kinds of poetry from the late eighteenth century onwards, and it affected the translation and composition of epic, ballads and romances, all of which became classified as antique forms. The problem provoked a range of responses, from forgery through imitation to the invention of antiquated-sounding prosodic forms. This fundamental sense of the archaism of epic, and with it other traditional forms of popular poetry, was the ultimate ground for the range of forged or imitated poetic productions which were associated with the rediscovery of epic and ballad from the outset in the 1760s; the same problematic continued to entail pastiche upon the poets of the nineteenth century. Consider the following list: Macpherson's *Ossian* poems in the 1760s; Percy's *Reliques of Ancient English Poetry* (1765) with its range of imitated ballads; Chatterton's 'Rowley' poems, also written in the 1760s; Cowper's toying with the idea of translating Homer into Chaucerian English; Scott's *Minstrelsy of the Scottish Border* (1802–3), with its creative editorial practice and its forged and imitated ballads. Forgery; imitation; pastiche: all were endemic to the problematic of epic primitivism, and all entail a complex negotiation between text and reader, in which there is a simultaneous recognition of the supposed antiquity of the verse form coupled with a knowledge of its actual contemporaneity (in the case of forgery, this knowledge is restricted to the author). The many nineteenth-century poems to be discussed in this volume had different ways of staging this negotiation, with more or less reference to the moment of actual composition, and more or less complete attempts at direct imitations of antiquated diction and prosodic forms. Epic primitivism resulted in epic pastiche.

But a further result springs from the ambivalent attitude to the heroic past that is built into the whole problematic – the sense that contemporary civility marks a real progression from the barbarous past, but also that there is a real loss of glamour, heroism or straightforward poetic interest in the decorous rationality of the present. A straightforward repudiation of the barbaric stage of society which produced epic poetry might result in a wholly rational poetry, but not a very exciting one; what epic primitivism tends to suggest, on the contrary, is the problem of the unsuitability of the modern world to poetry more generally. This will be a matter of dispute throughout the nineteenth century, but the difficulty of writing a modern epic when the form is strongly marked by its barbaric origins is one which will beset many poets; in this study I discuss *Aurora Leigh*, in which Barrett Browning vehemently repudiates the idea that the modern world cannot sustain heroic treatment. The structure of feeling, given its most powerful embodiment by Scott, by which the grandeur and affective power of epic and its close cousin romance are relegated to the past while modernity gets the prosperity without the affective glamour – this structure of feeling will create particular problems throughout the century for those who wish to find heroism in the contemporary world. Carlyle, as we shall see, will solve this problem in an influential but idiosyncratic way; William Morris will transform the whole problematic by a dialectical inversion which makes the epic appeal of barbarism the basis for a critique of the insufficiency of the contemporary world. The interdependence, which is to say the incompatibility, of modernity with epic results in a sense of the essentially unheroic nature of the civil society which has superseded the barbarous.

While the power and sublimity of epic, to use the categories suggested by Vico, might have been lost in contemporary civil society, that does not mean that they have been lost from the contemporary world altogether. On the contrary, epic primitivism suggests, as one possibility, that equivalents of the epic are to be found throughout the world in those societies or among those peoples who are still at the barbarous stage of their progress. But it also provides the seeds of a different account of epic as the necessary form to be rediscovered for the atavistic business of building an empire. In what follows, I will discuss these two contradictory entailments. On the one hand, there is what might be thought of as the traditional account of epic and empire: that there is a natural fit between martial epic and imperial attitudes. This is a view shared both by pro-ponents and critics of empire, as we shall see. On the other hand, epic primitivism can be deployed to understand the subject peoples of empire; this will be a widespread response in the nineteenth century, and its political ambivalence will be explored.

EPIC AND NOVEL, AND A GENERIC MAP OF THE WORLD

If epic as a mode is 'essentially archaic', then the mode most frequently adduced as fitted for modernity is the novel. The relationship between the two modes was a matter of scholarly controversy in the twentieth century, as theorists of the novel sought either to claim an epic inheritance for their form or to see it as repudiating its heroic forebear. While this debate has its intrinsic interest, and will be duly considered in what follows, it is introduced principally for the light it throws on two matters: how the assimilative power of the novel makes it the form most fitted for the modern world, and how the novel's assimilation of epic leads to a generic map of the world. In fact these two matters are inextricably related, since modernity in a world of uneven development is as much a spatial or geographical term as it is a temporal or historical one. That is to say, while society in the nineteenth century had progressed beyond the heroic or barbarous stage in most of Europe, on the European margins and throughout the world beyond Europe, vestiges or living fossils of heroic society persisted. The novel's partial recognition of this, in imperial tales at the end of the century, provides the topic for a concluding section of this book, where the trope of epic is pursued in novels by Stevenson, Haggard and Conrad.

The notion of a generic map of the world – a map of the world according to genre – needs some further explication. In a different, though related, context, such a map was beautifully articulated by Jane Austen in *Northanger Abbey* in 1818:

Charming as were all Mrs. Radcliffe's works, and charming even as were the works of all her imitators, it was not in them perhaps that human nature, at least in the midland counties of England, was to be looked for. Of the Alps and Pyrenees, with their pine forests and their vices, they might give a faithful delineation; and Italy, Switzerland, and the South of France, might be as fruitful in horrors as they were there represented. Catherine dared not doubt beyond her own country, and even of that, if hard pressed, would have yielded the northern and western extremities.[10]

'Mrs. Radcliffe's works': Austen is here of course concerned with Gothic fiction, which, although it is a characteristically modern form, is also one which is coded as archaic – that is to say, it is a form which deals with the horrors of a pre-modern world.[11] It has its own geography, as Austen suggests; Catherine's mistake in the novel is to expect to find the terrors which perhaps genuinely infest the Alps and the Pyrenees in the 'midland counties of England'. This is not just a generic map of Europe; it is also a generic map of these islands, and their northern and western extremities are the places where the Gothic might still be expected to lurk.

This book will argue a similar case in relation to epic as a genre. It is possible, of course, to overstress the coincidence between the 'northern' and 'western' parts of Britain as visualised by Austen, and the North and West of the Germanic and Celtic primary epics rediscovered in the eighteenth and nineteenth centuries. The West is clearly the same West; the gloomy Gothic possibilities of Wales, Ireland and Scotland are clearly associated with the underdevelopment which characterised those regions (or parts of those regions) in the nineteenth century; and one of the central features in the many episodes of the Celtic revival from *Ossian* to Yeats's 'Wanderings of Oisin' 130 years later was a rediscovery of a national epic. But this is a different North; for Austen the North means surely the Highlands, while for Morris and the other discoverers of the Nordic past the North meant the whole Germanic descent of a substantial section of the English population.

Nevertheless, the quotation from Austen is at least very suggestive – that the genres coded as archaic thus have simultaneously a geographical centre of gravity as much as a historical one. A map of the world, therefore, according to genre: in the nineteenth century, starting with the islands of Britain and then including the whole planet, certain regions of the world came to be strongly associated with certain genres coded as in some sense archaic. These were epic above all, but also Gothic, as we have seen, and romance as it is conceived in relation to epic. But these dispositions are reproduced within the novel; the way in which the latter form assimilates the archaic material of epic, and thus provides an implicit national geography, is the very matter of dispute between Mikhail Bakhtin and Franco Moretti to be discussed below. Hence the 'generic map of the world': the book will seek to trace these dispositions as they figure in the implicit or affective geography of the novel. As the protagonist of *Kidnapped* or *King Solomon's Mines* or *An Outcast of the Islands* makes his way across borders – the Highland Line provides the prototype for all these transitions – he makes his way into a world which is at once ethnically and generically distinct. The imaginative map of the world conveyed by the late nineteenth-century novel carries with it these presuppositions of epic primitivism.

I begin, however, with an account of the Homeric question as it was discussed in Britain, in conjunction with the Ossianic controversy, for in both cases the imbrication of the understanding of epic as an antique form with notions of modernity is evident. This leads on to a discussion of the role of Walter Scott, whose importance as the principal transmitter of this nexus of ideas into the nineteenth century cannot be overstated.

CHAPTER I

Homer, Ossian and Modernity

THE HOMERIC QUESTION

The Homeric question was set in train by the English traveller Robert Wood, whose 1769 *Essay on the Original Genius and Writings of Homer* initiated over two centuries of debate about the poet. Wood, among other things, asserted that the poet was probably illiterate; this was taken up by the German scholar Friedrich Wolf at the end of the eighteenth century and made the basis of the contention that he was not one single poet at all.[1] At its most obvious level, then, this was a controversy about whether 'Homer' was one poet or many – both whether the same poet composed the *Iliad* and the *Odyssey* and whether, more radically, either poem was composed by a single author at all: ought they rather to be thought of as compositions made out of multiple original shorter poems or lays? But to put the matter in this way is to lose sight of what was at stake in the controversy. The effort to dissolve the Homeric epics into constituent lays was only the most visible aspect of a line of argument which, in a manner broadly typical of a phase of the Enlightenment, as we have seen, sought to historicize them; in the words of Wood, reproducing one phase of that interpretative circle in which the poems came to be understood, 'it is principally from him [Homer] that we have formed our ideas of that sameness in the pursuits and occupations of mankind in the Heroic ages, which is the genuine character of an early stage of Society'.[2] The Homeric epics, but especially the *Iliad*, were thus to be seen as the products of an 'early stage of society' and could therefore appear to lose some of the authority which had accrued to them as the supreme monuments of classical civilisation – precisely because they emerged from a state of society which preceded the civilised state.

Wood claimed the authority of a traveller; he could partly base his claims for the historicity of Homer's writings on his experience of the East (by which he meant the area covered by the Ottoman Empire). This led him to make a point which would become characteristic of the radical side in the Homeric controversy: that the manners and customs in evidence in the early Greek epics can be found in the modern world among contemporary uncivilised peoples – though there was a long history already in place in the eighteenth century predisposing Wood to make this connection.[3] Wood's example of such a people is the Bedouin Arabs. Comparable claims, with examples chosen from across the many peoples encountered by eighteenth- and nineteenth-century imperialism, were to become a staple of subsequent arguments. In Wood's case, this was more than a passing claim; he developed seven distinct points of comparison between 'Heroic, Patriarchal, and Bedouin manners' (p. 156), including disguise, cruelty, hospitality and the unnatural separation of the sexes. This allowed him to assert that the fundamental source of these distinctive indications of a stage of humanity was being ruled by oriental despotism.

Wood's arguments in this area, however, reproduce exactly that interpretative circle which we have seen characterising epic primitivism from its inception. That is, Homer's poetry is itself the main source of evidence for the manners of the heroic age, of which the poetry of Homer is to be seen as the product. Our previous quotation ('it is principally from him . . .') indicates that, in his view, it was almost exclusively from Homer himself that we have formed our ideas of the 'character' of early mankind. This leads to a very particular reading strategy; we are to deduce the manners of the past from our reading of the poet, and then to understand the poetry in the light of those deductions. This is nevertheless a very persuasive and powerful strategy that will dominate one side of the Homeric controversy hereafter.

Wood's essay had Homer as its topic, as, naturally, did the Homeric controversy which it can be said to initiate. Beyond this, as we have already seen, Homer was a central figure in wider eighteenth-century debates about the progress of society and the transition to modernity. The controversy carries forward, in technical philological terms, just those large issues which preoccupied Ferguson and the philosophical historians; it is fair to say, however, that while these broader questions were ultimately at issue, it is not always possible to see them among the ferociously contested details of the Homeric controversy. This is in part the legacy of Wolf, whose originality lay, not in the claim to the pre-literate and bardic Homer, but in the willingness to found this claim upon textual scholarship.[4] This opened the way to endless and in some respects undecidable debates about the date of the introduction of writing into Greece, the

possible smaller units into which the texts of Homer should be broken
down and the authenticity of almost each and every line of the received
texts. Nevertheless, given what was ultimately at stake in the controversy,
it is not surprising, as Richard Jenkyns has pointed out, that the adherents
of the Wolfian or 'rhapsodic' view of the texts tended to be politically
radical, while the more conservative tended to seek to retain the authority
of both the traditional text and its individual authorship.[5]

Wolf's strength lay in his command of the scholarship pertaining to the
textual transmission of Homer; in effect, as Grafton has argued, he sought
to transfer the newly developing methods of biblical scholarship to
Homeric criticism. This analogy is not an innocent one; when Wolf
suggests that the way the ancient materials were brought together is
comparable in the works of Homer, the ancient German epic material,
the Bible and the Koran, the suggestion is an explosive one; subsequent
accusations of atheism against Wolf in relation to his attitude to Homer
are more, perhaps, than mere name-calling. At all events, Wolf also makes
the typical analogy, in considering Homer, to 'the bards, the scalds, the
Druids' (p. 109) – this in relation to the feats of memory necessary for oral
recitation. So while the general positions to which Wolf subscribed were
not necessarily original, their power to provoke lay in their being combined with a formidable array of textual scholarship.

The fullest expression in English of the Enlightenment historicising
tradition represented by Wolf is to be found in George Grote's massive
History of Greece, first published in 1846. The first part of this twelve-
volume history (taking up the first volume and a half) is entirely devoted
to 'Legendary Greece'; Grote is a strictly positivist historian, who argues
that nothing positive can be known about Greece before the first
Olympiad, and therefore that all that can be done about pre-historical
Greece is to set out the mass of legendary material, including the
Homeric, that has descended from it. This tells us nothing conclusive
about the actual history of Greece preceding the historical period, but it
does allow us to form a strong sense of the religious mentality which
produced these legends.

This leads to a very particular way of considering the legends of ancient
Greece, including the epic material:

The times which I thus set apart from the regions of history are discernible only
through a different atmosphere – that of epic poetry and legend. To confound
together these disparate matters is, in my judgment, essentially unphilosophical.
I describe the earlier times by themselves, as conceived by the faith and feeling of

the first Greeks, and known only through their legends – without presuming to measure how much or how little of historical matter these legends may contain. If the reader blame me for not assisting him to determine this – if he ask me why I do not undraw the curtain and disclose the picture – I reply in the words of the painter Zeuxis, when the same question was addressed to him in exhibiting his master-piece of imitative art – 'The curtain *is* the picture'. What we now read as poetry and legend was once accredited history, and the only genuine history which the first Greeks could conceive or relish of their past time: the curtain conceals nothing behind, and cannot by any ingenuity be withdrawn. I undertake only to show it as it stands – not to efface, still less to repaint it.[6]

In this spirit, Grote recounts at great length the legendary material, without ever presuming to trace in it even the echoes of actual historical events. But while he thus repudiates one version of the 'historical method', he is in fact advocating another and much more sophisticated historicism; for all this material can itself be understood as evidence of the religious mentality which produced it. He thus concludes of the Greek myths that they are the special product of the imagination and feelings, radically distinct from both history and philosophy; that we are not warranted in applying to the mythical world the rules either of historical credibility or chronological sequence; that the myths were originally produced in an age which had no records, no philosophy and no criticism, but which was full of religious faith. Therefore the myths were originally fully plausible, and the time came when the Greeks made important advances socially, ethically and intellectually; as a result the myths ceased to retain their previous plausibility (I, 598–600).

Grote was himself a radical and a utilitarian; his intellectual descent springs directly from the Enlightenment, and he explicitly and approvingly quotes both Vico and Adam Ferguson to substantiate his arguments. In this context it is worth noting that the history he traces in ancient Greece – in which the plausibility of mythical religious stories is gradually undermined by the advance of a sceptical and scientific spirit – exactly anticipates one way of understanding the intellectual history of the nineteenth century. This is another aspect of the appeal of a historicist method with respect to ancient Greece to radicals and progressives, since it appeared to validate their own rationalising project in the world contemporary to them.

What, however, can we learn about legendary or prehistoric Greece from a study of its legends – from treating them, that is, as 'unconscious expositors of their own contemporary society' (II, 79)? This was a society which was ruled by the personal ascendancy of a King. The state of moral and social feeling was equally rudimentary – 'either individual valour and cruelty, or the personal attachments and quarrels of relatives and war companions, or the feuds of private enemies, are ever before us' (II, 107). The virtues that accompanied this state of social feeling are just those recognised by Adam Ferguson in barbaric society: 'mutual devotion between kinsmen and companions in arms ... generous hospitality to the stranger, and ... helping protection to the suppliant' (II, 116–17). But these scarcely counterbalance the primitivism of the society revealed by the Homeric legends:

When however among the Homeric men we pass beyond the influence of the private ties above enumerated, we find scarcely any other moralising forces in operation. The acts and adventures commemorated imply a community wherein neither the protection nor the restraints of law are practically felt, and wherein ferocity, rapine, and the aggressive propensities generally, seem restrained by no internal counterbalancing scruples. (II, 120)

Grote here adumbrates the widest context in which the Homeric controversy needs to be seen: the attempt to understand in its fullest social particularity and historical difference the world from which ancient epic derived.

Grote duly extends his argument by making the comparison between the status of these epic stories in Greece and that of those of medieval Europe:

What the legends of Troy, of Thêbes, of the Calydonian boar, of Œdipus, Thêseus, &c. were to an early Greek, the tales of Arthur, of Charlemagne, of the Nibelungen, were to an Englishman, or Frenchman, or German, of the twelfth or thirteenth century. They were neither recognised fiction nor authenticated history: they were history, as it is felt and welcomed by minds unaccustomed to investigate evidence and unconscious of the necessity of doing so. (I, 630)

Grote's own ambitions as a historian are evident in passages such as these: his own project has emerged from an intellectual world which has passed beyond the stage indicated here. This is a transition of which all societies are capable, but which not all have yet made; elsewhere Grote makes the comparison of prehistoric Greece not to the European past, but to the social world of contemporary barbaric societies. Indeed, he argues that 'the popular narrative talk, which the Germans express by the significant word *Sage* or *Volks-Sage*' is a 'phaenomenon common to almost all stages of society and to almost all quarters of the globe. It is the natural effusion of the unlettered, imaginative and believing man, and its maximum of influence belongs to an early state of the human mind . . .' (I, 163). Thus there were a large number of contemporary societies with which to compare the Homeric: 'The Druze in Lebanon, the Arabian tribes in the desert, and even the North American Indians' (II, 117). In a later edition, Grote quotes a Colonel Sleeman, whose descriptions of the state of mind 'actually present among the native population of Hindustan' provide an enlightening picture for the modern reader of the mentality of the legendary period in Greece.[7] The intellectual framework of epic primitivism is laid out here in a relatively complete form, though given an especially Enlightenment and positivist slant.

This does not mean that Grote was an extreme Wolfian; in the chapters that he actually devotes to the controversy he takes what is in effect a middle way, accepting that the *Odyssey* and the *Iliad* might well have been written by different authors, but that they themselves bear the marks of having been formed as complete poems (this much is non-Wolfian) – only this was achieved well before the advent of writing in Greece (and this is pro-Wolfian). He also makes the telling and potentially self-destructive point that 'our knowledge respecting contemporary Homeric society is collected exclusively from the Homeric compositions themselves' (II, 218) – thus acknowledging the potential circularity of the historicist method. In sum, however, the first two volumes of Grote's *History* constitute a formidable exposition of the radically historicising account of Homeric epic in the context of a legendary, and to that extent prehistoric, world.

Against Grote, and adopting more conservative positions, were the literary historian William Mure and, considerably influenced by him, William Ewart Gladstone. Mure's *Critical History of the Language and Literature of Antient Greece* was first published in 1850; the discussion of Homer that it contains is mostly devoted to a long and detailed demolition of the Wolfian case. But reading Mure – a deeply conservative scholar – allows us to see what was at stake in the Homeric question, which, though it was fought over minute details of textual scholarship, was ultimately a battle over the historicity of the Homeric texts and thus over their possible place in modernity. For Mure, the heroes of the *Iliad* are morally exemplary; at the poem's heart is a kernel of historical truth, so that it commemorates the heroic deeds of national forebears.

Mure's account of the poems, therefore, is that of a traditional humanistic scholarship, stressing the continuing value of the heroic figures presented to their readers. He wishes to minimise the rudeness of the Homeric age:

> It will be necessary to discard, or greatly qualify, the epithets 'rude' and 'barbarous', so frequently bestowed on the age of Homer, and test it by his own descriptions. We there find a race among whom civilisation was sufficiently matured to impart splendour to the social fabric, without impairing their own martial ferocity or simplicity of habits.[8]

He also wishes to minimise the habitual comparison of the Enlightenment tradition (made, as we have seen, by Ferguson and Grote) of the heroic age of Greece to that of contemporary 'barbarous' peoples; to do this, he introduces a racialised theory to temper his apparent humanism. So while he asserts that he will elucidate the historicity of the poems by recourse to the 'first principles of human nature' (I, 19), the apparent universalism of this is immediately tempered by the contention that the disposition to preserve the memory of past events is more marked among the Indo-European branch of mankind than it is among Negroes or North American Indians. In short Mure so shapes the argument as to minimise the sense of historical distance from the poetry, and to emphasise their European specificity.

Mure nevertheless concedes this much to the Enlightenment case, in that he refers to epic poetry throughout as 'epic minstrelsy', and sees epic poetry as existing on a continuity of national song which rises from ballads at one end of the scale to the full-length epopee at the other. He is prepared to admit the comparison of epic to the Border Ballads (Mure was himself a Scot), and where necessary concede that some of the ferocity of the Greek heroes had to be explained as peculiar to the heroic age. But these concessions are made in the context of an argument that seeks to undo the revolutionary implications of the Wolfian hypothesis – asserted at one point to have the effect of a revolutionary pamphlet in a disturbed state – and to restore the discussion of Homer to its traditional bases.

This then is the scholar admired by Gladstone as providing the last word on the Homeric controversy. His own publications on the Greek poet are themselves deeply conservative; they too wish to stress the moral continuity between the ancient past and the contemporary world. And not just the *moral* continuity; the most fantastic moments in Gladstone's 1858 *Studies in Homer and the Homeric Age* come when he asserts that the spirit of ancient Greece breathes in modern English institutions – 'and, if I mistake not, even in the peculiarities of these institutions' – and when he compares the Grecian kings to the British peerage.[9] Gladstone's wish to make the study of Homer more central to British education becomes more intelligible in the context of this extraordinary assertion.

OSSIAN AND EPIC PRIMITIVISM

Cognate with the Homeric controversy, and relying on similar premises, was another large disagreement over an epic poem: the cultural battles fought out over Ossian in the latter half of the eighteenth century. In both cases, scholarly controversies revolved around the antiquity of the poetry, and what that revealed about the social orders from which the poems emerged. Indeed, if any single occurrence best demonstrated the dependence of progressive theories of human society upon the reading of epic poetry, it was the publication of Macpherson's 'translation' of Ossian's *Fingal* in 1761. One way of telling this story has been to see Macpherson's fabrications as *produced* in response to the promptings of Hugh Blair and Adam Ferguson; equally it has been argued that Ferguson might himself have been influenced by the poetry of Ossian.[10] The circulation of arguments between Ferguson, Blair and Macpherson is striking, all of them relying on progressive theories of human society as the appropriate context for the emergence of epic poetry. The key documents in this congruence of historical argument and poetic fabrication are Blair's 'A Critical Dissertation on the Poems of Ossian', first published in 1763 to accompany *Fingal*; Macpherson's own 'Dissertation', published in 1765 with *Temora* in the second volume of *The Works of Ossian*; and Ferguson's *An Essay on the History of Civil Society*, published in 1767.[11] However, the sentimental version of epic heroism introduced by Blair and Macpherson – and later to be mocked by Scott – was not reproduced by Ferguson, and his tougher account of the epic virtues allows us to recognise that Scott was a better philosophical historian than those defenders of Ossian who saw in the poems a vindication of their own version of philosophical history.

Here first then is Blair, in the 'Critical Dissertation', a document which was crucial in explaining the poems of Ossian, and in a sense creating a taste for them:

The compositions of Ossian are so strongly marked with characters of antiquity, that although there were no external proof to support that antiquity, hardly any reader of judgment and taste, could hesitate in referring them to a very remote æra. There are four great stages through which men successively pass in the progress of society. The first and earliest is the life of hunters; pasturage succeeds to this, as the ideas of property begin to take root; next, agriculture; and lastly, commerce. Throughout Ossian's poems, we plainly find ourselves in the first of these periods of society; during which, hunting was the chief employment of men, and the principal method of their procuring subsistence. Pasturage was not indeed wholly unknown; for we hear of dividing the herd in the case of a divorce; but the allusions to herds and to cattle are not many; and of agriculture, we find no traces. No cities appear to have been built in the territories of Fingal. No arts are mentioned except that of navigation and of working in iron. Everything presents to us the most simple and unimproved manners. At their feasts, the heroes prepared their own repast; they sat round the light of the burning oak; the wind lifted their locks, and whistled through their open halls. Whatever was beyond the necessaries of life was known to them only as the spoil of the Roman province; 'the gold of the stranger; the lights of the stranger; the steeds of the stranger, the children of the rein.' (p. 353)

The problem with this line of reasoning is evident enough: the characteristics of society in its first stage of existence are deduced from the poems, and then the authenticity of the poems is deduced from their conformity to the nature of that stage of society. It is indeed a malign form of the interpretative circle described in the previous chapter; the difficulty arises from the impossibility, for Blair, of acknowledging that the Ossianic poems as 'translated' by Macpherson were precisely designed to conform to notions of the earliest stage in the progress of society.[12]

Macpherson too believes in 'stages' of human society, but in his case this is not a matter of progress; on the contrary, it is rather one of decline and partial restoration:

It is in this epoch [i.e. fifth century AD] we must fix the beginning of the decay of that species of heroism, which subsisted in the days of Ossian. There are three stages in human society. The first is the result of consanguinity, and the natural affection of the members of a family to one another. The second begins when property is established, and men enter into associations for mutual defence, against the invasions and injustice of neighbours. Mankind submit, in the third, to certain laws and subordinations of government, to which they trust the safety of their persons and property. As the first is formed on nature, so, of course, it is the most disinterested and noble. Men, in the last, have leisure to cultivate the mind, and to restore it, with reflection, to a primæval dignity of sentiment. The middle state is the region of complete barbarism and ignorance. (p. 211)

Whereas for Blair, the heroic stage of society occurred when subsistence depended upon hunting, in Macpherson's account the crucial factor is 'consanguinity, and the natural affection of the members of a family one to another'. The recently destroyed clan society of the Highlands is not far behind this assertion. In both accounts, however, epic poetry emerges from a primitive stage of human society, and readers can explain the peculiarities of the poetry by the characteristics of that society.

Ferguson's *Essay on the History of Civil Society*, as we have already noted, gave an altogether tougher and more sophisticated account of the stages of human society, fortunately reliant much more on Homer than on Ossian, though his close connection with Macpherson's translation is undeniable.[13] Ferguson recognised the genuine *barbarism* of barbaric society, so that while he might have been content to believe in the authenticity of the Ossianic poems, and even to promote them, the actual account of the epic virtues to be deduced from his *Essay* is quite unlike the sentimental heroes of Ossian's verses in Macpherson's version. Ferguson, after all, had correctly observed that 'Hector falls unpitied, and his body is insulted by every Greek'[14] – a mode of proceeding unimaginable in the poems of Ossian. Nevertheless, despite the excessive sentimentality of these poems, they appeared to provide a striking confirmation of the notion of human society passing through several stages on its way to modernity.[15]

Ossian's poetry is invoked here for several reasons in addition to its importance to the intellectual history of the eighteenth century. It provides the exemplary instance of the invention of a national epic located in the less developed regions adjacent to a civil society which has passed beyond barbarism; in this respect it will function as one model of the rediscovered primary epic for many of the nations of Europe in the nineteenth century. But the poetry is also invoked to remind us of the centrality of the mode of pastiche entailed upon all translations and reforged epic by epic primitivism; that is, Macpherson's extraordinary invention of an idiom at once suggestive of, and distinct from, any actually existing models of heroic verse will prove to be the first of many solutions to the question of how to write or rewrite epic verse. Both the Homeric and the Ossianic controversies therefore entail particular ways of understanding the antiquity of epic, its relationship to modernity, and the possibilities for an heroic idiom. Walter Scott's ambivalent relationship to Ossian will therefore be the starting-point for a discussion of his own working-through of that entailment. His solutions, however, are especially important, for it is Scott who provides a central locus or way-station for the transmission of the problematic of epic primitivism into the nineteenth century.

CHAPTER 2

Walter Scott and Heroic Minstrelsy

THE NATIONAL MUSE IN ITS CRADLE

John Sutherland makes a straightforward distinction in his biography of Walter Scott: between Scott as 'philosophical historian' and as antiquarian.[1] In the first capacity, Scott is the heir of the Scottish Enlightenment, familiar with the notion of history as a series of stages progressing from the savage state through to modern commercial civilisation. Such ideas, indeed, were a central part of his education.[2] Scott's role as an antiquarian, by contrast – 'the hoarder of coins, suits of armour, old manuscripts and heroic relics', in Sutherland's words – was perhaps at least as important in his formation as a writer. But it is Scott as philosophical historian that I wish to discuss in this chapter, especially as his writings carry forward an aspect of the problematic described in the Introduction – that combination of ideas that associates epic with the barbarous stage of society and hence pushes it to the margins of contemporary civility. It is above all through the figure of Walter Scott, as ballad collector and poet as much as novelist, that the connections between epic, romance, national balladry and the pre-modern world were conclusively established for the nineteenth century. This chapter will trace the nature of those connections, and the centrality of the figure of the bard, in Scott's writings about ballads and related topics, and in his poems *The Lay of the Last Minstrel* and *The Lady of the Lake*. But I begin with his account of Ossian and the Ossianic controversy.

His fullest statement on Ossian is to be found in his review of the *Report of the Highland Society upon Ossian*, and of Malcolm Laing's debunking 1805 edition of Macpherson's poetical works, a review which Scott published in the *Edinburgh Review* in 1805.[3] Broadly speaking, he accepts the conclusions of the Highland Society: that there was a mass of Ossianic material circulating in Gaelic in the Highlands, but that Macpherson's claim that his poetry was a direct translation of such poetry, or that it ever existed as a connected epic, cannot be sustained. Part of the question that needs to be answered, therefore, is why such claims should have been accepted so widely in the first place. Here is part of the answer:

There was every reason to suspect the affected sentimentality of Macpherson's Ossian; but, on the other hand, it was but natural to suppose, that a nation of hunters and warriors, as the Highlanders remained, almost to our own day, – a nation, the government of whose tribes was patriarchal, and therefore depended upon genealogical tradition, – with whom poetry was a separate and hereditary profession, and whose language is a dialect of the ancient Celtic, must necessarily have possessed much original legendary poetry. (p. 437)

One of the principal reasons for accepting the authenticity of Macpherson's poems, it thus appears, was that the nature of Highland society was exactly of the kind that, according to the fundamental propositions of the philosophical historians, would have been rich in 'legendary poetry'. Yet what should have given people cause for doubt was the 'affected sentimentality' of Macpherson's version. Scott expands upon this point:

Still, however, the reader must have observed a prodigious and irreconcilable difference betwixt the Ossian of Macpherson and such of those ballads as come forward as altogether unsophisticated. The latter agree in every respect with the idea we have always entertained of the poetry of a rude people. Their style is unequal; sometimes tame and flat; sometimes turgid and highly periphrastic. Sometimes they rise into savage energy, and sometimes melt into natural tenderness. The subject of most is the battle or the chase: Love, when introduced, is the love of a savage state ... [By contrast in Macpherson's poetry], all is elegance, refinement and sensibility; they never take arms, but to protect the feeble, or to relieve beauty in distress; they never injure their prisoners, nor insult the fallen: and as to Fingal himself, he has all the strength and bravery of Achilles, with the courtesy, sentiment, and high-breeding of Sir Charles Grandison. (p. 446)

Scott thus proves himself a better philosophical historian than those such as Blair, for whom Macpherson, ironically, first produced his versions of the Ossianic stories; for Scott here effectively convicts the 'translations' of a profound anachronism. The problem for Scott, unlike for the uncompromising opponent of Ossian, Samuel Johnson, thirty years previously, is not the very possibility of poetry in such a barbarous society as that of the Highlands, it is rather that Macpherson's poetry is not sufficiently in character with the society that produced it: 'The passions and feelings of men in a savage state, are as desultory as their habits of life;

and a model of perfect generosity and virtue, would be as great a wonder amongst them, as a fine gentleman in a birthday suit' (pp. 447–8). Scott, in short, uses the very conceptual framework of philosophical history to detect anachronism in Macpherson's Ossian, when the antiquity of Ossian was fundamental to the founding conceptual problematic of that history.

Scott thus uses philosophical history to convict, wittily but almost regretfully, Macpherson of imposture. Elsewhere in his writings the same notions are used to advance his own theory of the origins of popular poetry, which links together an account of the primitive stages of society with the figure of the Bard or minstrel. The two most important essays on these themes are the article on 'Romance' that he wrote for the *Encyclopedia Britannica* in 1824 and the 'Introductory Remarks on Popular Poetry', which he added to the 1830 edition of the *Minstrelsy of the Scottish Border*. In both these substantial essays, Scott reproduces some of the classical positions of his Enlightenment forebears, but combines them with a bardic theory of popular poetry in a distinctive synthesis of ideas – which lies behind his own poetic practice from earlier in the nineteenth century.

The 1824 'Essay on Romance' begins with a distinction between the romance and the novel, in which the latter is defined as 'a fictitious narrative, differing from Romance, because the events are accommodated to the ordinary chain of human events, and the modern state of society'. The fundamental premise of the essay, therefore, is one which makes the distinction between novel and romance cognate with the distinction between the modern and the pre-modern world – a pattern which repeats the primitivist theory of epic and which Scott's own novels from *Waverley* onwards repeatedly enact. But Scott's account of the origins of romance makes it, in effect, a version of epic: it is to be traced back to the origins of society and the tales told of the legendary past of early nations. Consideration of these 'traditional histories' leads Scott to take in epic, which is to be distinguished from romance not generically but by virtue of the skill of the poet:

Verse being thus adopted as the vehicle of traditional history, there needs but the existence of a single man of genius, in order to carry the composition a step higher in the scale of literature than that of which we are treating. In proportion to the skill which he attains in his art, the fancy and the ingenuity of the artist himself are excited; the simple narrative transmitted to him by ruder rhymers is increased in length; is decorated with the graces of language, amplified in detail, and rendered interesting by description; until the brief and barren original bears as little resemblance to the finished piece, as the *Iliad* of Homer to the evanescent traditions, out of which the blind bard wove his tale of Troy Divine. Hence the opinion expressed by the ingenious Percy, and assented to by Ritson himself. When about to present to his readers an excellent analysis of the old romance of *Lybius Disconius*, and making several remarks on the artificial management of the story, the Bishop observes, that 'if an Epic poem may be defined a fable related by a poet to excite admiration and inspire virtue, by representing the action of one hero favoured by Heaven, who executes a great design in spite of all the obstacles that oppose him, I know not why we should withhold the name of *Epic Poem* from the piece which I am about to analyze'.[4]

The distinction between epic and romance, though great, is thus explicitly that 'betwixt two distinct species of the same generic class' (p. 139). Epic is in effect a worked-up version of the traditional histories which circulate in any society in a primitive state, and are produced by minstrels, bards or rhymers in relation to the heroic deeds of that nation.

There is indeed an imaginary anthropology underlying this notion, in which the moment of recitation or performance is central:

It is found, for example, and we will produce instances in viewing the progress of Romance in particular countries, that the earliest productions of this sort, known to exist, are short narratives or ballads, which were probably sung on solemn or festive occasions, recording the deeds and praises of some famed champion of the tribe or country, or perhaps the history of some remarkable victory or signal defeat, calculated to interest the audience by the associations which the song awakens. (p. 139)

This imagined situation – the bard addressing the tribe to sing its own immediate heroism – is what links together ballad, romance and epic; it is not that Scott fails to distinguish between them, but that they are all in effect comparable productions in terms of their origin; the appropriate distinctions are aesthetic not generic.

Furthermore, such productions are 'common to almost all nations' (p. 146). Scott can thus produce a comparative account of the traditional histories of several nations, in which the close relationship between heroic national song and heroic national action is central:

Chanted to rhythmical numbers, the songs which celebrate the early valour of the fathers or the tribe becomes [sic] its war-cry in battle, and men march to conflict hymning the praises and the deeds of some real or supposed precursor who had marshalled their fathers in the path of victory. (p. 158)

Thus the Norman minstrel Taillefer sang the *Song of Roland* before the host at the Battle of Hastings. Furthermore, all nations come to develop comparable cycles of national story:

> Each nation ... came at length to adopt to itself a cycle of heroes like those of the *Iliad*, a sort of common property to all minstrels who chose to make use of them, under the condition always that the general character ascribed to each individual hero was preserved with some degree of consistency. (p. 150)

The examples that Scott gives include the Arthurian cycle, the Paladins of Charlemagne, and the heroes and heroines of the Nibelung tales. Thus these cycles of romances differ only in their mode of poetic treatment from epic stories, with which they share a common origin; they have the same original function in primitive stages of society in celebrating heroic deeds; and they are crucial in the formation of a sense of national identity. The connections are here established in which ballads and romances are to be seen as a kind of precursor to epic, and indeed might be seen themselves as epics in little. In the terms of this argument, moreover, these archaic forms provide the origins of *national* poetry or song.

All of this is congruous with the philosophical historians, for whom, as we have seen, there is an essential fit between the manners evidenced by epic poetry and the manners of barbarous or heroic society. Clearly, those earlier writers were not primarily intent on producing a theory of the origin of poetry; but this certainly was a matter of intense controversy among the antiquarian collectors of ballads who preceded Scott. On this topic, Scott's sympathies were overwhelmingly with that theory of the origins of popular poetry which accorded a high place to the individual bard; in that respect he might appear to be at odds with Enlightenment notions of the *popular* character of poetry. He can nevertheless combine these two seemingly antipathetic theories in a way which preserves the sense of the pre-modern nature of poetic 'traditional histories' at the same time as evincing a low opinion of the mechanisms of poetic transmission in the oral tradition.

For Scott, the originating scene for traditional poetry is that moment of recitation: 'Indeed, the slightest acquaintance with ancient Romances of the metrical class, shows us that they were composed for the express purpose of being recited, or, more properly, chanted, to some simple tune or cadence for the amusement of a large audience' (p. 157). Minstrels were the depositories of national stories and reproduced them in these settings; they indeed wrote (or composed) them. In the 'Essay on Romance', Scott simply asserts that bards (a term used effectively synonymously with minstrels) were of high status and have gradually sunk in the scale; as they have sunk, the ballads and romances which they originally composed have been corrupted with them. In this context Scott quotes Joseph Ritson, with whom he nevertheless disagrees on the original status of the bards: 'Tradition, says Ritson, is an alchemy, which converts gold into lead' (p. 177). As we shall soon see, this is a theory which goes a long way to explaining Scott's own editorial practices; but in general it means that he can persist with the Enlightenment view of the congruence of popular poetry with its period of composition, while maintaining the high original status of the bard: the corruptions of popular transmission account for the degenerate state in which contemporary versions are found.

A comparable set of arguments appear in the 'Introductory Remarks on Popular Poetry', which Scott wrote in 1830 to accompany the reissue of the *Minstrelsy of the Scottish Border*, though here they are more specifically targeted on the ballads which make up the volume. Scott notes the philological equivalence between the ancient Greek Ποιητης and the Scottish 'Maker'; and in turn their relationship to the old French 'Trouver' (sic) or troubadour. It is due to the exceptional talents of such individuals that the traditional stories of each nation have been preserved:

But the progress of the art is far more dependent upon the rise of some highly-gifted individual, possessing in a pre-eminent and uncommon degree the powers demanded, whose talents influence the taste of a whole nation, and entail on their posterity and language a character almost indelibly sacred. In this respect Homer stands alone and unrivalled, as a light from whose lamp the genius of successive ages, and of distant nations, has caught fire and illumination; and who, though the early poet of a rude age, has purchased for the era he has celebrated, so much reverence, that, not daring to bestow on it the term of barbarous, we distinguish it as the heroic period. No other poet (sacred and inspired authors excepted) ever did, or ever will possess the same influence over posterity, in so many distant lands, as has been acquired by the blind old man of Chios; yet we are assured that his works, collected by the pious care of Pisistratus, who caused to be united into their present form those divine poems, would otherwise, if preserved at all, have appeared to succeeding generations in the humble status of a collection of detached ballads, connected only as referring to the same age, the same general subjects, and the same cycle of heroes, like the metrical poems of the Cid in Spain, or of Robin Hood in England.[5]

This appears to be a familiar restatement of the equivalence of 'popular poetry' with the materials of epic; but in fact there is a significant equivocation here which distinguishes this passage from comparable ones in the 'Essay on Romance'. Does Homer stand 'alone and unrivalled' or not? According to the first paragraph, and indeed to the 'Essay on Romance', he does: he transforms the materials made available by rude rhymers into the dignity of epic. But in the second paragraph, it would appear that if it were not for the editorial efforts of Pisistratus, the Homeric poems would now appear indistinguishable from such poems as the Cid and Robin Hood. This is beginning to sound dangerously like the arguments of Wolf; indeed Scott's first editor, Lockhart, had already spotted this danger and had added a footnote to the effect that 'He [Scott] said of the Wolfian hypothesis, that it was the most *irreligious* one he had ever heard of, and could never be believed in by any *poet*' (p. 3 fn.). Let us agree with Lockhart that the predominant emphasis in Scott's writing was on the distinguishing genius of Homer; he nevertheless restates in this passage the generic equivalence of epic poetry with the popular poetry of ballads.

Scott as philosophical historian re-emerges in these introductory remarks, though he is also interested in whether popular poetry – the ballad in this case – can be valid as historical sources:

Yet the investigation of the early poetry of every nation, even the rudest, carries with it an object of curiosity and interest. It is a chapter in the history of the childhood of society, and its resemblance to, or dissimilarity from, the popular rhymes of other nations in the same stage, must needs illustrate the ancient history of states; their slower or swifter progress towards civilisation; their gradual or more rapid adoption of manners, sentiments and religion. The study, therefore, of lays rescued from the gulf of oblivion, must in every case possess considerable interest for the moral philosopher and general historian.

The historian of an individual nation is equally or more deeply interested in the researches into popular poetry, since he must not disdain to gather from the tradition conveyed in ancient ditties and ballads, the information necessary to confirm or correct intelligence collected from more certain sources. And although the poets were a fabling race from the very beginning of time, and so much addicted to exaggeration, that their accounts are seldom to be relied on without corroborative evidence, yet instances frequently occur where the statements of poetical tradition are unexpectedly confirmed.

To the lovers and admirers of poetry as an art, it cannot be uninteresting to have a glimpse of the National Muse in her cradle, or to hear her babbling the earliest attempts at the formation of the tuneful sounds with which she was afterwards to charm posterity. (pp. 6–7)

The first paragraph here is an especially explicit statement of Scott as philosophical historian, in which ancient poetry is precisely mobilised in order to trace the 'slower or swifter progress towards civilisation' of particular states. Scott here briefly appears as the comparative or 'general' historian; in the next paragraph he figures as the historian of an individual nation, scouring the ballads to find in them corroborative evidence of historical evidence gathered elsewhere. Here Scott is still historian rather than antiquarian, though to be sure the distinction is less firm in this area. Finally he emerges as a lover of poetry, and the ballads have value to such a person insofar as they provide a glimpse of the 'National Muse in her cradle'; it is a powerful phrase, combining both the developmental sense of poetry in its relation to social progress and the specifically *national* aspect in which these ancient poems take on their significance.

Seen in these perspectives, then, popular poetry is the carrier or the embodiment of a *geist* at once historical and national. As in the 'Essay on Romance', however, Scott combines this 'philosophical' view with the potentially distinct idea of the powerful bard, whose original productions have been corrupted by the abrasions of successive generations. If in the earlier essay he had adopted Ritson's mordant description of tradition as a reverse alchemy which turns gold into lead, in this later piece Scott ventures a metaphor of his own: the action of transmission resembles the way in which the distinguishing impress upon coinage is worn away to near-invisibility by passing through innumerable hands:

Thus, undergoing from age to age a gradual process of alteration and recom-position, our popular and oral minstrelsy has lost, in a great measure, its original appearance; and the strong touches by which it had been formerly characterised, have been generally smoothed down and destroyed by a process similar to that by which a coin, passing from hand to hand, loses in circulation all the finer marks of the impress. (p. 12)

Though originally popular, therefore, in the sense of indicating the character of its age, popular poetry *now* is enfeebled by its popular nature, for transmission by oral tradition has effaced the marks of the original bardic inspiration which once characterised it.

Such a theory, of course, has immediate implications for Scott's practice as a ballad editor; in the light of this notion of oral transmission as corruption, the task of the editor is effectively to restore as good a version as possible of what ignorant transmitters have preserved.[6] In particular, it appears to give a licence to the editor to ignore differences between different versions, and to seek to supply the deficiencies of actually recorded copies with improvements that the greater historical knowledge of the editor suggests. Hence the extraordinary editorial practices of Scott – and, indeed, before him of Percy – in which different versions are collated, the style improved, and words, half-lines and whole stanzas are simply added without acknowledgement. At least, this practice seems extraordinary in the light of the scholarly standards established for ballad collection by Child later in the nineteenth century. Yet, in view of Scott's commitment to the notion of balladry as expressing a particular and earlier stage in the progress of society towards civilisation, his editorial practices take on a different character; they are part of the general problematic in which the reading of such ballads inevitably provokes a sense of the antique. There is thus a continuity between Scott's editorial practice, aimed at giving the reader a sense of the putative original, and his concomitant interest in the practice of ballad imitation, to which he devotes another essay in the 1830 edition of the *Minstrelsy*, and of which he gives various examples, of his own and others' composition, in various editions.

For, as I suggested in the Introduction, the primitivist theory of epic, and the accompanying notions of popular poetry that Scott espouses, entail a poetic practice of imitation and pastiche upon all writers who seek in any way to recapture the effects that they find in epic or in its lowly cousin the ballad. The rediscovery of popular poetry, from Percy onwards, is inextricably intertwined with ballad imitation, pastiche and forgery – both Percy's and Scott's ballad editions included explicit imitations, while Scott's later editions also included, unknowingly, some outright forgeries.[7] To read an ancient ballad, just as to read a primary epic, is to confront a world whose manners are radically distinct from one's own; in seeking to imitate such a ballad, one must seek to reproduce the same effect in the reader of historical distance. This is an aesthetic problem which haunts the ballad from the time of Chatterton, Wordsworth and Coleridge, in the period of Swinburne and Morris, through to Andrew Lang at the beginning of the twentieth century – just as the example of *Ossian* haunts the imitation of epic. As Malcolm Laws has perceptively written, the problem for ballad imitators is at once to reproduce faithfully the manner of their models and to indicate at the same time their own departure from it.[8] The horizon of this aesthetic problem is the recognition of the antiquity of both epic and ballad, provoking a complex interchange between text and reader; when reading an acknowledged Scott imitation of a ballad, for example, the reader is simultaneously aware of the modernity of the poem and of its effort to provide the reader with an equivalent experience to that of reading an actually ancient poem. Both the attempt to write an original epic in the nineteenth century and the effort at epic translation will be afflicted by a version of this more or less intractable problem.

Scott's 'Essay on Imitations of the Ancient Ballad' is to be read, according both to Lockhart and to the content of the two essays, as a direct continuation of the 'Introductory Remarks on Popular Poetry'.[9] It begins with an account of the progress of popular poetry, showing how the taste for it altered and refined with the advent of printing and the progress of society. It was only in ruder parts of the country (rural Scotland rather than England) that the 'ballad or popular epic' survived into the eighteenth century (p. 7). This history takes Scott up to the period of his own youth at the end of the eighteenth century, and the vogue for imitations of ancient ballads that was then widespread. He distinguishes two different problems: the attempt to pass off modern productions as antique (generally unsuccessful), and the 'fair trade of manufacturing modern antiques'. In this latter case, the object of the imitator is 'to obtain the credit due to authors as successful imitators of the ancient simplicity, while their system admits of a considerable infusion of modern refinement' (p. 13). Citing a variety of examples which include Burns, Coleridge and Hogg, he concludes that successful imitations in this mode do indeed manage to combine a sense of antiquity with 'modern refinement'. Interestingly, these are the very grounds on which Scott had earlier been able to detect the implausibility of *Ossian*. The essay thus articulates the problem which will dominate nineteenth-century poetry in imitative mode: how to provide in the contemporary present an equivalent experience to that provided when reading a genuine antique, while at the same time avoiding all the flatness and turgid qualities that occasionally afflict the originals. The paradox of the 'manufacture of modern antiques' is not solved by its witty invocation.

Superficially this may appear a problem endemic to epic since Virgil; that is, there is an element of pastiche built into all secondary epics, which attempt to do for Rome what Homer did for Greece, or for Italy what Virgil did for Rome. Epic poets are inevitably engaged in a complex interchange of authority with their epic forebears, and neoclassical writers are especially conscious of this generic inheritance. The crucial difference for the nineteenth-century writer, however, is the intervention of a sense of historical difference; while neoclassical imitation is founded on the continuity of past with present, however threatened by contemporary dullness or dunces, post-primitivist writers must necessarily be conscious of the categorically distinct historical stages which divide them from the heroic past. Thus there are certainly any number of would-be nineteenth-century epics written in more or less neoclassical mode; the particular problematic bequeathed by the philosophical historians, and mediated by Scott, will be how to write an epic in the antique mode when the naiveties of that neoclassical tradition are left behind. How, in short, to write a ballad, or more challengingly an epic, when such forms are precisely evidence of the difference, from our own modernity, of the social stage which produced them?

Scott begins the 'Essay on Imitations of the Ancient Ballads' with the invention of printing; it is this, he argues, that 'necessarily occasioned the downfall of the Order of Minstrels' (p. 1). But printing on its own was not sufficient, 'as even the popular poetry was now feeling the effects arising from the advance of knowledge, and the revival of the study of the learned languages, with all the elegance and the refinement which it induced' (p. 2). These combined influences Scott characterises as the 'general progress of the country' (p. 2). There is thus, it seems, an unpassable gulf between the situation of the modern poet and that of the ancient bard; for the modern poet is unavoidably committed to the culture of print, which is exactly what caused the demise of his minstrel forebears. This is a further aspect of the paradox of 'manufacturing modern antiques'. Scott's own poetry circulates almost obsessively around these paradoxes. His longer narrative poems typically alternate between the present moment of composition and the past story that they tell; in that past moment the scene of bardic recitation is repeatedly enacted, challenging comparison with the present moment of Scott's own bardic recitation – from which it is inevitably distinguished by the print medium which is what readers hold in their hands. Just as music on ancient instruments can never provide the same experience for modern audiences as it did for its original listeners, so the productions of modern bards can never be equivalent to the original putative experience of bardic recitation.

THE MANUFACTURE OF MODERN ANTIQUES

Scott's account of the composition of *The Lay of the Last Minstrel*, in his 1830 Introduction to the poem, is pertinent in this context; it may seem a curiously cold-blooded affair. It links his own personal and financial circumstances with his decision to become a full-time writer, as though the whole calculation were a matter of ensuring his financial security before even a topic or a manner for his writing should be established. The explicit materialism of this account – a note sounded again and again in his introductions to his other poems – makes absolutely clear the circumstances which surround the modern poet, writing for profit and an anonymous public. Yet his poems still claim bardic status for themselves. This gulf between the modern poet and the antique bard on which he models himself is one that Scott must somehow overcome; *The Lay of the Last Minstrel* and *The Lady of the Lake* revolve around this problem. In this respect, they set the scene for one strand of nineteenth-century poetry which harks back to bardic, or more specifically epic, models.

The problem is partly a technical matter, and these technical matters of poetic measure and style are another preoccupation of the Introduction. What would be the appropriate measure for a modern romance? Scott initially rejects the ballad measure:

The ballad measure itself, which was once listened to as an enchanting melody, had become hackneyed and sickening, from its being the accompaniment of every grinding hand-organ; and besides, a long work in quatrains, whether those of the common ballad, or such as are termed elegiac, has an effect upon the mind like that of the bed of Procrustes upon the human body; for, as it must be both awkward and difficult to carry out a long sentence from one stanza to another, it follows, that the meaning of each period must be comprehended within four lines, and equally so that it must be extended so as to fill that space.[10]

The history invoked here is not the short history from the rediscovery of the ballad from the time of Percy's *Reliques* to the moment at the beginning of the nineteenth century which Scott is recalling. Rather it is the much longer history which has led to the degradation of the national ballad metre from its heroic heyday to its present incarnation as the favoured measure of the commercial broadside ballad. Scott needed to find a measure which had the appropriate air of antiquity without the harrowing constrictions and vulgar associations of the ballad measure. The solution came thanks to hearing John Stoddart repeat the as-yet-unpublished fragment 'Christabel'. The measure of Christabel – described by Coleridge as 'founded on a new principle: namely, that of counting in each line the accents, not the syllables' – provided an apparent technical solution to the paradox of manufacturing modern antiques.[11] It provided, in short, the effect of antiquity without the constrictions of actually existing historic verse-forms.

Nancy Goslee has provided a sophisticated account of *The Lay of the Last Minstrel* partly in terms of the interplay of diegetic levels within it.[12] According to this schema, the structure of a 'tale within a tale' which characterises the poem can be described by making the story of the last minstrel himself, and his performance at Newark Castle at the end of the seventeenth century, the principal narrative or diegesis. The tale within this tale – the lay that he performs – becomes intradiegetic, while the moment of composition, Scott's moment at the beginning of the nineteenth century, becomes metadiegetic. Goslee's analysis of the poem turns on the interchanges of authority between these diegetic levels, whereby the book of spells which lies at the heart of the intradiegetic 'lay' provides an ambivalent token of Scott's own written 'bardic' authority at the metadiegetic level. I wish to supplement this analysis by pointing to the putative history of popular poetry which underlies the poem and which in effect it dramatises.

Such a history is indeed the opening premise of the poem, which sets itself at the moment of transition to a more modern world:

> The way was long, the wind was cold,
> The Minstrel was infirm and old;
> His wither'd cheek and tresses gray,
> Seem'd to have known a better day;
> The harp, his sole remaining joy,
> Was carried by an orphan boy.
> The last of all the Bards was he,
> Who sung of Border chivalry;
> For, welladay! their date was fled,
> His tuneful brethren all were dead;
> And he, neglected and oppress'd,
> Wish'd to be with them, and at rest.
> No more on prancing palfrey borne,
> He caroll'd, light as lark at morn;
> No longer courted and caress'd,
> High placed in hall, a welcome guest,
> He pour'd, to lord and lady gay,
> The unpremeditated lay:
> Old times were changed, old manners gone;
> A stranger fill'd the Stuarts' throne;
> The bigots of the iron time
> Had call'd his harmless art a crime.
> A wandering Harper, scorn'd and poor,
> He begg'd his bread from door to door,
> And tuned, to please a peasant's ear,
> The harp, a king had loved to hear.

(p. 7)

This is set at a specific historical moment at the end of the seventeenth century – Scotland, the Borders in particular, is ruled by the successors to the Stuarts, and extreme forms of Protestantism have criminalised the minstrels' music. More important than these specific historical references, however, is the assertion not only that 'Old times were changed', but also that 'old manners [were] gone'; it is not to overstate the case to say that philosophical history underlies the passage, so that the minstrel is a historical survival from an earlier period in which 'manners' permitted, or indeed dictated, the organic interchange between the minstrel's art and its immediate courtly context. The originating scene of recitation – softened and made more chivalric, to be sure, from its barbarous original – underlies the passage, and will serve as the fundamental scene of the poem. But in this modern recreation of the scene of recitation, the ladies of the court who will listen to the minstrel's lay will do so to humour him, re-enacting the organic situation of his youth with an inevitable air of irony.

The reference to 'manners', with all its implications of historical overview, sufficiently indicates that the writer of this introductory section of the poem, and indeed of all the sections of the poem which narrate the minstrel's story (Goslee's 'diegesis'), is writing in the contemporary moment – that is, the early nineteenth century, at least a hundred years after the time in which this story is set. This is despite the fact that the diction of the poem makes use of the occasional anachronism – 'welladay!' is the most visible in this opening section. In general, however, the poem at this point makes use of a regular octosyllabic couplet which, while it draws on a colourful and faintly anachronistic vocabulary ('caroll'd', 'palfrey' and so on, in addition to 'welladay'), makes no effort to manufacture a modern antique. This is in strong contrast to the minstrel's lay itself, where the 'Christabel' metre and manner immediately indicates that we now are in the presence of a recreated antiquated idiom:

> The feast was over in Branksome tower,
> And the Ladye had gone to her secret bower;
> Her bower that was guarded by word and by spell,
> Deadly to hear, and deadly to tell –
> Jesu Maria, shield us well!
> No living wight, save the Ladye alone,
> Had dared to cross the threshold stone.
>
> (p. 8)

This is definitely accentual rather than syllabic verse, and seeks to provide its readers with the sense that they are engaging with the very words and manner of the last minstrel as he sings his 'unpremeditated lay' in the company of the benign ladies of Newark Castle. The historical layering out of which the whole poem is constructed – a modern poet writes of a seventeenth-century minstrel who sings a medieval story which itself contains an even earlier Book of Spells – this historical layering entails the necessity of pastiche upon the modern poet as he seeks to recreate the necessary sense of antiquity.

However, this is a different kind of imitation than is to be found in the *Minstrelsy,* and which Scott will attempt again in *The Lady of the Lake* in the ballad of Alice Brand; that is, this is not an imitation of a Border Ballad, as the Introduction and the whole situation might lead the reader to expect. According to that opening section of the poem, 'The last of all the Bards was he / Who sung of Border chivalry', we might legitimately expect a riding ballad of the kind that Scott had so assiduously collected. Here indeed the claim for the organic relationship between popular poetry and historical stage or social situation could be grounded: the manners of rough and remote areas, such as the Borders, as late as the sixteenth and seventeenth centuries, promoted the survival of bardic relationships between poet and laird long disappeared elsewhere. Instead, Scott in *The Lay of the Last Minstrel* chooses to indicate the antiquity of the lay itself by imitating not 'The Battle of Otterbourne' or 'Johnnie Armstrang', but 'Christabel'. The pressure of the intervening history is strong here; it is precisely because subsequent popular tradition has so vulgarised and effaced the original bardic moment that Scott has to indicate the antiquity of his own poetry by imitating a form which at once suggests great age and retains a dignity now lost from the genuine antiques spoilt by their association with the popular ballad and broadside poetry.

Having suggested that the poem marks a clear break between the story of the last minstrel and the latter's own lay, it is also true to say that the poem seeks to efface this distinction; or rather, Scott lays claim to his own Bardic authority in the poem by blurring the very historical distances that the logic of the poem demands. This is part of the complicated inter-change of authority which the poem enacts. This blurring is most evident at the moments of pausing and resumption that occur between the six cantos. Each canto ends with a switch back into regular octosyllabics to mark the fact that the diegesis has been resumed; each ensuing canto reverts to the Christabel metre, but the minstrel takes the opportunity for some more general prologue-like or invocatory verses before taking up the narrative of the lay. The most famous of these verses – indeed, doubtless the most famous lines of the poem – occur at the beginning of Canto

Sixth, when the bard has been provoked by the ladies of the court asking him whether he would not make a better living south of the Border. He replies with the following invocation, which begins the final section of the poem:

> Breathes there the man, with soul so dead,
> Who never to himself hath said,
>   This is my own, my native land!
> Whose heart has ne'er within him burn'd,
> As home his footsteps he hath turn'd,
>   From wandering on a foreign strand!
> If such there breathe, go, mark him well;
> For him no Minstrel raptures swell;
> High though his titles, proud his name,
> Boundless his wealth as wish can claim;
> Despite those titles, power, and pelf,
> The wretch, concentred all in self,
> Living, shall forfeit fair renown,
> And, doubly dying, shall go down
> To the vile dust, from whence he sprung,
> Unwept, unhonour'd and unsung.
>
>   (p. 35)

It is hard to distinguish this from the voice of Scott himself; it has an especial reference in the heightened patriotic atmosphere of 1805. It can be described as an anti-Jacobin poem, inviting the reader to 'mark' the man who fails to make the connection between love of an immediate familiar landscape and a wider patriotism. But there is also a subdued reference to the scene of recitation; for 'Minstrel raptures swell' specifically for those listeners who make an untroubled connection between self and country – who participate, in fact, in that organic national situation that the moment of recitation enacts. The passage suggests, in short, an intimate relation between minstrelsy and patriotism which is underwritten by the scene of recitation in the past, and continues into the moment of patriotic crisis in the present.

The national dimension of this is complicated by the minstrel's immediate specification of his patriotism as directed to Scotland; indeed it had been provoked by the ladies' suggestion of England as a possible prosperous home for his last years:

> O Caledonia! Stern and wild,
> Meet nurse for a poetic child!

> Land of brown heath and shaggy wood,
> Land of the mountain and the flood,
> Land of my sires! What mortal hand
> Can e'er untie the filial band,
> That knits me to thy rugged strand!
> Still, as I view each well-known scene,
> Think what is now, and what hath been,
> Seems as, to me, of all bereft,
> Sole friends thy woods and streams were left;
> And thus I love them better still,
> Even in extremity of ill.
> By Yarrow's streams still let me stray,
> Though none should guide my feeble way;
> Still feel the breeze down Ettrick break,
> Although it chill my wither'd cheek;
> Still lay my head by Teviot Stone,
> Though there, forgotten and alone,
> The Bard may draw his parting groan.
>
> (p. 35)

Again the interchange between past and present moments is complicated, not least by the modernity of the sentiments here – Scott's contemporaneous dismissal of *Ossian* on the grounds of anachronism is relevant to his own imagining of a Border minstrel articulating the sentiments of a Lake poet. Still more significantly, the landscape he evokes here is of course Scott's own, though not so closely associated with him at this point in his career; this section of the poem serves to elide the difference between the last minstrel and Scott himself and thus tries to appropriate the authority of the bardic tradition for the modern poet.

The national question remains a troubling one, however, and will be a troubling aspect of Scott's inheritance in the nineteenth century, though other poems and the novels will suggest a powerful way of resolving it. Broadly speaking the difficulty is this: the logic of a poem like *The Lay of the Last Minstrel* and indeed of the *Minstrelsy of the Scottish Border* is to suggest a specifically local, Border or Scottish, national context for the poetry, while Scott also wishes to assert a wider British patriotism. In the particular context of this poem he fails to resolve this difficulty, and the invocation to Caledonia remains unchallenged, or unincorporated into any wider unity; elsewhere, and especially in *The Lady of the Lake*, Scottishness will be associated with a bardic, glamorous and potentially epic past.

In *The Lay of the Last Minstrel*, then, Scott seeks to achieve two potentially contradictory aims: to dramatise a moment of historical transition, when the social order or 'manners' which sustained minstrelsy definitively passed away; and to claim the authority of that bardic tradition in the present moment, a claim that naturally pushes him to eliding the historical distance he has been at pains to establish. The epic primitivist presumptions which underlie his understanding of popular poetry – epic, ballad and romance – have as a necessary consequence this gulf between the poetry of the past and the present moment, and it is around this gulf that the poem revolves.

The Lay of the Last Minstrel was Scott's first extended poem, and his first commercial success; it can be described as an act of local and familial patriotism, commemorating the deities of the Scott family and the Border landscape. The other of his long poems in which the figure of the bard plays a central role is *The Lady of the Lake*, published five years after *The Lay of the Last Minstrel* in 1810. By contrast with both the latter poem and *Marmion* (1808), *The Lady of the Lake* is a poem set in the Highlands, and concerns the society of the clans in the sixteenth century – an evidently more propitious context for the claims made on behalf of the origins of popular poetry by Scott as heir to the philosophical historians. Indeed, it is in the later poem that we can see laid down that generic map of the world which will be developed in *Waverley* and which associates epic with the heroic past and consequently with those regions of the world where the social forms of barbarous or heroic society persist.

The narrative of the poem consists of the adventures of King James V of Scotland as he makes his way in disguise through the Perthshire Highlands. Most of the interest of the poem comes from the depiction of Highland manners produced by Scott; he is careful to provide an almost ethnographic account of clan society. Thus in the second canto he describes the gathering of the clan on Loch Katrine (the lake of the title); the boatmen, as they row across the lake, sing an appropriate song:

> Hail to the Chief who in triumph advances!
> Honour'd and bless'd be the ever-green Pine!
> Long may the tree, in his banner that glances,
> Flourish, the shelter and grace of our line!
>   Heaven send it happy dew,
>   Earth lend it sap anew,
> Gayly to bourgeon, and broadly to grow,
>   While every Highland glen
>   Sends our shout back agen,
> 'Roderigh Vich Alpine dhu, ho! ieroe!'[13]

This last line is duly provided with a footnote by Scott explaining the use of patronymics in patriarchal societies such as that of the Highland clans. So here is a scene indeed full of romantic interest but grounded on a particular historical understanding of clan society, and producing a 'boat song' that demonstrates both the romance and the ethnography – it is a song which evinces particular clan loyalties to ancient symbols and the patriarchal chief. Of course the fact that it is in English rather than Gaelic renders it less ethnographically correct, though the heavily marked dactyllic rhythm may be read as an equivalent of the presumed Gaelic verse – a particular version of the difficulty of manufacturing modern antiques. In all, then, the poem is enamoured of clan society while seeking to represent their 'manners' in a historically accurate way.

John Sutherland points out that the poem was written on the basis of a tour that Scott made to the Highlands, at exactly the time of the clear-ances;[14] this remarkable ability to assign the glamour of Highland life to the past, while failing to make any connection to its destruction in the present, characterises Scott. It is a kind of bargain: the gentile society of the past (that is, the society of the *gens*) gets the glamour while modernity gets the unromantic prosperity, bought at however painful a cost. Sutherland also attributes the flattering portrayal of clan society to the success of the Highland regiments in the contemporary campaigns in Spain. Whatever the importance of this contemporary factor in influencing the poem, it certainly embodies a view of the clan society of the Highlands which fixes for the nineteenth century the unbreakable association between the Highlands and a heroic past, an association indeed which Scottish writers have been both perpetuating and resisting in equal measure ever since.

The poem is not made up of various diegetic levels in the manner of *The Lay of the Last Minstrel*, though it does repeatedly dramatise the scene of bardic recitation; in fact the poem is continuously interrupted by various songs, laments, ballads and other intradiegetic material. It too, in other words, is preoccupied with the matter of minstrelsy; one of the central characters is the minstrel Allan-Bane, who accompanies the Lady of the Lake and who sings or recites at several key moments in the poem. He is a Lowland bard, but he serves at will the function of heroic memorialist for Highland bravery. As Lowland bard he sings the ballad of 'Alice Brand' in the fourth canto, in a scene where Scott comes nearest to replicating the account of balladry that he had advanced, or was to advance, in his various prose writings; this is indeed an imitation of a traditional ballad, without the interposition of the Christabel metre which Scott had felt necessary for the longer 'lay' of the last minstrel. 'Alice Brand' is in a more familiar ballad metre:

> Up spoke the moody Elfin King,
> Who wonn'd within the hill, –
> Like wind in the porch of a ruin'd church,
> His voice was ghostly shrill.
>
> (p. 137)

Even here, in a stanza chosen to demonstrate the element of straight-forward ballad-imitation that characterises 'Alice Brand', one can note the essential modernity of the third line of the stanza; that simile is a piece of self-conscious Gothicism unlikely to be found in any historical ballad.

If the singing of 'Alice Brand' is to be read as Allen-Bane performing his function as Lowland minstrel, the recitation in the final canto, which accompanies Roderick's death, brings the poet nearer to heroic mem-orialist or bard of clan society. The only battle in the poem is here described; in this section Scott approaches most closely a heroic idiom cognate with epic. It is a remarkable set-piece in the poem and is indeed one of the few occasions in Scott's poetry when he attempts an account of a battle – *Marmion*, subtitled 'A Tale of Flodden Field', had famously relegated the battle itself to a small section of the poem. This, then, is Scott in full heroic mode:

> Bearing before them, in their course,
> The relics of the archer force,
> Like wave with crest of sparkling foam,
> Right onward did Clan-Alpine come.
>   Above the tide each broadsword bright
> Was brandishing like beam of light,
>   Each targe was dark below;
> And with the ocean's mighty swing,
> When heaving to the tempest's wing
>   They hurl'd them on the foe.
>
> (p. 156)

While this is broadly octosyllabic, the variations in rhythm and metre allow Scott to attempt heroic elevation, at the same time as including some archaic indications which mark this out as an 'unpremeditated lay' in full minstrel fashion. Even the epic simile ('Like wave with crest of sparkling foam') is muted and avoids the full elaboration of neoclassical verse. In short, Scott is once again involved in the manufacture of a modern antique, but he has achieved here whatever genuine *élan* the pastiched idiom permits.

So while the poem enacts a theory of epic minstrelsy, it is also possible to consider it in its entirety as a kind of degraded or romantic epic. It has several of the features of an epic poem: the gathering of the clan; the single combat; the games; the disguised hero. On the other hand, its plot is at best desultory; the only battle is based on a mistake, and there is no particular reason for the clan to gather at all. And some of the plot elements are absurd – all the male principals (the Douglas, Roderick Dhu and the King) spend much of the poem in disguise. Indeed the desultoriness of the poem rather underlines this account of it as epic than otherwise; the poem is on its way to transforming the multiple ballad and romance materials of traditional poetry into the connected art-work of the epic but finally fails to achieve this ambition.

The Lady of the Lake concludes with its author bidding farewell to the 'Harp of the North':

> Harp of the North, farewell! The hills grow dark,
>   On purple peaks a deeper shade descending;
> In twilight copse the glow-worm lights her spark,
>   The deer, half seen, are to the covert wending.
> Resume thy wizard elm! The fountain lending,
>   And the wild breeze, thy wilder minstrelsy;
> Thy numbers sweet with nature's blending,
>   With distant echo from the fold and lea,
> And herd-boy's evening pipe, and hum of housing bee.
>
> (pp. 159–60)

This sets the writing of the poem in the present, albeit a contemporary landscape refracted through a Gray-like melancholy. The 'Harp of the North' has a double referent: both to Allen-Bane's harp which has been so prominent in the poem, and to Scott's own 'harp', the task that he has just performed in his capacity as modern minstrel both seeking bardic authority and conscious of his inevitable distance from that role. The crepuscular melancholy of these lines marks not only the poem's conclusion but also provides the appropriate note by which to sound the passing of the Highland world which the poem had celebrated – at once enchanting, mournful and definitively past:

> Receding now, the dying numbers ring
>   Fainter and fainter down the rugged dell,

And now the mountain breezes scarcely bring
  A wandering witch-note of the distant spell –
And now, 'tis silent all! – Enchantress, fare thee well!

(p. 160)

What *The Lady of the Lake* provides for its readers, in short, is a particular generic map of the world, and in doing so it provides an affective history and geography also. The 'North' of the poem is a region of faded glamour, which is based on a particular and ethnographically established history. The price to pay for a prosperous modernity is a permanent and melancholy exclusion from that affectively charged past.

CHAPTER 3

Epic Translation and the National Ballad Metre

MACAULAY, MAGINN AND THE NATIONAL BALLAD METRE

Scott's relationship to popular poetry in *The Lay of the Last Minstrel* and *The Lady of the Lake* was partly conditioned by his own activity as collector and editor of ballads in *Minstrelsy of the Scottish Border* in 1802–3; this volume is itself one of the key documents in the revival of interest in traditional and non-elite forms that dates from Percy's *Reliques of Ancient English Poetry* in 1765. This important cultural current is contemporaneous with the developing Homeric controversy and shares some of the same assumptions. If the Homeric epics were made up of a combination of earlier lays, then those lays were presumably the equivalent of the ballads being rediscovered on the Borders. More than this; just as the *Iliad* emerged from an earlier, heroic, stage of human society, so the ballads too came out of the rough and primitive conditions of a society dominated by violence, feuding and warfare. This suggestive equivalence between the Border ballads and the pre-Homeric lays became the basis for a style of Homeric translation whose most notorious practitioner was Francis Newman.

Newman's predecessor in this line was the Irish author and journalist William Maginn; his *Homeric Ballads*, originally published in *Fraser's Magazine* (which he founded), were republished together, posthumously, in 1850. The topics of Maginn's ballads were taken from the *Odyssey*, and he used a variety of popular metres to set them; here is an example in ballad metre proper called 'The Return from Troy':

> [The tables were set where the salt-sea shore
>   Was washed by the flowing brine,]
> And all the guests, when the feast was o'er,
>   Were filled with meat and wine.
> Then the Knight of Gerene said, 'Tis fit
>   That we should truly hear

48

> Who are the guests that among us sit,
> Since now they are full of cheer'.[1]

This is preceded by a note in which Maginn sets out his reasons for choosing ballad forms for his translation. He is critical of Pope's translation because the age of *esprit* is so distant from the age of Homer. He continues:

Since that time we have had another school. We have found, that what chivalry inspired might be what the grammarians and men of *goût* rejected. *So we got back to Homer.* The *truly* classical and the *truly* romantic are one. The moss-trooping Nestor reappears in the moss-trooping heroes of Percy's reliques, and those whom those reliques inspired. (pp. 88–9)

– namely, Walter Scott himself. So there follows a long quotation from the *Lay of the Last Minstrel*, praised as 'Nestorian and Homeric' (pp. 89–90).

Newman's decision to opt for a version of the ballad metre for his translation – soon to be discussed – is therefore far from arbitrary or unprecedented. It derives from the epic primitivist view of Homer which, as we have seen, saw him as emerging from an earlier and indeed primitive stage of society; epic primitivism could see in the Border Ballads particularly a close cultural equivalent to the Homeric social and cultural milieu. This historicist position was certainly at stake in the controversy over Homeric translation between Arnold and Newman; while it may not be the case that it was the predominant view of Homer in the first half of the nineteenth century, it was certainly sufficiently prominent to inform writing other than Maginn's and Newman's.[2] It lies behind, for example, Macaulay's extraordinary pastiche, *Lays of Ancient Rome*, published in 1842. Along with most other nineteenth-century attempts at an heroic idiom, this long survived in school-room anthologies but was fatally wounded as serious poetry by the prodigious cultural effects of the First World War – a point to be discussed more fully in a later chapter.[3] The poems emerge directly, however, from the same aesthetic that informs Newman's translation, and from the same theory of epic primitivism. Macaulay makes clear in his Preface the very particular circumstances which he envisions surrounding the production of the four Roman lays – and the choice of title is significant, because it precisely alludes to songs of a traditional type. He presupposes these poems to have been written in the idiom of a pre-classical Latin poetry now lost, and indeed lost in Roman classical times also. Furthermore, all human societies are presumed to have gone through a similar stage in which traditional stories of a legendary and heroic type provide the subjects of national recitation.

Macaulay thus quotes examples from around the world (many from ethnographic sources), concluding thus:

This species of poetry ... attained a still higher degree of excellence among the English and the Lowland Scotch, during the fourteenth, fifteenth, and sixteenth centuries. But it reached its full perfection in ancient Greece; for there can be no doubt that the great Homeric poems are generically ballads, though widely distinguished from all other ballads, and indeed from almost all other human compositions, by transcendent sublimity and beauty.[4]

While it is true that the admission of so massive a distinction between Homer and the other writers of ballad poetry certainly distinguishes Macaulay from Newman or Maginn, the insistence on the generic identity of Homer to traditional recited forms puts him nevertheless in the same camp. It is inevitable, therefore, that the idiom that Macaulay chooses for his heroic lays should be that of the national ballad metre, as in the following extract from 'Battle of the Lake Regillus':

> Herminius beat his bosom:
> 　But never a word he spake.
> He clapped his hand on Auster's mane:
> 　He gave the reins a shake,
> Away, away, went Auster,
> 　Like an arrow from the bow:
> Black Auster was the fleetest steed
> 　From Aufidus to Po.
>
> 　　　　　　　　　　　(p. 94)

The oddness of Macaulay's project appears in these lines, in which the metre and the diction of the Border Ballads is combined with Latin proper names; but it is explicable if understood as a very particular scheme indeed, in which the modern reader is to see the poems as providing an English equivalent to what this now lost national Roman poetry would have been like – so justifying the description of the *Lays* as a pastiche. In reading these poems, the modern reader is to have an equivalent experience as a Roman of the classical period would have had in reading the (actually lost) poetic fragments of the Roman state's early history.

NEWMAN AND ARNOLD ON HOMERIC TRANSLATION

Preceding Newman's choice of ballad metre for his translation, therefore, was a whole scholarly and poetic tradition, and some of its habitual contentions appear both in the introduction to the translation and in his reply to Arnold's lectures, in which his version had been repeatedly ridiculed. Thus Newman writes:

The style of Homer is direct, popular, forcible, quaint, flowing, garrulous, abounding with formulas, redundant in particular and affirmatory interjections, as also in grammatical connections of time, place, and argument. In all these respects it is similar to the old English ballad, and is in sharp contrast to the polished style of Pope, Sotheby, and Cowper, the best known translators of Homer.[5]

Certain technical consequences follow from this decision: how best do you find a metrical equivalent to the hexameter? To which the answer is an unrhymed long line of four plus three beats (i.e. ballad metre), with an extra syllable thrown in to make up the deficiency that the absence of rhyme would create in an otherwise faithful reproduction of ballad metre. The rationale for this decision, however, is what matters; Newman wants a measure which will reproduce the 'moral genius' of Homer (p. v); as he writes, 'the entire dialect of Homer being essentially archaic, that of a translation ought to be as much Saxo-Norman as possible, and owe as little as possible to the elements thrown into our language by classical learning' (p. vi). Thus his problem is to find for the middle of the nineteenth century a style which will reproduce the same effect of anti-quity as the original does – a point to be pursued in the controversy with Arnold. Thus:

I am not concerned with the *historical* problem, of writing in a style which actually existed at an earlier period of our language; but with the *artistic* problem of attaining a plausible aspect of moderate antiquity, while remaining easily intelligible. Now, in doing this, I alight on the delicate line which separates the *quaint* from the *grotesque*. I ought to be quaint; I ought not to be grotesque. (p. x)

This is capable of even more extreme formulation, as when Newman asserts that he ought 'to retain every peculiarity of the original, so far as I am able, *with the greater care, the more foreign it may be,* – whether it be matter of taste, of intellect, or of morals' (p. xvi). In pursuit of this ideal of creating a sense of the foreignness and antiquity in the translation, he goes to the remarkable length of prefacing his translation with a glossary of the obsolete English words that he has used in the course of it.

Lawrence Venuti has helpfully discussed these matters in *The Trans-lator's Invisibility* and suggested a distinction between 'foreignising' and 'domesticating' styles of translation.[6] Newman's translation appears as a prime example of the 'foreignising' and historicist mode; that is, it seeks to make the poem seem strange rather than familiar to its readers, and thus resist its too-ready assimilation to models of a universal human nature whose primary exemplars are to be found in the here and now. Newman's decision to translate Homer into an English which itself needs a glossary is only odd if seen in the light of an ideology which privileges the active suppression of national and historical difference.

We can add to this analysis by noticing that Newman's practice as a translator evokes the problem of pastiche in an especially explicit way. Like Scott in his 'manufacture of modern antiques', Newman sees his problem as creating for the reader a 'plausible aspect of moderate antiquity'. So it is a complicated frame of mind that Newman seeks to create; readers are to recognise, as they read, the equivalence between their experience of reading poems like the Border Ballads and the experience of reading Homer. The equivalence between the historical character of pre-modern Britain and Homeric Greece is to be constantly evoked by the translation.

Given these notions, what sort of verse did Newman produce? The following lines give the famous exchange between Achilles and his two immortal horses at the end of Book 19 of *The Iliad*; they are set out as originally published, each line consisting of a four-stress and three-stress half, the gap between them typographically indicated, having the effect of a strongly marked caesura in a seven-stress line:

'*Chestnut* and *Spotted*, noble pair!   Far-famed brood of *Spry-foot*!
In other guise now ponder ye   your charioteer to rescue
Back to the troop of Danaï   when we have done with battle:
Nor leave him dead upon the field,   as late ye left Patroclus'
  But him the dapple-footed steed   under the yoke accosted,
And droop'd his auburn head aside   straight way; and thro' the yoke-strap
His full mane falling by the yoke   unto the ground was streaming:
(Him Juno, whitearm'd Goddess, now   with voice of man endowed:)
  'Now and again we verily   will save, and more than save thee,
Dreadful Achilles! Yet on thee   the deadly day o'erhangeth.
Not ours the guilt; but mighty God   and stubborn fate are guilty
Not by the slowness of our feet   or dulness of our spirit
The Troians did thy armour strip   from shoulders of Patroclus;
But the exalted God, for whom   brighthair'd Latona travail'd,
Slew him amid the foremost ranks,   and glory gave to Hector.

Now we, in scudding, pace would keep	even with breeze of Zephyr,
Which speediest they say to be:	but for thyself 'tis fated
By hand of hero and of god	in mighty strife to perish.'
So much he said: thereon his voice	was by the Furies stopped.
To him Achilles, fleet of foot,	responded, sore disdainful:
'*Chestnut*! Why bodest death to me?	from thee this was not needed.
Myself right surely know also,	that 'tis my doom to perish,
From mother and from father dear	apart, in Troy; but never
Pause will I make of war, until	the Troïans be glutted.'
He spake, and yelling, held afront	the singlehoofed horses

(pp. 345–6)

This is perhaps surprisingly effective; it is certainly rapid and flowing, though certain other characteristics meant that it especially appalled Arnold. At all events, Newman's use of ballad metre is part of the effort to reproduce the 'moral genius' of the original (he recurs to the phrase), and the context for this effort is the post-Enlightenment effort to view Homer as emerging from a primitive stage of society, for which the British equivalent is to be found in the Border Ballads. Walter Scott – 'by far the most Homeric of our poets' according to Newman (p. v) – makes an inevitable appearance in this connection.

Arnold's reaction to this comes in the context of a wider discussion of the *desiderata* for translating Homer. He advances four characteristics of the poet by which translations can be measured: 'he is eminently rapid'; 'he is eminently plain and direct ... in his syntax and his words'; 'he is eminently plain and direct in the substance of his thought'; 'he is eminently noble'.[7] Arnold does not, of course, only discuss Newman's translation; he also takes under review the translations of Chapman, Pope, Cowper and the later versions which scarcely deviate from the practice of the latter two. When he turns to Newman's version, however, it is above all the lack of nobleness that he uses to indicate its inadequacies. And this, indeed, is the main line of attack which he takes against the whole scholarly and cultural tradition that leads from the eighteenth century through Scott and his followers – for he also criticises Maginn and protests against the notion that Scott might be thought of as Homeric. What he objects to, at bottom, is just that notion of epic primitivism which underlies Newman's translation; he wants to find a poetic mode which is capable of reproducing those four characteristics of Homer without any distracting sense of quaintness, antiquity, or historical distance.

Arnold devotes the second half of his second lecture to disputing the notion that there is any equivalence between the genuine epic of Homer

and ballad poetry. He concedes that there may have been some value in
the comparison when it was used to discredit the artificial manner of
Pope and his school; but clearly for him the argument has been pulled
much too far in this direction, and he insists that the ballad manner and
the ballad measure are actually 'ten thousand times' less capable of the
grand manner than, especially, Milton. Newman's translation is only the
most egregious example of a widespread mistake: 'Homer's manner and
movement are always both noble and powerful: the ballad-manner
and movement are often either jaunty and smart, so not noble; or jog-trot
and humdrum, so not powerful' (p. 129).

Thus Arnold can make all sorts of incidental fun at the expense of
Newman's diction, at the absurdity of his deliberate archaisms; but it is
exactly the contention that ballad measure could *at all* be the carrier of
the 'moral genius' of Homer that he finally denies. In the broadest terms
we can characterise the difference between Arnold on the one hand and
the epic primitivists on the other as that between a humanist assertion of
possible continuity from the ancient world to the present and the
recognition that there is an unbridgeable historical gulf dividing then and
now.[8] Arnold seeks to find an idiom which, though distinctively poetic
and 'noble', nevertheless does not jar modern readers into any sense of the
fundamental difference dividing them from the distant past, while
Newman is insistent on the absolute antiquity of Homer and seeks to find
a poetic idiom which will constantly remind the modern reader of that
antiquity.

There are a couple of points at which Arnold's line of argument
appears to waver, or at least where he makes concessions which force him
into some interesting formulations. At one point he quotes Goethe to the
effect that reading Homer is a reminder that 'in our life here above
ground we have, properly speaking, to enact Hell' (p. 102) – which
Arnold cites to counteract a specifically Ruskinian sentimentalism with
respect to Homer. It is hard to insist on the 'nobility' of the poetry,
perhaps, in the face of such a recognition. At another moment, when he is
seeking to deny the equivalence between Homeric epic and ballad, he
quotes Maginn's characterisation of Nestor, which I quoted earlier, as the
'moss-trooping Nestor' (p. 135). So:

Therefore to call Nestor the 'moss-trooping Nestor' is absurd, because, though
Nestor may possibly have been much the same sort of man as many a moss-
trooper, he has yet come to us through a mode of representation so unlike that of
Percy's *Reliques*, that instead of 'reappearing in the moss-trooping heroes' of

these poems, he exists in our imagination as something utterly unlike them, and as belonging to another world. (p. 135)

This is surely a strong line of argument. It concedes the historical basis of the view that the social world of Greek epic might indeed resemble that which created the Border Ballads, but shifts the argument onto the 'mode of representation'. Such a contention is far from the unthinking humanism of contemporary caricature. Nevertheless, this position can perhaps only be sustained by unduly divorcing mode of representation from its historical ground, as though the genius of Homer had somehow hit on a mode unreachable to humanity in similar social states elsewhere in the world. It is therefore apt to rely too much on the notion of Homeric (or perhaps Greek) 'genius'; despite this, Arnold arrives at a position which enables him to encompass both a sense of the historical location of the Homeric epics and an appropriate attention to their style.

I quoted a section of Newman's translation to indicate where his principles led him; here is the same passage as translated by Arnold. For various reasons, he fixes on the hexameter as the poetic measure best able to allow the four Homeric characteristics. He offers a small number of passages as specimens, doing so, one should say, with due modesty. Thus:

> 'Xanthus and Balius both, ye far-famed seed of Podarga!
> See that ye bring your master home to the host of the Argives
> In some other sort than your last, when the battle is ended;
> And not leave him behind, a corpse on the plain, like Patroclus.'
> Then, from beneath the yoke, the fleet horse Xanthus addressed him:
> Sudden he bowed his head, and all his mane, as he bowed it,
> Streamed to the ground by the yoke, escaping from under the collar:
> And he was given a voice by the white-armed Goddess Hera.
> 'Truly, yet this time will we save thee, mighty Achilles!
> But thy day of death is at hand; nor shall we be the reason –
> No, but the will of heaven, and Fate's invincible power.
> For by no slow pace or want of swiftness of ours
> Did the Trojans obtain to strip the arms from Patroclus;
> But that prince among Gods, the son of the lovely-haired Leto,
> Slew him fighting in front of the fray, and glorified Hector.
> But, for us, we vie in speed with the breath of the West-Wind,
> Which, men say, is the fleetest of winds; 't is thou who art fated
> To lie low in death, by the hand of a God and a Mortal.'
> Thus far he; and here his voice was stopped by the Furies.
> Then, with a troubled heart, the swift Achilles addressed him:

'Why dost thou prophesy so my death to me, Xanthus? It needs not.
I of myself know well, that here I am destined to perish,
Far from my father and mother dear: for all that, I will not
Stay this hand from fight, till the Trojans are utterly routed.'
So he spake, and drove with a cry his steeds into battle.

(pp. 166–7)

If there were some absurdities in Newman's version, this too is not without
its difficulties, because in his desire to avoid the commonplace or the jog-
trot, Arnold seems to me to have fallen into the most inert academicism.

It can be compared also with the Earl of Derby's translation, written in
a rather casual blank verse, but retaining a broadly neoclassical manner
which is exactly what the ballad-Homers most disliked:

> 'Xanthus and Balius, noble progeny
> Of swift Podarge, now in other sort
> Back to the Grecian ranks in safety bear,
> When he shall quit the field, your charioteer;
> Nor leave him, as you left Patroclus, slain.'
>   To whom in answer from beneath the yoke
> Xanthus, the noble horse, with glancing feet:
> Bowing his head the while, till all his mane
> Down from the yoke-band streaming, reach'd the ground;
> By Juno, white-arm'd Queen, with speech endued:
>   'Yes, great Achilles, we this day again
> Will bear thee safely; but thy day of doom
> Is nigh at hand; nor we shall cause thy death,
> But Heav'n's high will, and Fate's imperious pow'r.
> By no default of ours, nor lack of speed,
> The Trojans stripp'd Patroclus of his arms:
> The mighty God, fair-hair'd Latona's son,
> Achiev'd his death, and Hector's vict'ry gain'd.
> Our speed of foot may vie with Zephyr's breeze,
> Deem'd swiftest of the winds; but thou art doom'd
> To die, by force combin'd of God and man.'
> He said; his farther speech the Furies stay'd.
> To whom in wrath Achilles swift of foot:
> 'Xanthus, why thus predict my coming fate?
> It ill beseems thee! Well I know myself
> That I am fated here in Troy to die,
> Far from my home and parents; yet withal
> I cease not, till these Trojans from the field
> Before me fly.' He said, and to the front
> His war-cry shouting, urg'd his fiery steeds.[9]

This too has its own strengths, but the persistence of certain classicisms in both diction and word-order means that this remains a translation within the broad neoclassical tradition from which Maginn and Newman had been trying to escape.

Arnold's lecture, when it was published, clearly drew blood; Newman replied to it with a pamphlet called *Homeric Translation in Theory and Practice: A Reply to Matthew Arnold, Esq.*, in which some of the arguments that I have already rehearsed were given a further airing. Arnold in turn replied to the reply, in the final section of the book *On Translating Homer* as it is now published. Several aspects of this controversy deserve further elucidation: the way that Arnold sets up the debate as one between the critic and the scholar; the manner in which Newman manages to insinuate that this is a debate about masculinity; and the less ideologically charged but central question of how to reproduce in the contemporary reader the same impression as the poetry of Homer would have had on the cultivated Greek of Sophocles' era.

The first two matters are connected in the following quotation from Newman's *Reply*: 'An intelligent child is the second-best reader of Homer. The best of all is a scholar of highly masculine taste; the worst of all is a fastidious and refined man, to whom anything quaint seems ignoble and contemptible.'[10] This is, obviously enough, a hit at Arnold; his problem is that he is insufficiently 'masculine' to appreciate the quaint, rough or barbaric aspects of the poetry. There is a larger question here of the way in which the epic poetry of the ancient world might have figured in the construction of masculine identity in the nineteenth century; but Newman's immediate polemical point in this context is to qualify negatively some of Arnold's defining characteristics as not appropriately masculine – so that to be 'fastidious' and 'refined' is also to disqualify your manliness.

This in turn relates to the way that Arnold essentially concedes the ground of scholarship in order to stand on the supposedly higher ground of criticism. Part of the problem for him is the very existence of the Homeric controversy – he needs to shift the discussion off that ground in order for his appropriation of Homer to have any force. Scholarship almost inevitably has the effect of locking the text back into its originating moment; Arnold's whole project is to release Homer into the contemporary world in a way that cuts off the trail of distracting historical allegiances to the barbarian past. He scarcely attempts to stand on scholarly ground, therefore, although he repeatedly concedes the value of scholarship; rather, he makes his judgments on questions of taste, upon which scholarship can make no claim to finality.

A connection from this point can then be made to one of the most interesting aspects of the controversy, which does indeed turn on critical judgments rather than scholarly ones. Since Newman believes that Homer is absolutely rather than relatively 'archaic', it becomes in practice impossible in the modern world to reproduce his original effect – since the modern world itself can never be 'archaic' by definition. It follows that the best that one can hope for in a translation is to seek to produce in a modern reader the same impact that a reading of Homer would have had on an Athenian of the age of Pericles, to whom epic poetry would have been as antiquated as the Border Ballads are to the nineteenth century. This judgment is one that Arnold has to controvert; he does so by asserting that the Homeric archaisms would have been no more noticeable than some of the poetic mannerisms of contemporary poetry such as the use of 'thou' or the verbal inflection 'eth'. Once again the dispute turns on the question of the 'nobility' of the poetry; for Arnold, the occasional archaism is to be permitted as creating an effect of heightened dignity without compromise to the essential contemporaneity of the poetry; while for Newman the archaism is an indication of the ultimate social and historical alterity of Homer, for his Periclean reader as much as for the nineteenth-century one. Arnold assumes that a language of poetic dignity is available without distracting historicising associations; Newman is caught up in the intractabilities of pastiche, of a language at once invented and antique at the same time.

THE GEOGRAPHY OF THE NATIONAL
BALLAD TRADITION

In following Scott's indebtedness to the philosophical historians and the theory of epic primitivism, and in his poetry, I sought to indicate some of the intellectual and aesthetic grounds of what Raymond Williams would describe as a structure of feeling – one which assigns the affective glamour of epic to the pre-modern world, while remaining unconsoled in a prosperous modernity. But 'Scott' here represents much more than the sum total of his writings; he ought rather to be thought of as providing a crucial cultural problematic for the whole nineteenth century, which enabled people to think and feel the nature of their sense of place and history. His is the unavoidable lens through which these matters are refracted. His 'influence', to that extent, was not only a matter of diverse, myriad, individual appropriations, but more importantly one which provided the ground-rules of an epochal version of the transition to modernity.[11]

But I wish to conclude this chapter by considering two aspects of Scott's inheritance which are especially relevant to this study, and which will lead back to the debate between Arnold and Newman as it turned on the question of the nationality as much as the antiquity of epic. The first is precisely that of the national question: which nation exactly owned the 'national ballad metre'? And the second concerns the ambivalent bestowal of affect or glamour upon a heroic past which is by the same token debarred from entry into modernity.

Early in the twentieth century, Swinburne was to publish a pugnacious edition of ballads – original and imitated – called *Border Ballads*, in which he sought to redress Scott's Scottishness, and to attack Andrew Lang for asserting that poets south of the Tweed had better leave these Scottish popular poems alone.[12] This was only the most combative episode in the war of the ballads, between those who sought to claim English or Scottish origins for them and, with this, rights on the national poetic past. Part of Scott's inheritance, in short, was an entailment of Scottishness upon the 'national muse in her cradle', which was to complicate matters for English poets throughout the century.

One way of understanding this question is to see it as an episode – admittedly a minor one – in the never-ceasing enterprise of nation building. The national question was an open one for the nineteenth century, and the negotiations between notions of Britain, Scotland and England were complicated. Though the structure of feeling that awarded the glamour of an heroic past to a particular version of Scottishness was given form and substance by Scott, the terms of this settlement were necessarily fluid and open to renegotiation. In particular, the nature of both an heroic English and an heroic British past were to remain uncertain in the light of Scott's inheritance; Swinburne's impatient claim on the Englishness of the ballads is but one small instance of the national conflicts that were entailed by *The Minstrelsy of the Scottish Border* and *The Lady of the Lake*. The very specificity of Scott's Scottishness was to leave the question of a national epic open, and in a subsequent chapter I discuss the search for one later in the nineteenth century.

The political ambivalence of the bestowal of affect or glamour on the heroic past of regions where pre-modern social forms persisted longest – the Borders, the Highlands – was a further entailment of Scott's inflection of the epic primitivist problematic as I have described it. For Scott enabled an epic or heroic history to be glimpsed among many of the peoples who were to be forcibly modernised by European imperialism in the course of the nineteenth century. The generic map of the world pioneered by Scott for the islands of Britain would be extended later in the century to encompass the whole planet. Scott's assimilation of distinct Border and Highland histories into a wider narrative of modernity is but a pale reflection of an altogether more brutal *aufhebung* in the actual history. The attribution, and the claim, of an heroic past to the many peoples so subsumed in the course of the nineteenth century will prove problematic, as I shall argue in a later chapter on the fictions of empire at the end of the century; but it nevertheless proved a resource as such peoples resisted their subsumption.

One hint of this large implication can be glimpsed in the Arnold/ Newman controversy. Near the beginning of his *Reply*, Newman makes this statement:

I have the conviction, though I will not undertake to impart it to another, that if the living Homer could sing his lines to us, they would at first move in us the same pleasing interest as an elegant and simple melody from an African of the Gold Coast. (p. 14)

Here epic primitivism takes a different though, as we have seen, a by no means unprecedented direction. It is not only the equivalence between Homeric epic and the 'national ballad metre' (p. 22) that is suggestive; if epic emerges from a primitive or heroic stage of human society, then, as Wood, Ferguson and Grote repeatedly emphasise, the place to seek modern equivalents for that stage will be not only the European past but the 'primitive' world currently undergoing conquest and colonisation. This is not an accidental moment in Newman's argument; he reverts to it later when he suggests, for instance, that Homer's quaintness, and his excessive love of simile, are evidence of 'a disturbance of the logical balance, such as belongs to the lively eye of the savage' (p. 56).

'Savage' and 'barbarian' were carefully distinguished in the more developed forms of philosophical history such as that written by Ferguson; Newman's usage here is casual rather than considered. There are precedents for this casualness; Margaret Rubel argues, for example, that the careful three-stage theory by which humanity progressed from savagery through barbarism to civilisation could co-exist with a cruder binary opposition between the 'rude' and the 'civilized'.[13] Certainly there is a crudeness which permits an equivalence to emerge between the rude society of the recent past in the Borders and the 'savage' of a wholly different anthropological character. Nevertheless, Newman has chosen this example to emphasise the pre-modern character of Homer's poetry in as dramatic a way as possible.

It is unclear how much significance to attach to Newman's choice of the Gold Coast – it may indeed be that he intends a specific reference to the Kingdom of the Ashanti, who were at least slightly known in Britain in the mid-century. It may be on the contrary that his choice here is more accidental and that the African of the Gold Coast stands in as a kind of generic primitive. However, Newman both alludes to an argument that was a staple of the radical side in the Homeric controversy and anticipates some of the modes of representation of the newly colonised peoples of the empire that will become more prominent as the century progressed. Built into that casual-seeming allusion is an equivalence between the epic-producing archaic societies of the ancient world and societies in a similar stage of development nearly three millennia later. When this trope reappears in much later nineteenth-century writing, for example in Rider Haggard's *King Solomon's Mines* (1886), the chosen African race will not be found on the Gold Coast but in the south of the continent among the Zulus – this cultural moment will be discussed in a subsequent chapter. Newman's allusion here has an ambiguous political charge. On the one hand it can be seen as a benign move, since it associates 'primitive' peoples with a high-prestige literary form. On the other hand, it con-tinues to give currency to a view of human history in which other peoples have to pass through various preliminary stages before they reach their consummation in resembling us.

Arnold quotes the phrase about the 'African from the Gold Coast' in his reply to the reply, without dwelling on it, but as further evidence of Newman's absurdity, as though, if he started from such false premises, it were not surprising that he should be led to such ludicrous conclusions. His antipathy to the general position that Newman glances at is a natural consequence of the general case that Arnold argues in *On Translating Homer*: anything that distracts from the essential continuity between the ancient Greek past and the present is to be avoided – and the analogy with contemporary Africans could certainly be seen as one such distrac-tion. Arnold's particular version of humanism is compromised by the analogy because it fails to admit historical difference; Newman's his-toricism is naturally drawn to it.

Built into Newman's translation, and his defence of it, is an implicit notion of modernity, produced out of its difference from the Homeric past. For Arnold too the notion of the modern was central, though it meant something very different for him – both when used as a diagnosis of contemporary ills and also as a permanent possibility in human affairs, a mentality in evidence as much in Sophoclean Athens as in nineteenth-century London. I discuss Arnold's views on these matters, especially as they relate to the possibility of contemporary epic, in a later chapter. In the context of his dispute with Newman, we can note that, far from distinguishing us from the epic past, for Arnold, our modernity, insofar as it links us to the age of Pericles, enables us better to connect with Homer.

I have suggested that it is possible to read the difference between Arnold and Newman as one that distinguishes, broadly, humanist and historicist impulses; scholarship is still caught between these two poles. Indeed, the Homeric controversy, and Arnold's reaction to it, can be seen as one of the testing grounds on which the contours of contemporary debates were first laid down. The very sense of modernity, which underlies our sense of the historical alterity of those texts which emerge from social worlds which precede our own, was in part created out of the recognition of the differences that divide the modern world from Homer. In addition, the historicist method – self-confirming circularity or benign interpretative circle, according to conviction – was most powerfully adumbrated with respect to Homer's poetry, tested against notions of the primitive or barbaric largely derived from that poetry itself.

In passing I suggested that Arnold himself construed this as a battle between scholars and critics – and he had the many years of the Homeric question behind him to remind him of the inadequacy of barren scholarship. This too is a battle that remains unresolved, and here again the Homeric controversy pioneered critical and scholarly differences that remain. For while the controversy turned on the unity or otherwise of the poems, a critical sense was inevitably called in to supplement purely scholarly procedures. Arnold himself was certainly happiest when discussing the poetry in ways which called upon questions of taste and judgment rather than scholarly expertise – or rather, he was obliged by the procedures of his own argument to subordinate scholarship to the higher considerations of criticism. It was over the body of Homer, therefore, that these familiar if intractable interdependencies and hostilities were first articulated.

Finally, the connection that Newman makes to the 'African of the Gold Coast' is one that contemporary scholars are far from likely to dismiss in the manner that Arnold does. In making that connection, Newman was articulating a possibility inherent in epic primitivism that surfaces frequently in the nineteenth century, and whose ambiguous political charge I have briefly indicated. For a simple illustration of the continuing currency of epic primitivism, readers may refer to the cover of Christopher Logue's wonderful version of Homer, where the 'War Music' of Homer is once again made equivalent to that of tribal African society – this time from the East Coast rather than the West, because the picture on the cover is that of a Kikuyu warrior.[14] While it may be that this equivalence emerges more from Faber and Faber than from Logue himself, it nevertheless suggests that the cultural conflicts fought out in the Homeric question, Homeric translation and the national ballad metre are still far from resolved: Newman may have lost the battle, but his successors have perhaps won the war.

CHAPTER 4

The Matter of Britain and the Search
for a National Epic

The previous chapter discussed the matter of translation: how to deal with the inevitable paradoxes created for the translator when dealing with epic material understood as emerging from a stage of society different from that of the present. Some of the same problems emerge, however, when an author seeks to write an original epic, or at least seeks to write in an heroic idiom in a world now defined as categorically unheroic. This is but the outward and visible sign of a deeper perplexity: how to create a national epic, or recast the materials of one, in a modernity that is bound to understand all such efforts as inherently anachronistic.

CARLYLE AND THE IDEA OF A NATIONAL EPIC

I start with the eccentric but unavoidable figure of Thomas Carlyle. Writing in *Past and Present* in 1843, he sought to found a viable vision of the future of 'Britain' (I put the word for the time being in scare quotes) on the capacity of its Captains of Industry (his coinage in this very text) to rediscover a heroic sense of the world beyond the essentially barbaric aim of making money. This will involve, he asserts, the reimposition of order and high purpose on the chaos of existing society:

Difficult? [he asks]. Yes, it will be difficult. The short-fibre cotton; that too was difficult. The waste cotton-shrub, long useless, disobedient, as the thistle by the way-side, – have ye not conquered it; made it into beautiful bandana webs; white woven shirts for men; bright tinted air-garments wherein flit goddesses? Ye have shivered mountains asunder, made the hard iron pliant to you as soft putty: the Forest-giants, Marsh-jötuns bear sheaves of golden-grain; Ægir the Sea-demon himself stretches his back for a sleek highway to you, and on Fire-horses and Wind-horses ye career. Ye are most strong. Thor red-bearded, with his blue sun-eyes, with his cheery heart and strong thunder-hammer, he and you have prevailed. Ye are most strong, ye Sons of the icy North, of the far East, – far marching from your rugged Eastern Wildernesses, hitherward from the gray

Dawn of Time! Ye are sons of the *Jötun*-land; the land of difficulties conquered. Difficult? You must try this thing. Just try it with the understanding that it will and shall have to be done. Try it as ye try the paltrier thing, making of money! I will bet on you once more, against all Jötuns, Tailor-gods, Double-barrelled Law-wards, and Denizens of Chaos whatsoever![1]

We could describe this as Carlyle seeking to re-enchant the world; to redescribe, that is, the disenchanted industrial landscape of modernity so as to make it continuous with an heroic national past. It is indeed a myth of origin that Carlyle provides here; a myth of national origins which, more ambitiously than all of his contemporaries, looks way beyond the Glorious Revolution of 1688; beyond the Protestant Reformation; beyond the Norman Conquest or even the Saxon settlements; beyond the Arthurian legends and the matter of Britain. Beyond all these way-stations Carlyle looks to the far-distant prehistoric past of the Northern and even Indo-European peoples and their presumed migration out of Asia. In short, what Carlyle provides here are intimations of a national epic.

He does this quite consciously, as can be seen from another quotation from *Past and Present*, this time from the book's concluding chapter, 'The Didactic' – though actually Carlyle can never write in any mode which is not didactic. Where, he wants to know, is an heroic life now to be led?

Not on Ilion's or Latium's plains; on far other plains and places henceforth can noble deeds be now done. Not on Ilion's plains; how much less in Mayfair's drawing-rooms! Not in victory over poor brother French or Phrygians; but in victory over Frost-jötuns, Marsh-giants, over demons of Discord, Idleness, Injustice, Unreason, and Chaos come again. None of the old Epics is longer possible. The Epic of French and Phrygians was comparatively a small Epic: but that of Flirts and Fribbles, what is that? A thing that vanishes at cock-crowing, – that already begins to scent the morning air ... (pp. 286–7)

As he puts it elsewhere, what is needed in England now is an epic, not of 'arms and the man', but of 'tools and the man'. Carlyle here implies that it is possible, indeed necessary, to rediscover the heroic virtues in the contemporary world, translated into the idiom of that contemporaneity; this is a task that presents itself to people as they live their lives now, for this is to be an epic that is to be acted out in deeds, not merely sung in verse or told in prose.

Carlyle's insistence on the impossibility of an old-fashioned martial-heroic epic in the contemporary world makes him consistent – unsurprisingly, given his intellectual indebtedness to German Romanticism – with other figures who draw their inspiration from the same source, notably with Karl Marx. This repudiation of the possibility of a contemporary martial epic, moreover, is conjoined with a specific understanding of the epic poetry from the past, and it is to the nexus of ideas that surround such poetry, and their consequences for the nineteenth-century poet, that this chapter is predominantly directed. What exactly are the consequences, for the poet of the period, of the insistent association of epic with the idea of nation? How do the intertwined ideas of epic and nation, and the accompanying tendency to think of epic poetry as primitive national song, affect the attempts at epic by Tennyson and Morris? This association was, after all, a European phenomenon (possibly an American one too); part of the difficulty for poets writing in English was that there was no obvious candidate, among the primary mythical materials available, for them to adopt as the national epic.

Once again, Carlyle provides a good introduction to the phenomenon of the rediscovered national epic, certainly as it concerns Germany. As part of the emergence of German Romantic nationalism, the old German epic stories of the *Nibelungenlied* were rediscovered and promoted at the beginning of the nineteenth century as an authentic epic for the German people. This is how Carlyle sardonically put it in an essay of 1831:

Learned professors lecture on the *Nibelungen* in public schools, with a praise-worthy view to initiate the German youth in love of their fatherland; from many zealous and nowise ignorant critics we hear talk of a 'great Northern Epos,' of a 'German Iliad;' ... the *Nibelungen* is welcomed as a precious national posses-sion, recovered after six centuries of neglect, and takes undisputed place among the sacred books of German literature.[2]

Carlyle's irony, however, is short-lived; by the end of the essay on 'The Nibelungen Lied' he is prepared to concede both that 'a true epic spirit lives in it' and that the stories collected in the *Lied* were indeed 'National Traditions', albeit 'common property and plebeian' (I, 261). Moreover, he contends that, unless the poems of *Ossian* turn out to be authentic, the *Nibelungenlied* are the most ancient poems available to us and thus provide an extraordinary and invaluable glimpse back into a very ancient past. He also contends that they are superior to the poems concerning the Cid in Spain, though he denies that they are indeed as great as Homer.

Mention of the poems of *Ossian* and the *Cid*, however, suggests something of the plethora of national epics that were being rediscovered or, if necessary, invented, at the end of the eighteenth century and the beginning of the nineteenth century. This is also the period which saw the rediscovery of the *Chanson de Roland* in France and of the *Kalevala* in Finland; it seemed as if no self-respecting or aspirant nation could be complete without its own national epic. *Hiawatha* perhaps needs to be added to the list; Longfellow certainly saw himself as writing poems modelled on the Northern *Edda* and was partly inspired by the *Kalevala*. This process is touched upon by David Quint in *Epic and Empire*, a book which mostly concerns the politics of earlier classical and neo-classical epics, but in a chapter on the idea of epic in the nineteenth century Quint recounts how French and German scholars continued the Franco-Prussian war of 1870 on another terrain – by arguing over the respective merits of the *Nibelungenlied* and the *Chanson de Roland*, and what each epic revealed about the national soul.[3]

So the nationalism of the nineteenth century seized upon epics – especially the old vernacular primary epics, if these were available – and made them an expression of the national spirit. How exactly this was achieved clearly differed in different national situations. The rediscovery of the *Nibelungenlied*, as we have seen, coincided with the birth of German nationalism under the impetus of the humiliations of the Napoleonic Wars. The very different national situation in France at the beginning of the nineteenth century can be gauged from the fact that Napoleon himself is said to have carried a copy of the poems of Ossian with him at the Battle of Austerlitz – modelling himself, as befits a child of the Enlightenment, not on Roland but on Alexander, who carried with him a copy of the *Iliad* on his journey of world conquest.

And for those nations struggling to define themselves as such, like Scotland or Finland, the rediscovery of a candidate for national epic was naturally of inestimable value in the process of nation building. Perhaps we need a Gramscian perspective to explain this: a primary epic is useful in the project of nationbuilding, that is in the task of establishing national ideas as the predominant way in which a people or a collection of peoples can understand themselves and their past. This is a *process* because it is permanently subject to challenge or revision as other possible ideas can be invoked to make sense of people and their world.

This matter is complicated, however, by the essentially primitive nature of epic as it came to be understood by epic primitivism – the fact that it is, in Newman's phrase, 'absolutely archaic'. This way of conceiving epic is not necessarily at odds with the nationalising conception that I have sketched in. Indeed, it can seem entirely compatible if one assumes a national or racial continuity between that distant heroic past, the seedbed of epic poetry and the actually existing nationalities of the present nineteenth-century day. Some such assumption underlies Carlyle's prose in the first extract from *Past and Present* that I quoted. But it does mean that the invocation of epic in the present is bound to be overlain with questions concerning the primitivism or essential antiquity of the epic material, and a variety of possibilities in relation to this then present themselves. That is, connections between that ancient heroic past and the present national moment can be based upon notions of racial continuity, or a wider human persistence, or alternatively such connections can be partly repudiated as atavistic.

What then of a national epic for any of the constituent parts of 'these islands'? I choose this awkward formulation as a way of avoiding 'Britain', or England or Scotland or Wales or Ireland. The whole question of Englishness and Britishness has become highly contentious in the light of the swirling controversies over the national question that have erupted in the course of the last twenty-five years – and because we may be witnessing the 'Break-up of Britain', in Tom Nairn's prescient phrase from the 1970s. In terms of historiography also, reflecting these concerns doubtless, the question of the invention of Britain has become a controversial topic. Thus in her influential book from the early 1990s, *Britons: Forging the Nation*, Linda Colley argued that the idea of Britain was essentially an eighteenth-century notion, crucially emerging in the 1740s and forged above all around a confessional – i.e. Protestant – identity; 'Britain' permitted a massive investment on the part of Scots in the British imperial project which in the later eighteenth and early nineteenth centuries was disproportionately officered by Scots. Against this view – or perhaps as a large corrective to it – Raphael Samuel's *Island Stories* (published posthumously in 1998) argued convincingly that the idea of Britain has in fact been repeatedly invented in the course of the history of these islands. It emerged around the time of the 1745 Jacobite rebellion, when the pugnacious sentiments of *Rule Britannia* were composed; a century and a half earlier, at the time of the accession of James I and VI of Scotland; under the Tudors; at the time of Edward III and his military adventures in the North; and indeed the notion of Britain was current in medieval Welsh bardic poetry, hence taking us back to the topic at hand.

The point of this little excursus into contemporary debates is to remind us of the provisional – the forged – nature of notions of nationality, especially of the idea of Britain. It might seem that in the nineteenth century such ideas were more secure than they are now, though in the century of the Act of Union, the Irish Question, the rediscovery of

Welshness and the restaging of the Eistedfoddau, the foundation of the national Association of the Vindication of Scottish Rights and the massive ideological work that had to go into the notion of the British Empire (British, naturally, and not English), this would surely be a mistake. The possibility of a national epic thus entered a charged area where questions of nationality, race and identity collided.

THE SOURCES OF A PRIMARY EPIC FOR BRITAIN

What candidates were there, then, for a national epic in 'Britain' in the nineteenth century? Soon I shall discuss the attempts to *write* a national epic, to make up for the deficiency of the primary material. But first I want to consider the available primary materials themselves, either as they were already cast in epic form or as they appeared to be available for recasting as such. People could look to two widely differing traditions, broadly Celtic and Germanic (though these titles too ought to go into inverted commas) to provide the materials of primary epic of the same order as the *Nibelungenlied* or the *Chanson de Roland*. On the one hand, there were the stories of Celtic tradition; not only the Arthurian materials available through Malory and other sources, but other Celtic narratives newly made available through Lady Charlotte Guest's translation of the *Mabinogion*, first published in 1838. And on the other hand there was a range of 'Germanic' material, both actual Anglo-Saxon poetry including *Beowulf,* but also the newly discovered and translated materials of the primitive North – the various Edda and Sagas that became increasingly available as the nineteenth century progressed, starting with a translation of Friðþjof's saga in 1839, but gaining much wider currency with William Morris's translations of three of the Icelandic sagas in the mid-1870s, *Three Northern Love Stories*.

Celtic or Germanic? What was at stake in this choice? It is important not to get misled in this matter by the subsequent baleful history of racialised accounts of the Nordic, Germanic or Teutonic past, though it is also important to recognise that the nineteenth century's understanding of itself, and indeed the history of the world, came to be overwhelmingly racialised. On the one hand, then, Matthew Arnold could invoke the Celtic spirit as embodied in its literature as an antidote to the bourgeois stolidity of the English. In 'On the Study of Celtic Literature' in 1867, where the Saxons are plodding, reliable and unimaginative, the Celts are spiritual with the qualities of sensibility and nervous exaltation, and have an affinity to the 'spell of the feminine idiosyncrasy'. But, as we shall see when considering Tennyson's use of Celtic material in *Idylls of the King*, the heroic as mediated through this particular prism turns out to have a range of other meanings as well. One obvious difficulty in using the Arthurian cycle as the basis of national epic is, however, ultimately insurmountable – that whatever way you tell the story, Arthur's principal enemies are the Saxons, and no matter how much you soften this by insisting on their paganness, this can never be a story of uncomplicated national or racial continuity for any of the populations of these islands outside of Wales.

This was a point made forcibly by the Christian Socialist J. M. Ludlow in the 1860s, after the publication of the first of Tennyson's *Idylls of the King*. The publication of the poem led him to write a book on the three great medieval epic cycles, though in fact he restricted himself to the Norse and the Carolingian stories. His reasons for repudiating the Arthurian material are interesting:

in its development it is the latest of the three great cycles, and courtly rather than popular, and that in no instance does any whole poem belonging to it rise to the height of a genuine epic. Nor can this be wondered at, since it does not appeal, if I may so speak, to the epical passions of mankind, – patriotism, religious zeal, love, hatred, revenge, – in their singleness or their breadth, but only to the sentiments and to the fancy. We can only make Arthur epical by making him more and more unreal; the only patriotism he appeals to is a microscopic Welsh or Breton patriotism; no religious fervour can be kindled in his favour by making him a Christian hero against certain paynim Saxons, long converted into good Catholics by the time the first minstrel sang of him, in any but a Kymric dialect.[4]

Welsh or Breton people might have excellent reasons for objecting to their patriotism as 'microscopic', and indeed to hearing their languages described as dialects. Nevertheless, Ludlow's point is a strong one; the Arthurian material did not lend itself readily as the basis for a British national epic, precisely because it told of the battles between the ancestors of different populations in these islands.

The Germanic stories, on the other hand, can be invoked for a range of perhaps surprisingly popular and even democratic meanings; in a myth of origin which starts the history of the English people with the Anglo-Saxon forest clearings (as in J. R. Green's 1874 *Short History of the English People*) the Germanic people are the basis of democracy in their folk-motes or trial by jury, and their stories could be made to yield comparable democratic meanings. But other meanings could cluster around these stories also; Vansittart Conybeare, writing an essay on *The Place of Iceland in the History of European Institutions,* again in the 1870s, could assert that 'it is to the seafaring instincts of the [Viking] race that England owes the naval supremacy which has long been her glory, and is still her strength' – so swashbuckling politics and imperialism could take comfort from the old Nordic stories also.[5]

The choice between Celtic and Germanic primary epic material was not, therefore, simply a matter of choosing between mythical racialised histories which would lead uncomplicatedly to 'British' or 'English' national epics. It was *further* complicated by the relative antiquity of the material. We have seen Carlyle invoking Norse mythology to hint at the far distant past of the race. Broadly speaking, the Germanic or Northern material could certainly be understood as emerging from an earlier social state than the Celtic stories. While many of the Icelandic Sagas are rugged familial histories, they also contain what is clearly some very early material in the Eddas, and in the *Volsungasaga* there is a version of the same narrative that is to be found in the German *Nibelungenlied*. In the light of notions of epic primitivism, there is undoubtedly here the stuff of a national epic, emerging from a Barbarian stage of society, with tanta-lising hints of the heroic migrations and battles of the Dark Ages – one of the central characters in the *Volsungasaga*, for example, is Atli, otherwise the historic Attila. By contrast, the Celtic stories, overwhelmingly the Arthurian corpus and the matter of Britain itself, came to the nineteenth century in very much more mediated form – a point made by Ludlow in that quotation above. Not only because of Malory, but also because of all the other medieval retellings, including some parts of the *Mabinogion*, these stories arrived already cast in the form of romance; that is, they are the characteristic tales of a chivalric court culture very different from the epic barbarism carried in places by the Germanic material.

This contrast immediately needs to be complicated, for several reasons. In the first place, there is the constant possibility of the Ossianic material, which may have been controversial, but which indubitably intimated some very ancient heroic material, however much it may have been fab-ricated by Macpherson. Secondly, many of the stories in the *Mabinogion* were not cast as romances, were not indeed Arthurian, but looked as though they contained echoes of primitive, pre-medieval matter. And as far as the Germanic narratives were concerned, these too had been partly mediated by medieval, Christian and romancing intermediaries. But in general it remained the case that for the nineteenth century (and indeed for us now) the Arthurian cycle arrived as a series of romances, while the Northern stories seemed more readily assimilable to an epic model.

WRITING A NATIONAL EPIC: TENNYSON VS. MORRIS

Insofar as anybody might wish to promote any of these stories *as they stood* as the basis for a national epic, this matter of the national and historical location of the narratives was clearly important. But what of those poets who wished to write an epic poem of their own? Does the relative antiquity of the narratives seized upon make much of a difference? Perhaps we should think of the stories themselves as indifferent or entirely malleable and conclude that, for those who sought to write an epic poem in the nineteenth century, it was all a question of the manner or idiom that the poet managed to forge. This was, indeed, the opinion of Matthew Arnold. As we saw in the previous chapter, he conceded that the historical Nestor, for example, may not have been much different from a sixteenth-century moss-trooper celebrated in the Border Ballads but powerfully asserted that Homer's manner had decisively elevated his heroes above the level attained by the balladeers or their nineteenth-century imitators. If, on the contrary, one takes the theories of epic primitivism seriously – that epic emerges from a distinctive barbaric or heroic stage of society – then one would be inclined to argue that chivalric romances come marked with their historical location also. In this case, that material would be far from plastic or indifferent, and whatever the manner adopted, no nineteenth-century poet could make the story of Arthur, Lancelot and Guinevere into an epic equivalent to the story of the *Iliad*, or make the narrative of Sigurd, Regin and Fafnir the Serpent into a romance.

A whole series of issues are raised here. One concerns the very possibility of an heroic idiom in nineteenth-century poetry. There was, after all, no shortage of models for such an idiom, including the neoclassical heroic couplet, Miltonic blank verse and, as we have seen, the so-called national ballad metre, the vogue for which flowed strongly from Percy's *Reliques* in the eighteenth century through Walter Scott and his successors. A second issue concerns the historic weight or centre of gravity of distinctive genres – epic or romance – and the persistence of generic meanings beyond their moment of origin. These avenues are pursued elsewhere in this book; here I contrast the use made of all this potentially epic material by Tennyson and William Morris in, respectively, *Idylls of the King* and *Sigurd the Volsung*.

Idylls of the King is widely familiar and has a substantial scholarly literature devoted to it; Morris's *Sigurd the Volsung* has had less of a readership since its publication in 1876. The following extracts provide a good idea of the contrasting aesthetics ruling both poems. The first passage is from the first of the *Idylls*, 'The Coming of Arthur'; somewhat uncharacteristically, it describes a battle scene (most of the fighting in the poem-sequence concerns either jousts or single combat):

> Thereafter – as he speaks who tells the tale –
> When Arthur reached a field-of-battle bright
> With pitched pavilions of his foe, the world
> Was all so clear about him, that he saw
> The smallest rock far on the faintest hill,
> And even in high day the morning star.
> So when the king had set his banner broad,
> At once from either side, with trumpet blast,
> And shouts, and clarions shrilling unto blood,
> The long-lanced battle let their horses run.
> And now the Barons and the kings prevailed,
> And now the King, as here and there that war
> Went swaying; but the Powers who walk the world
> Made lightnings and great thunders over him,
> And dazed all eyes, till Arthur by main might,
> And mightier of his hands with every blow,
> And leading all his knighthood threw the kings
> Carádos, Urien, Cradlemont of Wales,
> Claudias, and Clariance of Northumberland,
> The King Brandagoras of Latangor,
> With Anguisant of Erin, Morganore,
> And Lot of Orkney. Then, before a voice
> As dreadful as the shout of one who sees
> To one who sins, and deems himself alone
> And all the world asleep, they swerved and brake
> Flying, and Arthur called to stay the brands
> That hacked among the flyers, 'Ho! They yield!'
> So like a painted battle the war stood
> Silenced, the living quiet as the dead,
> And in the heart of Arthur joy was lord[6]

Compare this with another bloody extract taken from *Sigurd the Volsung*; this also comes from near the beginning of the poem, but this time it concerns a king's last battle, not his first. The king in question is Sigmund, Sigurd's father; he has just got married (though he is old) but an ousted suitor is angered and wants to win the bride by force; a battle ensues:

> White went his hair on the wind like the ragged drift of the cloud,
> And his dust-driven blood-beaten harvest was the death-storm's
>   angry shroud,

When the summer sun is departing in the first of the night of wrack;
And his sword was the cleaving lightning, that smites and is hurried
    aback
Ere the hand may rise against it; and his voice was the following
    thunder.
Then cold grew the battle before him, dead-chilled with the fear and
    the wonder:
For again in his ancient eyes the light of victory gleamed;
From his mouth grown tuneful and sweet the song of his kindred
    streamed;
And no more was he worn and weary, and no more his life seemed
    spent:
And with all the hope of his childhood was his wrath of battle blent;
And he thought: A little further, and the river of strife is passed,
And I shall sit triumphant and the king of the world at last.
But lo, through the hedge of the war-shafts a mighty man there came,
One-eyed and seeming ancient, but his visage shone like flame:
Gleaming-grey was his kirtle, and his hood was cloudy blue;
And he bore a mighty twi-bill, as he waded the fight-sheaves through,
And stood face to face with Sigmund, and upheaved the bill to
    smite.
Once more round the head of the Volsung fierce glittered the
    Branstock's light,
The sword that came from Odin; and Sigmund's cry once more
Rang out to the very heavens above the din of war.
Then clashed the meeting edges with Sigmund's latest stroke,
And in shivering shards fell earthward that fear of earthly folk.
But changed were the eyes of Sigmund, and the war-wrath left his
    face;
For that grey-clad mighty helper was gone, and in his place
Drave on the unbroken spear-wood 'gainst the Volsung's empty
    hands:
And there they smote down Sigmund, the wonder of all lands,
On the foemen, on the death-heap his deeds had piled that day.[7]

The contrast between the two poems is, evidently, very considerable, most visibly concerning such technical matters as diction and versification. These, however, are manifestations of a profound contrast: Morris is seeking to provide a nineteenth-century equivalent of the poetry of the heroic ages, while Tennyson is seeking to provide a highly moralised story or set of stories which can prove exemplary in the present day. Tennyson's poetry is mellifluous, aristocratic and melancholy; Morris's is rugged, popular (in a very special sense), and tragic.

As efforts at epic poetry, those technical matters certainly merit attention. Tennyson opts for the 'natural' verse-form for high matter in English, the iambic pentameter; despite his many experiments with quantitative metre, he distrusted the hexameter and wrote a burlesque of the attempts at hexameter translations of Homer which were made after Arnold had recommended the form in his lectures 'On Translating Homer'.[8] Morris by contrast opts for the hexameter, but it is basically dactylic; in addition he makes heavy use of alliterative formulations, which contribute to the archaic impression created by the poetry. Indeed his diction altogether is extraordinary; he naturally eschews latinate vocabulary where possible, but also produces many coinages of his own, most visibly those noun phrases such as 'death-storm', 'war-shaft', 'fight-sheaves', 'spear-wood' and 'death-heap', which are partly nonce coinages, but also allude to Old Norse and Old English poetic kennings. Tennyson's verse, in short, while wonderfully accomplished, basically remains within the predominant tradition in English poetry as it was available in the nineteenth century; Morris was clearly attempting a radical break with that tradition (in this poem at least) and sought to found his poetic practice on allusions to an older and more popular (i.e. not learned) style.

A further contrast is immediately apparent if we compare the two poets' alternative uses of the epic simile. Thus Tennyson seeks a simile to enhance the force of Arthur's command to his knights to stop pursuing the defeated enemy:

> Then, before a voice
> As dreadful as the shout of one who sees
> To one who sins, and deems himself alone
> And all the world asleep, they swerved and brake
> Flying, and Arthur called to stay the brands
> That hacked among the flyers, 'Ho! They yield!'

Though this has the outward form of an epic simile, nothing could be more unheroic; the allusion here is to conscience and the moral world, to the inward life of moral decisions, sin and guilt. Morris's similes, by contrast (in the first five lines of the extract), though scarcely developed to the extent usually characteristic of 'the epic simile', nevertheless seek unequivocally to heighten and elevate Sigmund's battle-prowess by allusions to the dramatic phenomena of the natural world; it is not that Sigmund has no inner life but that Morris seeks to find the grounds of comparison from within the heroic world he is seeking to recreate.

The contrast between the two poets extends far beyond these two poems; I have chosen not to counterpose, for example, Morris's 'Defence of Guinevere' with Tennyson's 'Guinevere' from the *Idylls*, though the contrast is striking and both poems were written within a couple of years of each other (Morris's was written first). But their opposite attitudes to Guinevere's transgression is only symptomatic of a whole range of differences, above all in their politics, where Tennyson's conservatism contrasts with Morris's revolutionary socialism (though he was still only an 'advanced liberal' when he wrote *Sigurd the Volsung*). This has a bearing on their choice of a national epic; but it would be possible also to compare the two poets in a different way by considering, instead of *Sigurd the Volsung*, Morris's *The Earthly Paradise*, the massive rescension of poetic stories which include many retold romances as well as some Northern narratives. Nevertheless, the differences between the two poets are strikingly evident when they attempt specifically epic poems.

Yet it may be objected that *Idylls of the King* neither is nor was intended to be an epic poem. It is true that Tennyson himself wished to play down the idea that it might be. He wrote to his American publishers shortly before the publication of the first four poems in the series thus: 'I wish that you would disabuse your own minds and those of others, as far as you can, of the fancy that I am about an Epic of King Arthur. I should be crazed to attempt such a thing in the heart of the 19th century.'[9] This view is the exact corollary of epic primitivism; it partly reflects the impact of a review of 'Morte d'Arthur' by James Sterling in the 1830s. This latter poem had been prefaced by a mock-serious introductory poem called 'The Epic', in which the Arthurian fragment is supposed to be merely one book snatched from the bonfire of a whole twelve-book epic on Prince Arthur, a project hedged about with uncertainty also:

> 'Why take the style of those heroic times?
> For nature brings not back the Mastodon,
> Nor we those times; and why should any man
> Remodel models? These twelve books of mine
> Were faint Homeric echoes, nothing-worth'[10]

For all its self-deprecation, these lines here do actually amount to saying that 'Morte d'Arthur' is a fragment of an epic. Tennyson's very uncertainty about styling the poem an epic, then, is based not upon modesty about his own powers but about the anachronism of such a project.

On the other hand, Hallam Tennyson unequivocally referred to the whole sequence as an epic in his chapter on the *Idylls* in the *Life*, while

Tennyson's brother-in-law, the classical scholar Edmund Lushington, was unhappy with the designation 'idylls' and suggested 'epylls or little epics' instead.[11] The question is partly complicated by the protracted composition history of the poems (which extended more or less across the whole of Tennyson's poetic life, since 'Morte d'Arthur', which eventually became the final book, was one of his earliest poems). This in turn is related to the fact that the poem obviously brings together a number of different stories which can be quite successfully read on their own. I do not wish to enter the scholarly controversy over the 'unity' or otherwise of the poem-sequence, since the question of the poem's 'epic' status certainly does not depend on this (that is, 'epic' poetry is not usefully defined as being long and consisting of a unified action – though some of the accounts of the relation between epic and the presumed pre-existing constituent lays would push you in this direction). It is, however, the case that Tennyson was interested in the unity of the whole action, a concern visible in his desire to include stories from the innocent phase of the Round Table to balance out the later stories – a problem for him since 'Guinevere' was one of the first *Idylls* published as such in the late 1850s. In other words, as he continued with the project and tried to weld his disparate narratives together, he was very conscious of the overall narrative shape of the sequence and wanted to ensure that the reader emerged with an appropriately balanced sense of one single progression or direction in the way the successive stories were placed.

It does, nevertheless, seem useful to me to consider the poem as a national epic and ask what consequences flow from viewing it as such. This question can be approached by pointing to those aspects of the poem which do not appear to be 'epic'. I have already alluded to one: that if anything Tennyson is rather embarrassed about the heroic (understood as the martial) virtues. Heroism is constantly to be redefined in moral terms. This leads us to some of the biggest questions about the poem, which are to do with its Christian, theological and allegorical aspects. In fact these turn out to be closely related. The Arthurian cycle becomes thoroughly Christianised by Tennyson – though this was a process which was already underway in the medieval world. We have already seen something of this at work in that short extract quoted earlier, insofar as the poem is centrally concerned with matters of individual moral choice. Still more, there is an understated Christian allegory at work in the poem, by which the figure of Arthur is quietly proposed as a Christ-figure whose ability to redeem the world is betrayed by the treachery of those he loves. This makes the whole poem into a theodicy, an attempt to explain man's fallen state and the presence of evil in the world. Another argument might – instead of comparing *The Idylls of the King* with nineteenth-century efforts to create a national epic from primary epic materials – compare the poem with *Paradise Lost*.

However, these specifically nineteenth-century aspects of the *Idylls* are precisely what make it unlike 'epic' in the heroic sense; and therefore Tennyson's attempt to recast his material in these Christianising and 'moral' ways makes the project of a national epic (if it is such) inevitably into a moral and individualist one.[12] The nation is to form itself not around a martial-heroic sense of its past, or at least only in a very subsidiary way; rather its national story tells of moral heroism but also of the inevitable defeat of high endeavour.

Turning to Morris and *Sigurd the Volsung*, it is easier to make the claim that the poem is to be conceived as a national epic, if only because, though not quite directly in relation to his poetic version of the story, Morris said as much. Before writing the poem, he translated in 1870 the prose *Volsunga Saga*, including in the translation some versions also of relevant Edda where necessary. In the Preface to the translation, he referred to the story as the 'great Epic of the North', and concluded his introduction with the following interesting comments:

In conclusion, we must again say how strange it seems to us, that this Volsung Tale, which is in fact an unversified poem, should never before have been translated into English. For this is the Great Story of the North, which should be to all our race what the Tale of Troy was to the Greeks – to all our race first, and afterwards, when the change of the world has made our race nothing more than a name of what has been – a story too – then should it be to those that come after us no less than the Tale of Troy has been to us.[13]

Morris offers here a characteristically straightforward assertion of epic primitivism and with it the assertion that this primary epic should have the same significance for 'us' that the Tale of Troy had to the Greeks – though he immediately qualifies this with an extraordinary anticipation of 'our' eventual disappearance. This raises the question of who the race is exactly that Morris imagines this story to fit. It is the Great Story of the North – so perhaps it is the common heritage of all the Northern peoples, starting with the Icelanders themselves, in whose language the story is preserved, and extending outwards to include all the Germanic peoples. In case this makes you feel a little queasy, the final anticipation of 'our' eventual disappearance may perhaps restore your equilibrium; the Great Story of the North will in some scarcely imaginable future become the common inheritance of humanity, just as the Tale of Troy has now become. Nevertheless, Morris is certainly intent on offering the story as the material for a national epic, and *Sigurd the Volsung* is his attempt to versify what he describes here as 'an unversified poem'.

What then would it mean for this story, versified in the way that Morris undertakes in *Sigurd the Volsung*, to become a national epic? As I suggested in looking at the extract from the poem, Morris is here attempting something quite different from Tennyson; he is trying to give readers some sense or experience of antique or barbaric poetry. He is, for example, rigorously self-denying in the references he makes to the contemporary (nineteenth-century) world; there is only one moment in which he alludes to the modern age as a comparison. And his poetic practice, as we saw, emphatically eschewed the predominant traditions of English heroic poetry. This is not to say that in any way he is providing, or could provide, the same experience as reading the original Saga or the Edda which it partly incorporates; Morris's poetry can only ever allude to or suggest the poetic practices which they naturally include. But we could nevertheless sum up the differences between the two poets' epics by saying that Tennyson wants his *Idylls* to be morally exemplary, while Morris evokes the barbaric world to insist on its historic distance from modernity.

So while Morris's claim that this is the 'Great Story of the North' would appear to suggest some continuity between that distant past and the present, in fact the almost ethnographic care he takes to recreate the atmosphere and mentality of the heroic age leads, on the contrary, to a sense of its difference, even of its exotic strangeness. Indeed, when the poem was published, the reviews commented overwhelmingly on its violence, finding it more like the stories that were becoming known from different parts of the empire than the dignified epic material with which classically trained nineteenth-century scholars were familiar. And the effect of that exotic strangeness is for the poem to act in some way as an implicit critique of the paltriness of modernity, a standing rebuke to the outcome of the national story whose beginning the poem recounts. The cultural politics of such a gesture, as I have described it, are perhaps ambiguous; shortly after the publication of *Sigurd the Volsung*, however, Morris would commit himself to a revolutionary socialism largely inspired, as he himself admitted, by a hatred of the modern world, and inspired also by the social forms which the barbaric world suggested were at least possible.

'The leading passion of my life has been and is a hatred of modern civilisation'; looking back on his conversion to socialism in the 1890s, Morris would thus describe the state of mind that underlay his rediscovery of hope in a possibility of a transformed future. This is his sense of that modernity:

Think of it! Was it all to end in a counting-house on top of a cinder-heap, with Podsnap's drawing-room in the offing, and a Whig committee dealing out champagne to the rich and margarine to the poor in such convenient portions as would make all men contented together, though the pleasure of the eyes was gone from the world, and the place of Homer was to be taken by Huxley.[14]

I take that closing opposition as more than a casual one; here is another statement of the opposition of epic to modernity, this time with a more thoroughly positive valuation on the epic side of the opposition. It is a moot point whether Morris's understanding of the epic past is properly dialectical – that is, whether his understanding of the passage to socialism via the barbaric past can be genuinely thought of as a dialectical advance or whether it is really no more than an impossible act of nostalgic return. We can nevertheless see the outline of an aesthetic for *Sigurd the Volsung* here, insofar as Morris's evocation of the epic past stands as the positive pole against which 'modern civilisation' is measured and found wanting.

There is an obvious danger of pastiche inherent in the manner that Morris chooses to recreate the epic past. As we have seen, that is a danger which is inherent in the very problematic of epic primitivism as it comprehends the production of new poetry; Morris, perhaps more than any other nineteenth-century writer, was involved in the 'manufacture of modern antiques'.[15] This is less of a risk for Tennyson, largely because he writes in a manner in the *Idylls* which is the continuation of the predominant tradition of educated English poetry. By contrast, Morris's choice of verse-form, his attempt to recreate the effects of an antique mode, inevitably involves him in the problem of pastiche, understood as the imitation of a style without critical distance from it. His consistent refusal to acknowledge the modernity of the moment of composition adds to this sense of the poem as a sustained imitation or recreation of one that should have been written as a primary epic but unfortunately never was. In this respect only, *Sigurd the Volsung* resembles the elaborate pastiches of Macaulay's *Lays of Ancient Rome*.

Nevertheless, Morris inevitably transforms his source material in ways that go beyond the evident necessities laid upon any writer who expands a prose saga into an epic-length poem. This involves both some rationalising and softening of his barbaric material – though the poem remains an extremely bloody one which retains much of the mythic material preserved in the saga. Thus the killing of the nine brothers of Sigmund by a she-wolf as they are held in stocks attached to a massive oak is retained by Morris, along with the eventual killing of the she-wolf by Sigmund. However, this latter is given a more plausible explanation in *Sigurd the Volsung*; whereas in the saga Sigmund kills the wolf by biting her tongue and eventually ripping it from her throat, in the poem the deed is accomplished by simple brute strength. More generally, the poem has a sustained psychological power which is not one of the saga's characteristic effects. So the mutual jealousy and hostility of Brynhild and Gudrun is kept up over a whole book of the poem's four books; this is present in the saga but is scarcely developed as more than a necessary element in moving the plot forward. I am reluctant to say that the poem is therefore 'novelised'; however, it does sustain a sense of psychological depth and complexity which are more characteristically novelistic than epic effects.

This is evident, for example, in the changes that Morris makes to the story in the concluding book, 'Gudrun'. This deals with the slaying of the Niblungs by Atli, and the part played in the slaughter by Gudrun herself, the Niblungs' sister and wife of Atli. In the saga her role is scarcely ambivalent: she is on the side of her brothers, to the extent of arming herself and actually fighting with them against Atli's warriors. In *Sigurd the Volsung*, however, her motivation is far more ambivalent: she continues to harbour massive resentment against her brothers for the slaying of Sigurd, and presides stony-faced over the battle with, and eventual massacre of, the Niblungs. It is not therefore that Morris has modernised the poem by introducing anachronistic psychological motives; rather he has expanded the material to make for artistic effects that are certainly not present in the saga and for which the model could be Shakespeare as much as Homer.

Another aspect of Morris's transformation of the saga is the way that his poem supplies at least suggestions of the society and the economy from which the epic has emerged. In this respect Morris is certainly the heir of the historicising tradition of epic criticism which began in the eighteenth century. Morris supplies a landscape and an implicit ethnography for the people of his poems, both features which are of course absent from the saga. Consider, for example, the following passage, in which Morris imagines a winter landscape and call to arms:

> Now gone is the summer season and the harvest of the year,
> And amid the winter weather the deeds of the Niblungs wear;
> But nought is their joyance worsened, or their mirth-tide waxen less,
> Though the swooping mountain tempest howl round their ridgy ness,

Though a house of the windy battle their streeted burg be grown,
Though the heaped-up, huddled cloud-drift be their very hall-roof's
      crown,
Though the rivers bear the burden, and the Rime-Gods grip and strive,
And the snow in the mirky midnoon across the lealand drive.
But lo, in the stark midwinter how the war is smitten awake,
And the blue-clad Niblung warriors the spears from the wall-nook take,
And gird the dusky hauberk, and the ruddy fur-coat don,
And draw the yellowing ermine o'er the steel from Welshland won.
Then they show their tokened war-shields to the moon-dog and the
      stars,
For the hurrying wind of the mountains has borne them tale of wars.
Lo now, in the court of the warriors they gather for the fray,
Before the sun's uprising, in the moonless morn of day;
And the spears by the dusk gate glimmer, and the torches shine on the
      wall,
And the murmuring voice of women comes faint from the cloudy hall:
Then the grey dawn beats on the mountains mid a drift of frosty snow,
And all men the face of Sigurd mid the swart-haired Niblungs know;
And they see his gold gear glittering mid the red fur and the white,
And high are the hearts uplifted by the hope of happy fight;
And they see the sheathed Wrath shimmer mid the restless Welsh-
      wrought swords,
And their hearts rejoice beforehand o'er the fall of conquered lords:
And they see the Helm of Aweing and the awful eyes beneath,
And they deem the victory glorious, and fair the warrior's death.[16]

Initially we can notice the sheer pleasure in landscape that such writing
expresses; it is a tour-de-force on Morris's part that he can find a suitably
archaic idiom to evoke the winter landscape. In particular, the success of
such conceits as the burg being the location for a 'windy battle', and the
landscape being in the grip of the 'Rime-Gods', is dependent on the
reader's sense at once of these being archaic ideas, and also of them genuinely evoking the harshness of the winter season. Set in this landscape,
Morris is careful to indicate or suggest a particular social organisation, with
its appropriate architecture of hall and burg. Even that classical marker of
elevated diction, noun plus epithet ('dusky hauberk', 'ruddy fur-coat',
'yellowing ermine'), is used to specify some ethnographic detail, as in the
'tokened war-shields' seized by the Niblung warriors.

   Implicit throughout Morris's version of the poem, then, is an understanding of the social roots of primitive epic, an understanding which is
visible not in any modern framing device but in the social landscapes
that are included in the poem, and in a thousand unobtrusive details of

vocabulary. However, while the poem is deeply 'historicist' in this respect, it eschews that simpler historicism which seeks to trace a real history behind mythical or legendary events. You could not tell from Morris's version where in the world the poem is set, nor that the story has been identified with the migrations of the Burgundians, nor that the characters of Gunnar, Atli and Jormunrek can be identified with the historical Gundaharius, Attila and Ermenrichus.[17] It is as though Grote's belief that you cannot trace any historical actuality 'behind' the mythical material of ancient Greece had here been acted upon by Morris in the way that he translates this ancient Germanic material. This is a historicism which seeks to recreate a *geist*, not one which is especially interested in tying the poem down to a 'real' history. Morris even goes so far as to exclude those references which in the saga can be used to give the story more precise geographical locations.

Morris's effort to rewrite the 'Great Story of the North' for the nineteenth century, and thus to provide a national epic, was fraught with difficulties created by the story's antiquity. On the one hand, Morris's hatred of modern civilisation led him to propose the values of epic barbarism as a counterweight to the paltriness and ugliness of the contemporary world. On the other hand, his unwavering historicism led him into a kind of pastiche of primary epic; the poem is undoubtedly a virtuoso exercise in an astonishing idiom, but it is both wonderful and a poetic dead-end. Oddly enough, the embarrassments attendant upon the poem do not accompany Morris's translations (he is the nineteenth century's most prolific translator). Just as in the parallel case of Newman's translation of Homer, the reader can negotiate the archaism of the translations as providing an equivalent of the 'absolutely antique' character of the original poems. But in the case of an original epic, the reader has to understand the archaism as emerging from a particular stage of society and at the same time recognise it as an elaborate exercise in historical reconstruction. There is no doubting the energy and élan, and the extraordinary facility, of Morris as he writes in this mode; it is just that the mode itself is almost self-defeating: no one in the nineteenth century can write a primary epic, just as no one now can be a skald. *Sigurd the Volsung* springs out of this fundamental impossibility, as though the whole poem were in inverted commas or was prefaced by an 'as if'. Later in his life Morris was amused to receive a letter from a German scholar who wanted to know what were his sources for the prose romance *The House of the Wolfings* (1889). Morris was doubtless right to be amused; yet a similar anthropological premise, that this is how matters might have been, underlies the poem as it does the romance, and suggests both its strength and the ambivalence of Morris's achievement in it.

CHAPTER 5

'As Flat as Fleet Street': Elizabeth Barrett Browning, Matthew Arnold and George Eliot on Epic and Modernity

The impossibility of a primary epic in the nineteenth century was not a consideration that impressed Elizabeth Barrett Browning, who announced an aesthetic in *Aurora Leigh* (1856) diametrically opposed to that which dominates *Sigurd the Volsung* and was equally opposed to the aesthetic notions underlying *The Idylls of the King*. This chapter will discuss what is in effect the inverse of the problems discussed in the previous one. The search for a national epic, for Tennyson and Morris at least, necessarily meant writing poetry set in the past. I have suggested how ideas of modernity were intertwined, by negation, with a historicised notion of epic. This interdependence entailed particular problems for those poets and writers who wished to write in an elevated or unironic mode about the contemporary world. For Barrett Browning herself, for Matthew Arnold and for George Eliot, the possibility of a valid aesthetic addressed to their contemporaneity involved a negotiation with the model of epic poetry. Inevitably, this topic, as the inclusion of George Eliot sufficiently indicates, involves the transition from epic to novel, whose relationship is discussed more fully in the following chapter.

The phrase 'as flat as Fleet Street' in the title of this chapter comes from Book V of *Aurora Leigh*, in a passage in which the poet is considering the possibility of writing heroic poetry set in the contemporary world.[1] The poet is Aurora Leigh herself, though there seems little invitation in the poem at this point to distinguish her opinion from that of the 'E.B.B.' who appended her signature to the Dedication, informing her cousin John Kenyon, and the world at large, that this was the poem 'into which my highest convictions upon Life and Art have entered'. Here at all events is the passage:

> King Arthur's self
> Was commonplace to Lady Guenever;

> And Camelot to minstrels seemed as flat
> As Fleet Street to our poets.[2]

'As flat as Fleet Street' – contemporary poets are deeply mistaken to consider the contemporary world inimical to poetic treatment, for even the epitome of modern urban flatness is as illusory in its prosaicness as Camelot would have appeared to the minstrels of King Arthur's court.

It is here, and in the passages which precede and follow my brief quotation, that Barrett Browning takes up most explicitly the themes of the interlinked nineteenth-century debate about modernity, the place of poetry in the modern world and the meaning and possibility of heroic action. Her immediate antagonist here would appear to be Tennyson; that at least was his own opinion, and Margaret Reynolds, in her edition of *Aurora Leigh*, quotes his comment to the effect that this passage in the poem was a version of the answer he would have given if he had continued the short poem 'The Epic', first published in 1842 to frame 'Morte d'Arthur'. Since Barrett Browning's poem was published in 1856, and the first of *The Idylls of the King* was not published until a year later, she cannot have had the latter in mind, but she is certainly in disagreement with the mentality that produced it. My short quotation is preceded thus:

> I do distrust the poet who discerns
> No character or glory in his times,
> And trundles back his soul five hundred years,
> Past moat and drawbridge, into a castle-court,
> To sing, – oh, not of lizard or of toad
> Alive i' the ditch there, – 'twere excusable,
> But of some black chief, half knight, half sheep-lifter,
> Some beauteous dame, half chattel and half queen,
> As dead as must be, for the greater part,
> The poems made on their chivalric bones;
> And that's no wonder: death inherits death.
> Nay, if there's room for poets in this world
> A little overgrown, (I think there is)
> Their sole work is to represent the age,
> Their age, not Charlemagne's, – this live, throbbing age,
> That brawls, cheats, maddens, calculates, aspires,
> And spends more passion, more heroic heat,
> Betwixt the mirrors of its drawing-rooms,
> Than Roland with his knights at Roncesvalles.
> To flinch from modern varnish, coat or flounce,

> Cry out for togas and the picturesque,
> Is fatal, – foolish too.
>
> (pp. 148–9; V, 189–210)

Then come the lines about 'King Arthur's self'.

This whole passage is partly an argument specifically about medievalism rather than the heroic in general; in making a case for the heroic potential to be found in the present age, Barrett Browning partially debunks the claims made for the chivalric world, which appears to have been peopled by 'some black chief, half knight, half sheep-lifter', and 'some beauteous dame, half chattel and half queen'. Both these characterisations have their own history behind them; the 'half knight, half sheep-lifter' alludes to the Scottian equivalence of heroic poetry with the Border Ballad, while the 'half chattel and half queen' glances at the position of women in heroic poetry, a matter to be discussed more fully later. The aesthetic ruling this passage invites comparison with Robert Browning in poems like 'Love among the Ruins', in which Browning explicitly counterposes the chivalric and martial virtues to the more pacifically erotic – to the advantage of the latter. An echo of Browning can be heard, too, in the vivid evocation of lizard and toad 'alive i' the ditch there'. Like Browning's poem, this passage is a repudiation of the chivalric version of the heroic. Unlike the poet of 'Love among the Ruins', however, the poet of *Aurora Leigh* goes on from this negative moment to propose an alternative heroic aesthetic for the present. The task of the contemporary poet is not to pore over that bygone time but to represent the contemporary world in all its immediacy and confusion.

So, if the poem repudiates the chivalric version of the heroic, and in doing so the aesthetic represented by the Tennyson of *Idylls of the King* (though not the more exactly contemporary *Maud*), it certainly does not reject the heroic in general. On the contrary, the whole point of the passage at large is to lay claim to the category of the heroic for the contemporary world. Here Barrett Browning's explicit reference point is not Tennyson but Carlyle, mentioned in this long passage which precedes the one I have quoted so far:

> Ay, but every age
> Appears to souls who live in't (ask Carlyle)
> Most unheroic. Ours, for instance, ours:
> The thinkers scout it, and the poets abound
> Who scorn to touch it with a finger-tip:
> A pewter age, – mixed metal, silver-washed;

An age of scum, spooned off the richer past,
An age of patches for old gaberdines,
An age of mere transition, meaning nought
Except that what succeeds must shame it quite
If God please. That's wrong thinking to my mind,
And wrong thoughts make poor poems.
                     Every age,
Through being held too close, is ill-discerned
By those who have not lived past it. We'll suppose
Mount Athos carved, as Alexander schemed,
To some colossal statue of a man.
The peasants, gathering brushwood in his ear,
Had guessed as little as the browsing goats
Of form or feature of humanity
Up there, – in fact, had travelled five miles off
Or ere the giant image broke on them,
Full human profile, nose and chin distinct,
Mouth, muttering rhythms of silence up the sky
And fed at evening with the blood of suns;
Grand torso, – hand that flung perpetually
The largesse of a silver river down
To all the country pastures. 'Tis even thus
With times we live in, – evermore too great
To be apprehended near.
              But poets should
Exert a double vision; should have eyes
To see near thing as comprehensively
As if afar they took their point of sight,
And distant things as intimately deep
As if they touched them. Let us strive for this
                        (pp. 147–8; V, 155–88)

In this passage, the heroic features of the contemporary world are a matter above all of perspective: a failure to see the grand outlines of the present because you are up too close and can only see the detail. Lincoln's or Jefferson's faces, too, would be inscrutable to anyone crawling over the surface of Mount Rushmore. If the poet takes her cue from Carlyle, her task becomes akin to reading the riddle of the Sphinx – the metaphor from *Past and Present* not dissimilar in its implications from Barrett Browning's use of Mount Athos. Every age has to struggle with its own perplexing features to discover its particular heroic duty.

This is why this section of the poem ends with the ringing call to poets to write grand poems – 'unscrupulously epic' – about the contemporary world:

> Never flinch,
> But still, unscrupulously epic, catch
> Upon the burning lava of a song
> The full-veined, heaving, double-breasted Age:
> That, when the next shall come, the men of that
> May touch the impress with reverent hand, and say
> 'Behold, – behold the paps we all have sucked!
> This bosom seems to beat still, or at least
> It sets ours beating: this is living art,
> Which thus presents and thus records true life.'
>
> (p. 150; V, 213–22)

The claim, then, is that it is possible to write about the contemporary world in a mode that captures its grand heroic heartbeats. Later in this chapter I will discuss the question of whether *Aurora Leigh* carries out the aesthetic programme laid out here in its Fifth Book. But first I want to ask, into what context of argument, in addition to those suggested by Tennyson and Carlyle, was Barrett Browning directing her polemic?

EPIC AND CONTEMPORANEITY

One immediate contemporary comparison is provided by the writings of Matthew Arnold, whose 1853 Preface to his poems argued through this same set of questions with almost diametrically opposite conclusions. The Preface begins by justifying Arnold's exclusion of his own 'Empedocles on Etna' from the volume; it goes on to argue that the main aim of poetry is to give pleasure by the representation of an action that will provide interest to the reader. Such an action can be taken from any age in human history, and given the basic continuities of human nature, can as well be taken from the past as the present. This is an argument that Arnold expanded in 1857, in the Oxford lecture subsequently known as 'On the Modern Element in Literature'; in this account, Greek literature is more appropriately described as modern than Elizabethan, because the Greeks had a manner of writing that was adequate to the great actions of their age. In the earlier Preface, however, while it is certainly true that his argument does not *exclude* poetry set in the contemporary world, he provides sufficient grounds to be sceptical of it:

They [people who constantly practice commerce with the ancients] do not talk of their mission, nor of interpreting their age, nor of the coming poet; all this, they know, is the mere delirium of vanity; their business is not to praise their age, but to afford to the men who live in it the highest pleasure which they are capable of feeling. If asked to afford this by means of subjects drawn from the age itself, they ask what special fitness the present age has for supplying them. They are told that it is an era of progress, an age commissioned to carry out the great ideas of industrial development and social amelioration. They reply that with all this they can do nothing; that the elements they need for the exercise of their art are great actions, calculated powerfully and delightfully to affect what is permanent in the human soul; that so far as the present age can supply such actions, they will gladly make use of them; but that an age wanting in moral grandeur can with difficulty supply such, and an age of spiritual discomfort with difficulty be powerfully and delightfully affected by them.

A host of voices will indignantly rejoin that the present age is inferior to the past neither in moral grandeur nor in spiritual health. He who possesses the discipline I speak of will content himself with remembering the judgments passed upon the present age, in this respect, by the men of strongest head and widest culture whom it has produced; by Goethe and by Niebuhr. It will be sufficient for him that he knows the opinion held by these two great men respecting the present age and its literature; and that he feels assured in his own mind that their aims and demands upon life were such as he would wish, at any rate, his own to be; and their judgment as to what is impeding and disabling such as he may safely follow. He will not, however, maintain a hostile attitude towards the false pretensions of the age: he will content himself by not being overwhelmed by them. He will esteem himself fortunate if he can succeed in banishing from his mind all feelings of contradiction, and irritation, and impatience; in order to delight himself with the contemplation of some noble action of a heroic time, and to enable others, through his representation of it, to delight in it also.[3]

This seems to anticipate exactly, and to counter, the case made by Elizabeth Barrett Browning only two years later, who appears precisely as one of those voices raised in indignant rejoinder with respect to the 'moral grandeur' of the present age – though her voice appears to be discounted in advance by the insistent masculinism of this passage. Arnold's lordly scepticism is certainly an antidote to Barrett Browning's enthusiasm; the man with a thorough knowledge of classical culture will content himself by 'not being overwhelmed' by the false pretensions of the present age. So while it is true that logically Arnold does not exclude the possibility that the modern world might provide a 'noble action', the whole tone of the passage sufficiently suggests his fundamental scepticism on that score. It is hard not to read the conclusion to the first paragraph without assuming that it is the *present* age that is 'wanting in moral grandeur', and is equally an 'age of spiritual discomfort'. So Arnold's contemporaneity is hostile to poetry; he is sceptical of the claims made on behalf of the modern world; and poets, far from having as their over-whelming responsibility 'to represent the age', ought, by contrast, to seek out those actions which are permanently interesting. Such actions – 'the noble action of a heroic time', a phrase with tacit epic implications – are inevitably more likely to be drawn from the past than the present. In his controversy with Francis Newman, Arnold appeared as the opponent of the implications of epic primitivism; here, in his implicit disagreement with Barrett Browning, he equally opposes the obverse case, which repudiates the exclusive epic pretensions of the past and insists that the heroic can be discerned in the features of the present.

Oddly enough, this makes his argument partly cognate with that of J. A. Froude in his essay on Homer – oddly, because Froude was a disciple of Carlyle, and Arnold showed an enduring hostility to Carlyle, with whom he characteristically disagreed. Froude's essay represents another possibility in the range of positions that might be taken with respect to epic and modernity. He denies outright, on humanist grounds which partly align him with Arnold, that Homer's poetry shows any evidence of subsequent historical progress to justify the modern world talking of the childhood, still less the barbarism, of the early Greek world. On the contrary, Homer's poetry shows evidence of a civility much more developed than the genuine savagery of the *Nibelungenlied*:

War, of course, was glorious to him – but war in a glorious cause. Wars there were – wars in plenty, as there have been since, and as it is like there will be for some time to come; and a just war, of all human employments, is the one which most calls out whatever nobleness there is in man. It was the thing itself, the actual fighting and killing, as apart from the heroism for which it makes opportunities, for which we said that he showed no taste. His manner shows that he felt like a cultivated man, and not like a savage. His spirit stirs in him as he goes out with his hero to the battle; but there is no drunken delight in blood; we never hear of warriors as in that grim Hall of the Nibelungen, quenching their thirst in the red stream; never anything of that fierce exultation in carnage with which the war poetry of so many nations, late and old, is crimsoned. Everything, on the contrary, is contrived so as to soften the merely horrible, and fix our interest only on what is grand or beautiful.[4]

Froude thus denies one of the central contentions of that Enlightenment tradition which had precisely seen in Homer's delight in warfare primary evidence of the barbaric alterity of the world view which his poetry was taken to represent. As a consequence, Froude's own reading of Homer involves him in searching through both *The Iliad* and *The Odyssey* for evidence of behaviour immediately similar to that of people of the nineteenth century. This is what makes his position cognate with that of Matthew Arnold; in both cases the continuing appeal of the poetry is founded on the continuity of human experience, which joins the ancient with the contemporary world.

Furthermore, as befits the future biographer of Carlyle, Froude discusses Carlyle's notion, alluded to by Barrett Browning, that the future epic will be an epic of labour and not of arms – indeed, he finds such a project already partly realised in Homer's poetry, where the heroes (and even some of the heroines) are happy to engage in manual labour. This scarcely means that *The Iliad* would make an appropriate model for Barrett Browning; however qualified the savagery of the poem (and there is plenty of scope for doubting Froude's reading of it), it remains primarily a martial epic and subject therefore to her profound hesitation. Like Arnold, nevertheless, and for similar reasons, Froude sees no barrier in the archaism of Homer's poetry to prevent it serving as a model for a contemporary epic; what divides the two writers is not their attitude to the ancient poet but their estimation of the possible heroic potential of the contemporary world.

We can step back momentarily from these arguments and bring forward another voice into the discussion, the very famous one that introduces *Middlemarch* fifteen years after the publication of *Aurora Leigh*:

Who that cares much to know the history of man, and how the mysterious mixture behaves under the varying experiments of Time, has not dwelt, at least briefly, on the life of Saint Theresa, has not smiled with some gentleness at the thought of the little girl walking forth one morning hand-in-hand with her still smaller brother, to go and seek martyrdom in the country of the Moors? Out they toddled from rugged Avila, wide-eyed and helpless-looking as two fawns, but with human hearts, already beating to a national idea; until domestic reality met them in the shape of uncles, and turned them back from their great resolve. That child-pilgrimage was a fit beginning. Theresa's passionate, ideal nature demanded an epic life: what were many volumed romances of chivalry and the social conquests of a brilliant girl to her? Her flame quickly burned up that light fuel; and, fed from within, soared after some illimitable satisfaction, some object which would never justify weariness, which would reconcile self-despair with the rapturous consciousness of life beyond self. She found her epos in the reform of a religious order.

That Spanish woman who lived three hundred years ago, was certainly not the last of her kind. Many Theresas have been born who found for themselves no epic life wherein there was a constant unfolding of far-resonant action; perhaps only a life of mistakes, the offspring of a certain spiritual grandeur ill-matched with the meanness of opportunity; perhaps a tragic failure which found no sacred poet and sank unwept into oblivion. With dim lights and tangled circumstance they tried to shape their thought and deed in noble agreement; but after all, to common eyes their struggles seemed mere inconsistency and formlessness; for these later-born Theresas were helped by no coherent social faith and order which could perform the function of knowledge for the ardently willing soul.[5]

This provides another working-through of some of the same questions that engage Barrett Browning. For the poet, the failure to understand the contemporary world in heroic terms was a failure of perception; the present age was as fully heroic as any that preceded it, but, crawling across its countenance, we failed to perceive it. For Arnold, the present age was in principle as possible of providing a noble action as any other, but his scepticism led him to doubt it. George Eliot appears to be the most sceptical of the three; the possibility of an epic life depends upon the existence of a 'coherent social faith and order' to shape that life and give it both opportunity and meaning; since Saint Theresa's day such a coherent faith and order has been absent. Moreover, in a reference to the nationalising notion of epic, the hearts of the two children in Eliot's 'Prelude' are 'already beating to a national idea'; epic and nation are momentarily linked here, though that association will soon be superseded by the *epos* of religious reform. This is not to say that *Middlemarch* the novel simply bears out the Prelude; but it is the case that one way of reading the novel is that Dorothea's 'mistakes' are accountable because the contemporary world offers her no context in which her heroic virtues can find fit expression in action.

It is striking that in all these poems, arguments and novels, in Tennyson, Carlyle and Froude as much as in Arnold, Barrett Browning and Eliot, are a set of contentions about epic poetry and its possibility in the modern world. Thus the poet of *Aurora Leigh* bids poets to be 'unscrupulously epic'; in the most modernist of all these opinions, she assumes that it is possible, in some form or other, to achieve epic elevation and seriousness in writing about the modern world. Eliot too discusses Saint Theresa's life in terms of 'epic'; to live such a life would involve a 'constant unfolding of far-resonant action' to inspire a 'sacred poet'. The case of Arnold is more complicated, though he too is certainly concerned with the possibility of 'some noble action of a heroic time'. The complication comes because in 'On the Modern Element in Literature' he contends that the dramatic rather than the epic form is suited to writing about the past, and that epic is better fitted for the present:

The epic form, as a form for representing contemporary or nearly contemporary events, has attained, in the poems of Homer, an unmatched, an immortal success; the epic form as employed by learned poets for the reproduction of events of a past age has attained a very considerable success. But for *this* purpose, for the poetic treatment of events of a *past* age, the epic form is a less vital form than the dramatic form ... But the epic form takes a wider range [than the dramatic form]; it represents not only the thought and passion of man, that which is universal and eternal, but also the forms of outward life, the fashion of manners, the aspects of nature, that which is local or transient. To exhibit adequately that which is local or transient, only a witness, a contemporary, can suffice.[6]

This does not make him an advocate of the possibility of a contemporary epic; what is at stake in this passage is the density or specificity of reference that epic requires. Precisely because the dramatic form can exclude those outward matters, the 'fashion of manners', it is better placed to render past actions, while the absence of contemporary famil- iarity would be a disablement in the attempt to write an epic. But this does not mean that Arnold is advocating epic as an appropriate form for the present age, since all his previous strictures, with respect to its debilitating absence of interesting actions, still apply. The attempt to find the appropriate form for the present, for Arnold as much as for Barrett Browning and Eliot, still requires consideration of the epic.

It might be thought, given Barrett Browning's liberal politics and her feminism, that she would be the writer least likely to countenance the possibility of a contemporary epic. For her to be able to imagine or promote such a notion, 'epic' as a term has to be used loosely, as indeed it does for it to make sense in the passage from the Prelude to *Middlemarch*. Epic can no longer mean an extended narrative poem with a heroic theme, but has to be translated in some way to connote high seriousness in art; the heroic theme must no longer be narrowly defined as martial heroism, but be extended to include other kinds of heroism also. In *Casa Guidi Windows* she makes just such a translation, proposing a new form of epic for the contemporary world:

> Drums and battle cries
> Go out in music of the morning star –
> And soon we shall have thinkers in the place
> Of fighters, each found able as a man
> To strike electric influence through a race,

> Unstayed by city-wall and barbican.
> The poet shall look grander in the face
>   Than even of old (when he of Greece began
> To sing 'that Achillean wrath which slew
> So many heroes'), – seeing he shall treat
> The deeds of souls heroic toward the true –
> The oracles of life – previsions sweet
> And awful, like divine swans gliding through
> White arms of Ledas, which will leave the heat
> Of their escaping godship to endue
> The human medium with a heavenly flush.[7]

This certainly concludes with an extraordinary image; poets will be like Ledas, the 'oracles of life' to which they are turned will be like divine swans, and their encounter will leave the mediums (doubtless a spiritualist allusion also) with a 'heavenly flush'. The poet has been eroticised here, but also feminised. Furthermore, this conception of the future epic poet manages to acknowledge the historicity of the Homeric poet while seeing that history transcended in a future ruled by thinkers, not by fighters.

AURORA LEIGH AS EPIC POEM

The question remains whether *Aurora Leigh* itself bears out the aesthetic announced so boldly in the central section of the poem. Barrett Browning is under no responsibility to make it do so, though naturally an extended discussion of epic poetry in the middle of a long narrative poem is bound at least to provoke comparisons in the reader's mind. Equally, the poem challenges comparison with the novel; indeed, Barrett Browning herself described it as a 'novel-poem'. Is it possible for the poem to be at once epic and novel; if so, how do these generic dispositions collaborate or compete?

It is undoubtedly possible simply to contend that the poem lives up to the claims about epic which it contains. Holly Laird, for instance, concludes a discussion of the poem with a straightforward assertion of its epic qualities: 'Aurora is witness to the fact that Browning, at least, knew her achievement for what it was even as she wrote it: an unscrupulous epic by a woman poet.'[8] However, wishing does not make it so – for even though Laird conducts an interesting discussion of the aesthetic which Barrett Browning proposes in Book V of *Aurora Leigh*, it scarcely does justice to the formal variety of the poem simply to assert that it is an epic. Furthermore, to claim epic status for the poem in this way is to engage in an act of generic translation; the implications of this claim need further consideration.

The subtlest discussion of these matters is that provided by Herbert Tucker, who recognizes epic as one generic possibility among others that the poem draws upon; the poem is also indeed novel and autobiography:

> For epic offered nineteenth-century writers a set of story-telling conventions that were arguably more flexible than those of popular prose forms like fiction, (auto)biography and history. From Homeric rudiments, writers of epic from Virgil to Milton and Wordsworth had with increasing address developed means of playing against one another the different immediacies of present tense narration and of invocation or apostrophe. Where epic paused from singing the story to sing about the song instead, and urged not the hero's concerns but the poet's, it made an opening that Barrret Browning was quick to occupy and distend for purposes of her own. One of the ways in which she feminized so famously masculine a genre was by exploiting internal differences between its narrative and narratorial, epic and poetic, registers. She found in epic models a traditional means to an untraditional, genuinely novel end, by crossing the linear plot of the *Künstlerroman* with desultory devices drawn from women's traditions of epistolary and diaristic narrative.[9]

In this account, the poem is to be seen as a generic combinatory, in which the genres act and react upon one another to destabilising effect. Epic emerges with its own subversive capacity; or rather, in an implicit challenge to Bakhtin, its invocation in a world dominated by novelistic realism makes it so. It is not therefore that the poem is straightforwardly an epic; more precisely, in it Barrett Browning draws upon some of the conventions of epic to enable her to reach beyond the constrictions imposed by the narrowly realist register indicated by the novel.

I think it is possible to extend this line of argument – while leaving open the large question of the relationship of epic to novel in the nineteenth century – by considering not only the narratological features of the poem, but also its poetic texture. There are certainly moments in it when Barrett Browning seeks a kind of epic elevation, so that the claim to epic status can rest upon more than mere assertion and is actualised in the poetry itself – though in the nature of things different readers will judge her success in this enterprise variably. One such moment is the remarkable account of the train journey south from Paris to Marseilles undertaken by Aurora and Marian Erle in the Seventh Book:

> I just knew it when we swept
> Above the old roofs of Dijon: Lyon dropped

A spark into the night, half trodden out
Unseen. But presently the winding Rhone
Washed out the moonlight large upon his banks
Which strained their yielding curves out clear and clean
To hold it, – shadow of town and castle blurred
Upon the hurrying river. Such an air
Blew thence upon the forehead, – half an air
And half a water, – that I leaned and looked,
Then, turning back on Marian, smiled to mark
That she looked only on her child, who slept,
His face toward the moon too.
So we passed
The liberal open country and the close,
And shot through tunnels like a lightning-wedge
By great Thor-hammers driven through the rock,
Which, quivering through the intestine blackness, splits,
And lets it in at once: the train swept in
Athrob with effort, trembling with resolve,
The fierce denouncing whistle wailing on
And dying off smothered in the shuddering dark,
While we, self-awed, drew troubled breath, oppressed
As other Titans underneath the pile
And nightmare of the mountains. Out, at last,
To catch the dawn afloat upon the land!

(pp. 227–8; VII, 417–41)

This is surely an impressive effort at an idiom for a contemporary epic. The passage is driven by excitement at the new technology of rail travel, but combines this with a very traditional poetic manner, even making use of the epic simile to provide some sense of the grandeur of the experience. Indeed, Barrett Browning is rather insistent upon this epic dimension here; she alludes both to the 'Thor-hammers' and to the Titans in this passage, and immediately afterwards brings in 'Charlemagne's knightly blood' and 'Odyssean ghosts' to reinforce the heroic frame of reference that the description of the journey aspires to. The strikingly modern and transforming experience of the railway, its capacity to shrink international distances and to revolutionise the traveller's perception of the relations of landscape, time and place, has found its appropriate expression in a transformed epic idiom.

So much is this the case that the passage can be described as pro-gramatically Carlylean; at least, its aesthetic impulse is directly cognate with that announced by Carlyle in *Past and Present*.[10] Epic here is indeed not 'Arms and the man' but 'Tools and the man' – quite literally so in the celebration of the steam-hammers which have bored the tunnel through which the train is travelling. Modernity has been poetically seized to emphasise its own characteristic heroic features, which are necessarily not the martial ventures of an antique heroic world, but are equivalent in their scale and grandeur – and require description in an idiom which makes that equivalence explicit. Yet Carlyle too has been transformed, as his emphatically masculine idiom has given way in Barrett Browning's writing here to a passage in which the bearers of this epically described experience are two women joined by bonds of tender concern for each other and for a child. So not 'Tools and the man' after all, but 'tools and the women'.

This is one sense, therefore, in which *Aurora Leigh* can be described as an epic poem in its own right – in places the poem seeks to take the manner of epic and redescribe the contemporary world using its distinctive generic resources. A complex set of aesthetic endeavours underlie this project even in its intermittent realisation; Barrett Browning has genuinely had to forge a new heroic idiom in making this effort, and the work involved has taken her via Carlyle's translation of an archaic vocabulary into one fit for the modern world and required her own further transformation of that vocabulary to make it fit for a woman-centred poem.

Nevertheless, this recognition that the poem seeks to draw upon the generic resource of epic serves to reinforce the point that the poem as a whole can scarcely be described as an epic and is better thought of as generically hybrid, moving in and out of the various idioms which it deploys. Herbert Tucker's point that this generic hybridity destabilises the ideological implications of a dominant novelistic realism can be allowed to stand, especially since it has the virtue of reversing the usual easy assignment of values attached to the epic and novel. Yet it needs to be supplemented by an acknowledgement of Barrett Browning's capacity, intermittently though emphatically, to forge an epic idiom that is adequate to the contemporary world.

THE TRANSFORMATION OF EPIC

A principal context for *Aurora Leigh*, therefore, is a large debate about the possibility of epic in the contemporary world. Implicit in all the positions that I have set out, and in Barrett Browning's own poem, are several overlapping and contending axes of opposition, which are difficult to disentangle. First there is the presumed hostility between epic and the modern world, a presumption that in different forms underlies all the positions that I have quoted. Related to this, though certainly not overlapping with it precisely, is the opposition between epic and novel – given categorical status in the twentieth century by Mikhail Bakhtin, and the topic for discussion in the next chapter. And also at issue here is an argument about gender, since traditional epic overwhelmingly tells stories of masculine heroism; for Barrett Browning and George Eliot, therefore, to lay claim in some form to the heroic in the contemporary world is at the very least going to involve some negotiation with this gendered inheritance.

If, as I have been arguing, the categorical opposition between epic and modernity underlies these debates, then Barrett Browning's belief in the possibility of a contemporary epic requires some transformation at least of one side of this opposition. The contrast with Morris in this respect is illuminating. His embrace of epic entailed the repudiation of modernity – and a commitment to its transformation. Barrett Browning's embrace of modernity, *per contra*, implies the transformation of epic, to retain those of its features which could survive into the contemporary world, and to repudiate the indications of its barbaric or martial origins. An epic for the modern world is possible, but only on the basis of this etiolating generic transformation.

Concomitant with this is Barrett Browning's rejection of the Wolfian side of the Homeric controversy despite her liberal credentials, which, according to Richard Jenkyns, might have predisposed her to take the more radical scholarly position.[11] Wolf gets a specific mention in *Aurora Leigh*; towards the end of Book Five, Aurora is strapped for cash, needs to sell one of her dead father's books and chooses Wolf's splendid edition of Homer:

> The kissing Judas, Wolf, shall go instead,
> Who builds us such a royal book as this
> To honour a chief-poet, folio-built,
> And writes above, 'The house of Nobody!'
> Who floats in cream, as rich as any sucked
> From Juno's breasts, the broad Homeric lines,
> And, while with their spondaic prodigious mouths
> They lap the lucent margins as babe-gods,
> Proclaims them bastards. Wolf's an atheist;
> And if the Iliad fell out, as he says,
> By mere fortuitous concourse of old songs,
> Conclude as much too for the universe.
>
> (p. 180; V, 1246–57)

There is another strikingly maternal image for poetic and intellectual succession here; this is the second occasion on which Barrett Browning has figured the act of reading heroic poetry as sucking rich milk from heroic breasts. This is an image I will return to. In the immediate context of the Homeric controversy, however, she here aligns Wolf's scepticism about the historic Homer with atheism, and thus aligns herself with those who insisted on the actual existence of the Greek poet. Her position at this moment consequently buttresses her assertions earlier in the Fifth Book about the possibility of a contemporary heroic poetry, since in both cases she postulates an elevated, even sacred, role for the heroic poet.

There is a congruence, therefore, between Barrett Browning's rejection of the Wolfian hypothesis and her demand that contemporary poets should be 'unscrupulously epic'. While her explicit mention of the Homeric controversy indicates her consciousness of the debates of epic primitivism, we can see *all* these positions – Arnold's and Eliot's as much as Barrett Browning's – as different responses to the secular effort to historicise epic and to see it as generically unsuited to modernity.

Arnold's particular combination of humanism with historicism sceptically repudiates the view that the modern world can produce potentially epic actions to match those of the ancient world. His position is humanist, as we have seen, insofar as it founds the interest of any poetic action upon the permanent continuities of human life which persist beneath the transient and changing fashion of manners or the local aspect of nature. This appears to suggest that a contemporary epic would be possible, except that a kind of historicism intervenes to suggest that the conditions of social life in the middle of the nineteenth century are peculiarly unpropitious for permanently interesting, and hence epic, action. These conditions are indeed the confusions and divisions of the contemporary world, which prevent its actors connecting their deeds with wider or grander motives. In this respect, the problem with the contemporary world, unlike a phase of ancient Greek life, is that it is not modern enough.

George Eliot's negotiation with the claims of the epic genre are equally complex. She does wish to appropriate the categories of epic for her contemporaneity, but recognises there is something in the very nature of the contemporary world which militates against that epic congruence of action with wider significance. St Theresa could successfully aspire to, and realise, an epos; Dorothea, given 'no coherent social faith and order', cannot. In both cases, however, epic action will undoubtedly not mean the martial-heroic action of primary epic. Insofar as epic is possible in the contemporary world – and the caveat is substantial – it will involve its translation into terms appropriate to our modernity.

This aspiration, minimal as it is, appears to put her in the same camp with Barrett Browning, for in both writers we see an effort to translate the old and grand aesthetic categories into a contemporary idiom. To this extent both writers are engaged upon an honourable bourgeois aesthetic project, which takes the class-based 'high' genres and seeks to redefine them as appropriate to the lives of ordinary people. Epic can go alongside tragedy as a genre which can be reclaimed for a democratic modernity, as it is in another of George Eliot's novels, *The Mill on the Floss*. Here – though not consistently – the category of tragedy is brought down from its elevated position, where it used to 'sweep the stage with regal robes', and made to serve as the appropriate way of understanding the life of an 'insignificant miller and maltster'. Epic likewise is being reclaimed by both Eliot and Barrett Browning as a genre which might be transformed for a modernity quite other than the heroic world from which it originated.

In Eliot's case, this act of possible reclamation can be described as Feuerbachian, for it is cognate also with her persistent effort to reclaim the categories of religion for a secular and humanist understanding of the world. Such a description sharply distinguishes her from Barrett Browning, however, whose liberalism was never secular and whose principal charge against Wolf was that he was an atheist. For Barrett Browning, to retain a sense of the original genius of Homer was cognate with retaining a sense of religious belief; both these commitments assured a sense of the divine purposefulness of the world:

> Wolf's an atheist;
> And if the Iliad fell out, as he says,
> By mere fortuitous concourse of old songs,
> Conclude as much too for the universe.
> (p. 180; V, 1254–7)

This remarkable assertion makes the stakes in the Homeric controversy especially high; a contemporary epic, far from requiring a Feuerbachian translation in the manner of Eliot, requires on the contrary a theistic insistence upon design cognate with a belief in the authority of the original Homer.

Nevertheless, both writers did seek to appropriate those historic 'high' genres for contemporary and 'ordinary' life, in a way that required at the very least some class and gender negotiations. What did such a project involve in the effort to translate epic into modern dress? For Barrett Browning, as we have seen in the earlier quotation from *Casa Guidi Windows*, that translation had to involve a repudiation of the old martial-heroic virtues in favour of liberal and high-minded intellectual aims – such as the abolition of slavery, or support for the liberation of Italy. Indeed, the context in the earlier poem makes explicit that in both the English and Italian national situations, what is required is not more of the martial virtues, but more of the specifically Christian and pacifist ones.

Such a translation would create a space for both the woman writer, and for women themselves to act in the epic mode. Those striking maternal images of the transfer of the heroic sense from one generation to the next are especially relevant in this context. Here are the lines which imagine how a possible epic of the present might be received by future generations:

> Never flinch,
> But still, unscrupulously epic, catch
> Upon the burning lava of a song
> The full-veined, heaving, double-breasted Age:
> That, when the next shall come, the men of that
> May touch the impress with reverent hand, and say
> 'Behold, – behold the paps we all have sucked!
> This bosom seems to beat still, or at least
> It sets ours beating . . .
>
> (p. 150; V, 213–20)

In these lines it is the age itself which is 'double-breasted'; a poetry adequate to it will catch its impress, which future generations may touch 'with reverent hand' – though there is sufficient ambiguity about whether it is the impress or the breasts themselves which are being reverently handled. Extending the metaphor, however, those future men will proclaim that they have sucked from the paps; in other words, the sense of high heroic transition from one age to another, carried by a putative epic song, is figured as the act of breast-feeding – a radical rewriting of a masculine poetic inheritance. The image reappears a thousand lines later to describe the treachery of Wolf:

> [Wolf], who floats in cream, as rich as any sucked
> From Juno's breasts, the broad Homeric lines,
> And, while with their spondaic prodigious mouths

They lap the lucent margins as babe-gods,
Proclaims them bastards.

(p. 180; V, 1250–4)

Here it is Homer's lines themselves which are the breast milk (though especially rich); but then the lines become babies, and the breast-milk the rich margin of white paper that surrounds the lines in Wolf's magnificent edition. In this complicated and shifting metaphor, Wolf's treachery is to refuse to recognise that there is a legitimate line of maternal succession from Homer to his baby-gods: again the transmission of the heroic is refigured in unembarrassedly feminine terms.

All this, however, is a statement of intent rather than a realised contemporary epic in itself; and indeed this is an aesthetic difficulty with *Aurora Leigh*, in that much of the poem is poetry about poetry, and it does not – cannot – realise in itself the aesthetic doctrines that it announces. A similar point can be made in relation to George Eliot's writing, which, at least in *Middlemarch* and *Daniel Deronda*, appears to aspire to the status of epic but manifestly fails to realise that aspiration in the body of the novels themselves. But it is worth dwelling on what would be involved if that ambition could have been realised; epic would come to mean any account of a 'far-resonant deed', and could thus include the actions of a spiritual provincial girl and a tubercular Jewish intellectual. What appears to prevent its realisation under modern conditions is the absence of that coherent social faith and order; this is Eliot's Comtean recognition of the anarchy of the contemporary world which fails to provide the context in which heroic action can take on meaning. But the aspiration remains in the case of both Eliot and Barrett Browning: both writers negotiate with the claims of epic understood in a transformed or translated way that would allow space for wholly different class, racial and gender characterisations.

Dorothea's failure to live out the epic life announced as an aspiration in the Prelude to *Middlemarch* points in two possible directions for explanation. One answer we have just suggested – that the contemporary world is too confused, too far away from that Positive state prefigured by Saint Theresa's Catholicism, to provide the coherent social faith and order which are the preconditions of an epic life. Such an answer provides another version of the notion of the inadequacy of modernity, the idea against which Barrett Browning was complaining. The alternative answer is more generic – that the ironies which are generated around Dorothea's life, and which are concerned with her inability to lead a grand heroic life, are more to do with the fact that she inhabits a novel than they are to do with the status of the contemporary world. In short, if Eliot is to be true to her generic inheritance as a novelist she is bound to undercut the claims to epic status that she announces in the Prelude. To follow this kind of explanation affords powerful formative capacity to the genres themselves, and makes writers little more than the puppets of the epochal generic dispositions that speak through them.

These questions are pursued more fully in the next chapter. However, I wish to anticipate it by taking one particular generic distinction suggested by Bakhtin, namely the 'zone of epic distance', which he sees as characterising the older form and which the novel typically abolishes. In this view, even if epic treats of contemporary events it does so via such a zone; events have always to appear as though from a distance, completed and whole in themselves, and closed off from the unfinished business of contemporaneity. The novel, by contrast, precisely inhabits the contemporary moment; or rather, even if it deals in past events, it does so in a way that is open to the constantly changing possibilities of a world in motion.

This is at least suggestive in thinking about that passage from *Aurora Leigh* that I quoted at such length earlier. Barrett Browning had complained that the difficulty about seeing the contemporary world in heroic terms was precisely one of perspective; we are like the ignorant shepherds crawling across Mount Athos putatively carved into a likeness of Alexander – just not far enough away to perceive the grand outline. It is not that *Aurora Leigh* is an epic poem, but that it represents a constant struggle to comprehend contemporaneity in epic terms. The task for the modern writer, in short, is just to establish the zone of epic distance of which Bakhtin writes. *Aurora Leigh* is a poem whose alternation between epic and novel can be seen in its intermittent capacity to hold its action at a suitably epic distance.

A comparable point may also be made with respect to *Middlemarch*. We could complement that earlier assertion that the novel constantly undermines its own epic pretensions (an argument which has a tendency to turn into another statement of a traditional conservative hymn to irony and small ambitions) by asserting rather that the novel enacts the effort to find a zone of epic distance. This is a matter of its formal organisation more than of the substance of Dorothea's story – or Lydgate's, for that matter. The most sustained consideration of the 'epic' in the novel occurs in the Prelude, with the narrator recurring to this topic in the novel's Finale. Thus the effort to find an epic perspective on Dorothea's life, in particular, is conducted above all by the organising consciousness of the author rather than by Dorothea herself, and is realised in the framing moments at the beginning and end of the book. The negotiation between epic and novel that *Middlemarch* enacts is thus inherently unstable, as the substance of the book threatens to spread beyond the aspiration to epic that seeks to frame it. In recognising this, however, one need not opt too simply for the Bakhtinian ideological preference of novel over epic.

One reason for hesitation in this matter is precisely because of the gender negotiations that both Barrett Browning and Eliot are conducting in relation to epic. Epic is an overwhelmingly male form, in the sense at the very least that the martial-heroic virtues which it celebrates are ones which are usually the prerogative of men. It is naturally possible to find moments of feminine tenderness even in the bloodiest of epic poems, such as *The Iliad*; Barrett Browning herself translated one such moment, the famous scene involving Hector, Andromache and their infant son Astyanax. Nevertheless, the question of gender renders particularly acute the difficulty of claiming epic status for the events of modernity while simultaneously repudiating the blood-soaked virtues associated with actual epic poems.

Perhaps at its most basic the claim to heroic status comes down to an assertion that 'this *matters*': the events and people with which this poem or novel deals are as important as any of the heroic affairs of antiquity. Arnold was surely right to be sceptical of some of the claims made for itself by a boastful mid-nineteenth century – 'an era of progress, an age commissioned to carry out the great ideas of industrial development and social amelioration', and all that. There is indeed a little bit of such stuff in *Aurora Leigh*, though it is ironic that Arnold should presume the man with a classical training to be especially immune to such cant, when Elizabeth Barrett Browning, the woman of remarkable scholarly attainments, should come closest to it. But much more importantly, the claim she makes in *Aurora Leigh*, even while the poem itself does not lay claim to epic status, is that the life of a woman can matter in just the way that epic has traditionally asserted. Such also is the potential claim made by George Eliot in *Middlemarch*, on behalf of Dorothea via Saint Theresa. In making this assertion, the novelistic virtue of irony, so often invoked in this context against the epic or the heroic, is insufficient. In seeking to assert a possible claim to the historic prestige of epic for the fortunes of their heroines, therefore, George Eliot and Barrett Browning were engaged in an effort which involved them not only in reclaiming the generic past, but also and in the same gesture translating that masculine epic past into a feminine epic present.

CHAPTER 6

Mapping Epic and Novel

To include discussion, in a book on epic in the nineteenth century, of *Middlemarch* and *Aurora Leigh* is an indication, it might be thought, of the overwhelming predominance of the novel in the period. Certainly the pull of the novel form – its massive cultural and social presence as much as its specific gravity as a mode – makes any discussion of contiguous genres necessarily involve some negotiation with its characteristic procedures. Not only epic in the nineteenth century but also romance, the drama and painting (to restrict examples to the aesthetic sphere) were dragged into the orbit of the novel. On the other hand, an opposite usage has taken the transformations of epic, envisaged by such writers as Barrett Browning and George Eliot, and used the word to describe almost indiscriminately the novel itself, so that it has become possible to speak with apparent appropriateness of the novel as providing the epic of bourgeois life, or more generally the epic of ordinary lives. It is not far from here to contemporary usages of the term in which epic is simply equivalent to 'long'.

Behind these usages are various and complex generic negotiations such as those which I sought to describe in the previous chapter. But the relationship of epic to novel, in large terms, was also the subject of considerable and fruitful debate in the twentieth century; the critical and theoretical arguments to be considered in this chapter were not, however, mere acts of retrospective reflection on an inert literary history, but more importantly constituted a way of arguing through questions of modernity, nationality, and – latterly – the phenomenon we have come to know as globalisation. I review this critical history, therefore, both to gain some perspective on the literary histories I have been discussing and to make the transition to the account of some more explicitly novelistic material in the remainder of the book. I begin with a discussion of Hegel, whose consideration of the epic in his *Aesthetics* is the fountain-head of many of the twentieth-century debates, and whose writings resume and carry forward those eighteenth- and early nineteenth-century discussions of the genre with which this book began.

HEGEL ON EPIC: TOTALITY, NATION AND MODERNITY

Hegel's discussion of epic in the *Aesthetics* makes up only a small portion of a massive purview of aesthetic forms. As such, it is necessarily reliant on the scholarship of others and, as far as epic is concerned, represents his own particular transformation of the tradition of primitivist scholarship on epic. Three themes will prove especially important for subsequent discussion: Hegel's sense of epic as a 'primitive' form, linking this, in his own way, to the concomitant understanding of modernity; his related insistence upon the *nationality* of epic; and his very distinctive deployment of the category of totality as the distinguishing formal feature of epic as a genre.

Hegel's assertion of the emergence of epic from an earlier, distinct, civilisation can be taken as a *locus classicus* of this position in nineteenth-century thought, underlying Marx's views on the subject as much indeed as Ferguson's arguments did:

All the truly primitive epics give us the vision of a national spirit in its ethical family life, in states of national war or peace, in its needs, arts, usages, interests, in short a picture of a whole way of thinking and a whole stage of civilization.[1]

Although Hegel's historicism is of an especially idealist kind – the key word in this quotation is 'spirit' – this assertion provides the central contention of his chapter on the epic insofar as it is addressed to 'primitive' epics. By this Hegel alludes to what, in a later vocabulary, will be described as 'primary' rather than 'secondary' epics; to those poems, in short, which emerge from societies at one with the spirit celebrated in the poetry, as opposed to those epics written at some historical distance from them. The essential distinction here is that between Homer and Virgil, and in expressing a strong aesthetic preference for Homer, who emerges as the typical epic poet according to a range of criteria, Hegel shows himself the heir of eighteenth-century epic primitivism. This preference leads him to articulate precisely the problem that I earlier identified as central to neoclassical epic: its inevitable distance from its primary model. For Hegel, the problem emerges most visibly in relation to the question of the representation of the gods:

But, especially in relation to the entire world of gods, an aspect of epic comes into view which I have indicated already, namely the contrast between primitive epics and those composed artificially in later times. This difference is most pronounced in the cases of Homer and Virgil. The stage of civilization which gave rise to the Homeric poems remains in beautiful harmony with their subject-matter, whereas in Virgil every hexameter reminds us that the poet's way of looking at things is entirely different from the world he intends to present to us, and the gods above all lack the freshness of individual life. (II, 1073)

Although Hegel discusses a number of neoclassical epics, his clear preference is for primitive epics in which there is an organic unity joining the outlook of the poet with that of the poet's subject matter. Only thus does the fundamental unity of the epic poem manifest itself, a unity expressing at once an aesthetic and a social wholeness.

While it is true that Hegel resumes earlier eighteenth-century scholar-ship in his view of epic as expressing the spirit of a 'whole stage of civili-zation', he nevertheless disagreed with the more extreme or Wolfian version of that tradition. In particular, he is insistent upon the individual com-position of the Homeric poems, though he can adroitly indicate how it is possible both to repudiate any notion of collective composition while at the same time insist that the poems are the expression of a collective spirit:

Nevertheless, an epic poem as an actual work of art can spring from *one* indi-vidual only. Although an epic does express the affairs of an entire nation, it is only individuals who can write poetry, a nation collectively cannot. The spirit of an age or a nation is indeed the underlying efficient cause, but the effect, an actual work of art, is only produced when this cause is concentrated into the individual genius of a single poet; he then brings to our minds and particularizes this universal spirit, and all that it contains, as his own vision and his own work. (II, 1049)

Thus Hegel makes the organic unity of the epic dependent on its being produced by a single author expressing or 'concentrating' a national or folk consciousness. In this way Hegel carries forward into the nineteenth century, and subsequently, the essential insight of the historicist tradition which precedes him, without being enmeshed in the particularities of the Homeric controversy.

A further aspect of the historicist tradition which Hegel continues is that necessary imbrication of notions of antiquity with concomitant notions of modernity, though again this is given a very particular slant. Just as much as for Ferguson or other more obviously Enlightenment figures, the assertion of the primitivism of epic produces a contrasting sense of modernity. In Hegel's case, however, we can see in his particular version of this argumentative trope a formulation of the Romantic critique of modernity, in which the modern world is measured by its failure to reproduce the unalienated unity of the world depicted in epic:

For his external life man needs house and garden, tents, seats, beds, swords and lances, ships for crossing the sea, chariots to take him to battle, kettles and roasting-tins, slaughter of animals, food and drink, but none of these and whatever else he may need, should have been only dead means of livelihood; on the contrary he must still feel himself alive in them with his whole mind and self, and therefore give a really human, animated, and individual stamp to what is inherently external by bringing it into close connection with the human individual. Our modern machines and factories with their products, as well as our general ways of satisfying the needs of our external life, would from this point of view be just as unsuitable as our modern political organization is for the social background required by the primitive epic. For just as the intellect with its universals and that dominion of theirs which prevails independently of any individual disposition must not yet have asserted itself in the circumstances envisaged in the whole outlook of the epic proper, so here man must not yet appear cut adrift from a living connection with nature and that link with it which is powerful and fresh, be it friendly or hostile. (II, 1053)

This is a powerful vision of a social world characterised by a direct and unmediated relationship both to its own necessary means of survival and to the natural world that surrounds it. It stands in implicit critique of a modernity where man is indeed 'cut adrift from a living connection with nature', thanks both to the progress of industrial production and the dialectical progressions of the spirit. Once again, epic has been invoked as the touchstone or most significant indicator of an antiquity categorically opposed to the present.

Concomitant with his understanding of epic as expressing the spirit of a stage of civilisation, Hegel also contends that it should be seen as the indicator of a distinctive *national* spirit. This is an emphasis that it would be easy to overlook, since in the case of primitive epics (Hegel's preferred category) it may be presumed that the world of the nation and that of civilisation are the same. Indeed, in the quotation above, when Hegel talks of 'a whole way of thinking and a whole stage of civilization', he makes this a summation of 'a national spirit in its ethical family life, in states of national war or peace, in its needs, arts, usages, interests'. However, while it is true that nationality is partly synonymous with the whole of an early stage of society, Hegel also has some specific claims for epic as the expression of particular national conflicts, in which the contribution of nations to a more universal human spirit is crucial.

Thus he is impressive in the range of primary epics that he takes under review, including, in addition to Homer, Virgil and the neoclassical epics, the *Nibelungenlied* and, most strikingly, the Indian epics. Yet the capaciousness of his aesthetic sympathies has its limits: although the Indian epics are sympathetically described, ultimately he asserts that they are so specialised to Indian life that they cannot be characteristic of 'what is really and truly human' (II, 1058). Still more remarkably, he is prepared to read the Trojan War as itself evidence of the working-out of the national principle, so that the victory of the Greeks over the Trojans is to be justified in world-historical terms:

It is not any ordinary war between nations hostilely disposed to one another that as such is to be peculiarly regarded as epical: a third aspect must be added, namely the justification claimed by the people at the bar of history, a claim which one people pursues against another. Only in such a case is the picture of a new higher undertaking unrolled before us. (II, 1061)

Thus in the *Iliad* 'the Greeks take the field against the Asiatics and thereby fight the first epic battles in the tremendous opposition that led to the wars which constitute in Greek history a turning-point in world history' (II, 1061). Homer therefore expresses the triumph of European moderation over Asiatic brilliance, described as 'the world-historically justified victory of the higher principle' (II, 1062). This too is a way for Hegel to link together the particularities of a national history with the progression of the universal spirit, yet it plainly involves the ruthless exclusion of non-European history, and its associated epics, as the condition for constructing its vision of the progress of the world-spirit.

Nevertheless, this exclusionary moment is not accompanied by any predilection for the German-national rediscovery of the *Nibelungenlied*, which had preceded Hegel's lectures by a few years. On the contrary, Hegel is sharply critical of this narrowly nationalist enthusiasm:

The story of Christ, Jerusalem, Bethlehem, Roman law, even the Trojan war have far more present reality for us than the affairs of the Nibelungs which for our national consciousness are simply a past history, swept clean away with a broom. To propose to make things of that sort into something national for us or even into the book of the German people has been the most trivial and shallow notion. At a time when youthful enthusiasm seemed to be kindled anew, it was the sign of the grey hairs of a second childhood at the approach of death when an age reinvigorated itself on something dead and gone and could expect others to share its feeling of having its present reality in that. (II, 1057)

Hegel here mobilises notions of epic primitivism against the revival of the old German epic material; a moment earlier he could draw on the antiquity of epic as an implicit critique of modernity. The apparent contradiction can be resolved by recognising that the whole account of epic is subservient to a grand narrative of the progress of the spirit, and in the light of this, the limitations of the German national song strike Hegel more strongly than any possible contribution it might make to that progressive story.

Infused into Hegel's position both with respect to nationality and modernity, and in some ways his central category both aesthetically and historically, is his insistence on the totality of epic – that is, the view that a genuine epic poem is both an all-encompassing form in its own right and achieves a summation of a whole and undivided social unity:

> Thus viewed, the rounding off and the finished shape of the epic lies not only in the particular content of the specific action but just as much in the entirety of the world-view, the objective realization of which the epic undertakes to describe; and the unity of the epic is in fact only perfect when there is brought before us in all their entirety not only the particular action as a closed whole in itself but also, in the course of the action, the total world within the entire circumference of which it moves; and when nevertheless both these principal spheres remain in a living conciliation and undisturbed unity. (II, 1090)

This powerful conception, which is mobilised to conciliate the conflicting demands of part with whole, operates at all levels of Hegel's analysis. It informs his notion of the unity of the epic poem itself (and thus predisposes him to an anti-Wolfian position, as we have noted); it underlies the way that he conceives of the social world from which epic emerges; and it also indicates the way that he conceives of the principal actor in epic:

> Now precisely because these chief epic figures are whole and entire individuals who brilliantly concentrate in themselves those traits of national character which otherwise are separately dispersed, and who on this account remain great, free, and humanly beautiful characters, they acquire the right to be put at the head of affairs and to see the chief event conjoined with their individual selves. The nation is concentrated in them into a living individual person and so they fight for the national enterprise to its end, and suffer the fate that the events entail. (II, 1068)

This is much more than the mere assertion of typicality; or, rather, it permits an understanding of 'typicality' by which the protagonists of epic become, by virtue of the resolved complexity of their characters, the epitome of their social world. Totality thus conjoins characterisation, action and social world; at each level of the analysis Hegel celebrates epic as the successful realisation of diversity held together in unity.

Hegel, to conclude, provides a rich and complex inheritance to his successors: he carries forward into the nineteenth century and beyond the central historicist insight of eighteenth-century discussions of epic; he insists upon the peculiarly national character of epic poetry; and informing both these positions is his particular philosophical and aesthetic predisposition which makes the epic the form that pre-eminently realises, at all levels, a totality of form and content. A. N. Whitehead once famously described the whole of Western philosophy as 'footnotes to Plato'; in the same vein the remaining arguments in this chapter are footnotes to this multiple Hegelian legacy of reflection on epic.

EPIC, NOVEL, MODERNITY

I have been arguing that built into post-eighteenth-century discussion of epic as a mode has been an argument over the nature of modernity, an argument which has at intervals surfaced with more or less explicitness. As a striking confirmation of this contention, twentieth-century debates about the relationship of epic to novel have repeatedly reprised or presupposed arguments about the transition from the pre-modern to the modern world, whether or not such contentions are explicitly tied to notions of progress in the Enlightenment manner. Thus Lukács's account of the novel in *The Theory of the Novel* (written before its author embraced Marxism) sees the novel as the form best suited to the fallen modern world, in which the totality of epic, after the manner of Hegel, has been lost. Bakhtin's categorical opposition of novel to epic, above all in the essay 'Epic and Novel', makes the contrast between the two forms in effect the marker of the transition to modernity. Franco Moretti, in *The Modern Epic*, contends that epic is the form best suited to the modern world-system first apparent in the nineteenth century. And Horkheimer and Adorno, in *The Dialectic of Enlightenment*, also make epic central in their account of the progress of reason, in which regulative reason always has the capacity to overtake or dominate reason's emancipatory ambition or potential; the decisive characteristic of the modern world has been just that disastrous fall from grace.[2]

This last example, however, indicates an instability at the centre of many arguments about the nature of modernity: it is characteristically unclear whether the transition to modernity is to be conceived as a once-only historical event or rather as a recurrent possibility or socio-cultural potentiality present in a variety of different societies or historical moments. Horkheimer and Adorno offer a reading of *The Odyssey* as a kind of exemplar of the operation of regulative reason: epos and mythos, far from being synonymous as might be assumed, are in fact antagonistic, and the Homeric spirit organises and regulates the primordial energies of myth in ways which act as an allegory of the operation of regulative reason in the modern world. The reading suggests that the possibility of regulative reason taking over the liberatory functions of enlightenment is one that has always existed in Western culture – indeed that it is a kind of original sin or wound which has marked the progress of reason since the Greeks, and which is re-enacted, with differing rhythms, intensities and scope, throughout subsequent history. Modernity has always-already been present in Western history.

A cognate instability affects Bakhtin's compelling account of the relationship of epic and novel in the essay of that name. The two forms are juxtaposed across a range of characteristics to demonstrate their mutual exclusion; the novel indeed is constituted out of its systematic repudiation of the fixities of epic. Thus the epic is closed, the novel is open; the epic is fixated on the past, the novel is directed to the present; the epic is marked off from the reader by a zone of epic distance, while the novel presents no barrier; the characters of epic are completed, while those of the novel are always open to the possibility of change. This set of formal differentiations can be read in two ways. On the one hand, it provides a history of the transition of a world dominated by epic to a world dominated by the novel. Though this appears to have happened twice, once in the classical and once in the modern world at the end of the Middle Ages, these would nevertheless be singular historical events, albeit similar in their terms, and their repetition could be explained along classic Viconian lines as the Middle Ages repeating the characteristics of a heroic prehistory. On the other hand, another possible reading of Bakhtin's essay suggests, on the contrary, that 'epic' and 'novel' are more like permanent generic principles which battle it out across time; the novel's struggle is not to represent modernity so much as con-temporaneity (by definition the state which all peoples actually inhabit at all times), while epic is either fixated on a heroic national past or, if it tries to address the present, seeks to memorialise it.

The implications of this instability are profound, not least for our understanding of the role of epic and novel in the nineteenth century. Are we to conceive epic and novel as transhistorical generic possibilities that reappear to battle it out on this particular historical terrain? Or is the nineteenth century irreversibly modern, and therefore so thoroughly novelised that any attempt at epic is bound to be defeated from the outset? The problem is not necessarily readily resolved, for any answer that suggests a permanent and once-only historical location for the transition from epic to novel is bound to do so in terms of formal characteristics that can always be found in the writing of other periods.

Bakhtin's account of these matters in 'Epic and Novel' is open to both emphases; the same cannot be said of Lukács's *Theory of the Novel*, the book written during the First World War which carries on Hegel's account of the epic in the *Aesthetics* into a theory of the novel. In brief, the novel is offered as the form best suited to a modern world whose organic unity and coherence have been irretrievably lost. The whole book is therefore an implicit lament for the lost world of epic; the novel is the successor form, but it is inherently flawed, the best that can be managed in an age of 'absolute sinfulness' (p. 153). Lukács can figure the transition from one form to another as equivalent to the passage from youth to adulthood; in paragraphs which deal with the presence of the gods in the worlds of epic and novel respectively, the nostalgia for the elder form is apparent:

> The heroes of youth are guided by the gods: whether what awaits them at the end of the road are the embers of annihilation or the joys of success, or both at once, they never walk alone, they are always led. Hence the deep certainty with which they proceed: they may weep and mourn, forsaken by everyone, on a desert island, they may stumble to the very gates of hell in desperate blindness, yet an atmosphere of security always surrounds them; a god always plots the hero's paths and always walks ahead of him.
>
>   Fallen gods, and gods whose kingdom is not yet, become demons; their power is effective and alive, but it no longer penetrates the world, or does not yet do so ... (p. 86)

A world without God, therefore, or even without the gods of the old epics, is doomed to irony; the disjunction between the aims of the hero and the world that can accommodate him is structural:

> Irony, the self-surmounting of a subjectivity that has gone as far as it was possible to go, is the highest freedom that can be achieved in a world without God. That is why it is not only the sole possible *a priori* condition for a true, totality-creating objectivity but also why it makes that totality – the novel – the

representative art-form of our age: because the structural categories of the novel constitutively coincide with the world as it is today. (p. 93)

The novel is thus doomed to the paradox of being a form that undoes itself from within; while the epic, in an analysis that recalls Hegel at every point, creates a totality unmarked by internal contradiction.

Lukács regards the novel, in sum, as the form best suited to modernity, but since we inhabit a fallen world, that is at best an ambivalent form of praise. Epic always stands to hand in *The Theory of the Novel* as the master-genre by which the novel can be measured; the passage to modernity is indicated by the differences between the two genres. Remarkably, these categorical preferences survive into Lukács's Marxist maturity; Galin Tihanov has demonstrated the persistence of the same arguments about epic and novel in the debates about the form that Lukács was conducting in the thirties in Moscow – debates which were the immediate context for Bakhtin's 'Epic and Novel'.[3] Where the earlier Lukács felt that he inhabited a world of absolute sinfulness, for which Dostoevsky might be the appropriate Homer or Dante, a vein of Marxist utopianism now permits him to anticipate a realised socialist future in which the novel will regain the unity and totality of epic. The novel in its current form is as transitional as the social stage which it seeks to represent.

Bakhtin and Lukács therefore stand opposed to each other in fundamental ways on the question of the novel and modernity; while both see the novel as the form best suited to modernity, their accounts of the relationship between the forms are categorically opposed. For Bakhtin the novel is most itself when it repudiates the epic, while for Lukács it should aspire to the condition of the older form. For the Russian thinker, the novel's openness to modernity, understood as the always-unfinished heterogeneity of the present moment, is cause for celebration; for the Hungarian, its immersion in the present should not prevent it acquiring the finish and totality of epic. As far as this aspect of Hegel's legacy is concerned, this is all to say, both accept the categorical alignments that he proposed but accord them opposing valuations.

Lukács's more rigid Marxist chronology – the pre-modern world of epic giving way to feudalism, capitalism and then socialism – makes it difficult to resolve the instability of the category of the 'modern' as I have described it: its capacity to allude to a once-for-all historical transition, and its simultaneous reference to ever-possible formal or rational capabilities existing in many periods of history. We have noticed Bakhtin's own version of this instability. Nevertheless, it is perhaps possible to suggest a resolution to these alternative ways of conceiving epic and novel, especially in the light of the discussion of the epic, transformed epic and novelistic writing considered in previous chapters. The tradition of criticism that has been one of the central topics of this book has been unanimous in asserting the historical ground of primary epic to be the heroic world which precedes modernity (whether or not immediately). It is fully in keeping with this fundamental insight to acknowledge that epic can establish itself as a genre, and can continue to exist as a set of generic possibilities, even beyond its historical originating moment. It will then remain to be actualised in succeeding periods, both according to the social possibilities of that period and according to the layered and complex nature of historical time, in which no socio-historical possibility is ever absolutely lost. If this is the case, then the dominance of the novel in the nineteenth century need not be denied, but it can be seen as co-existing with the epic in various relations of transformation, conflict and attempted assimilation. These relations can either exist between conflicting forms or within the capacious ambit of the novel itself which reproduces the historical layering of the world that surrounds it. This indeed will be the assumption in the discussion that follows.

EPIC, NOVEL AND NATIONALITY

Arguments over the temporal location of epic and novel, that is over their historical and social ground, inevitably have a spatial dimension also, though one that is more visible in some writers than in others. In this section, I discuss this necessary concomitant to the historical understanding of the modes, in particular in relation to the way that they can figure questions of nationality. That is, I ask how both epic and novel were, or might be, mobilised to articulate the contours of the nation-state, both within its borders and across them in relation to the peoples beyond those borders. This large question reappears under the more general-seeming but ultimately congruent rubric of the relation of centre to periphery. Bakhtin's arguments about epic and novel, as much in 'Discourse in the Novel' as in 'Epic and Novel', form the basis of this discussion; the challenge to these arguments posed by Franco Moretti, in *Modern Epic* (1996) and *Atlas of the European Novel 1800–1900* (1998), will lead to a developed sense of the dynamic relationship of epic to novel in the nineteenth century.

Starting with 'Epic and Novel', we are confronted with the assertion that 'the world of the epic is the national heroic past: it is a world of "beginnings" and "peak times" in the national history, a world of fathers and of founders of families, a world of "firsts" and "bests"' (p. 13). There are several aspects of this assertion, and the argument from which it is drawn, to comment upon. First, it might appear that the account of the epic provided by Bakhtin is overwhelmingly a temporal one; that is, the *problem* with the epic is its fixation on the past: it is cut off from the incompleteness of the present by this inevitable orientation. The novel, by contrast, because it inhabits the present and is open to it, has a spatial existence; where the epic is confronted only by one aspect of experience, the novel can move around its object, can inspect it from all sides and indeed can dismember it and peer at the results of its dismemberment.

More importantly, Bakhtin's association of the epic with nationality is striking. For at this point the Russian thinker is effectively resuming, and reversing the valuations of, the tradition of nineteenth-century scholarship which sought to make the association of epic with national origin the central element of its account of the mode. In this context, Bakhtin's association of epic with the national imaginary is significant not because it denies the association of epic and nation, but because of the way it reverses those nineteenth-century evaluations. In this account, and following on from one aspect of Hegel, epic is indeed the national form, or the form in which national consciousness gets its fullest or most typical enunciation; but this is, as it were, a matter of regret – this is the problem with epic, an indication of its categorical limitation. By virtue of the ineluctable binary logic of his argument, the novel inevitably becomes the form which challenges or subverts this nationalising impetus realised in epic.

It might be thought that this is little more than a gestural alignment in 'Epic and Novel'. Certainly, to flesh it out we need to supplement that essay with Bakhtin's account of the evolution of language, and its relations to the artistic forms, from 'Discourse in the Novel'. It is in this essay that the notion of 'heteroglossia' appears most fully – *raznorečie*, 'many-speechedness'. This is far more than a simple celebration of linguistic diversity. The notion includes a critique of the tradition of rationalist linguistics which Bakhtin sees as culminating in Saussure, and includes also an incipient social history of the great European national languages. For our purposes here, the crucial aspect of this account of language is its fundamentally spatial character, and its alignment of artistic forms (poetry and the novel) with opposed tendencies in language. On the one hand are a series of unifying or centripetal forces which act to create the illusion and prestige of a single national language, and which provide the real social ground for unitary or norm-based linguistics:

> The victory of one reigning language (dialect) over the others, the supplanting of languages, their enslavement, the process of illuminating them with the True Word, the incorporation of barbarians and lower social strata into a unitary language of culture and truth, the canonization of ideological systems, philology with its methods of studying and teaching dead languages, languages that were by that very fact 'unities', Indo-European linguistics with its focus of attention, directed away from language plurality to a single proto-language – all this determined the content and power of the category of 'unitary language' in linguistic and stylistic thought, and determined its creative style-shaping role in the majority of the poetic genres that coalesced in the channel formed by those same centripetal forces of verbal-ideological life.[4]

Here, the poetic genres are aligned with the centripetal forces that are drawing together a national language. Taken in conjunction with the quotation from 'Epic and Novel' – the world of the epic is that of the national heroic past, etc. – one might say that of all the poetic genres it is epic above all which performs the centralising and unifying function in the history of national languages. This would certainly coincide with a rough-and-ready sense of European linguistic history, in consideration of the central role of, say, Dante in the history of Italian, or perhaps Chaucer and Early Modern English. In addition, the poetic genres, in this account, are responsible for 'the incorporation of barbarians and lower social strata into a unitary language of culture and truth' – though given the nature of many epics (and the way they pit their heroes against barbarians of one kind or another), this incorporation might take a rather literal form. The poetic genres, in short, and among them epic above all, act to draw together national languages and with them nationality itself.

The novel, in Bakhtin's conception of it, works in ways that are categorically opposed to all this at all points. Where the poetic genres are centripetal, the novel is centrifugal, taking its energy from all those forces which oppose, undermine or ridicule the pretensions of unitary national languages. Where the epic incorporates barbarians and the lower social strata, the novel is the form which springs from them – or at least, from the lower social strata of fairgrounds and the comic-parodic genres. Where the poetic genres unify language, the novel delights in all the variousness of language: dialects, socially and professionally distinct jargons, the thousand idioms that pull a language (and with it a nation) apart. Bakhtin's categorical juxtaposition of the two forms is complete.

A principal implication from this argument is that Bakhtin's mode of analysis has the effect of linking the form of both the poetic genres and the novel (form understood as the relations of whole to parts) to the dispositions of national languages and hence of nations. Form here means the architectonics of the genres, the ways in which they incorporate, subsume or assimilate the various generic and linguistic materials from which they are constituted. Because of this, these genres are intimately linked to the national imaginary, but overwhelmingly by their formal dispositions, which in some sense mimic or echo the dispositions of the linguistic and national tendencies on which they draw.

This large implication, of a linkage between formal disposition and the national imaginary, will continue in Moretti's two books. However, the specific judgments that he makes about the forms directly contradict Bakhtin's central contentions and valuations. Starting with *The Modern Epic* of 1996, Moretti effectively disputes the whole relationship of epic to novel that Bakhtin proposes. The book is nothing less than a history of modern literature, from the late eighteenth century to the present. It starts from Hegel's account of epic, but the emphasis that Moretti takes from Hegel's *Aesthetics* is above all the stress on totality; he leaves to one side Hegel's simultaneous stress upon the nationality of the epic. This is important because it is precisely the inclusiveness of epic, its capacity to include rather than to exclude, that Moretti wishes to stress. But the inclusiveness of his texts, their epic quality – the epic ambitions of a series of what he calls 'world texts' – lies precisely in their capacity to sum up and to speak to, not the national imaginary, but the *world system*. The texts in question are *Faust, Moby Dick, The Ring Cycle, Ulysses, The Waste Land* and *One Hundred Years of Solitude*, which are 'more than' novels or 'more than' poems, according to Moretti; their characteristic difference from their apparently related forms requires them to be described as modern epics. Moretti has annexed the Hegelian notion of the totality of epic in order to make it speak to a set of texts which are potentially at least adequate to a world moving beyond the confines of nationality. In the process of doing so, he contradicts Bakhtin by making the novel the form which expresses most thoroughly the homogenising impulses required to sustain the nineteenth-century nation-state.

Moretti is a stylish and suggestive writer who works more perhaps by assertion and suggestiveness than by sustained and long-developed argument. This can be very impressive – the whole account of stream of consciousness, for example, taking *Ulysses* for its primary example but alluding as happily to Woolf and Musil and Faulkner, among others, is a *tour de force*. In this analysis, we start from a representation of the modern metropolis as the epitome of the world, move to an account of the department store and the experience of shopping as an epitome of the metropolis and move to stream of consciousness as the subjective form of shopping – understood as the repeated and discontinuous shocks of the metropolitan experience. Against this is juxtaposed that other aesthetic experiment of *Ulysses*, namely polyphony – that is, the unmediated presence in the text of a variety of styles. The imbalance between these two aesthetics provides a rich and suggestive version of this phase of modernism.

However, Moretti's whole notion of epic effectively empties the idea of any substantive content other than its world-ambition; the particular national or heroic ideas that are carried by the term are lost. In taking up Hegel's category of totality as the central distinguishing feature of the mode, Moretti has simultaneously abrogated the significant accompanying terms which give the totalising capacities of epic their force and meaning in Hegel's account – such as the expression of a significant world-historical national idea or the unifying force of a whole way of life expressed in the multiplicity of poetic details. Moretti's decision to cast these 'world texts' as epic has at the very least an arbitrary character.

Related to this is his cognate recasting of Bakhtin's account of the novel to the national question, the area in which his direct contradiction of Bakhtin emerges most sharply. Moretti reverses Bakhtin's opposition of epic and novel for the nineteenth and twentieth centuries, seeing epic as the mode of difference while the novel becomes the homogenising form, in the following way:

The nineteenth-century novel ... with its dialectic of provinces and capital pinning the story at the centre of the nation-state, acts in the opposite way to a centrifugal force. And the same holds for novelistic conversation, or the impersonal voice of the narrator: rather than nourishing polyphony, they impose a drastic *reduction* of it, giving birth to a more compact and homogeneous 'verbal-ideological world' in each new generation.

Pace Bakhtin, in short, the polyphonic form of the modern West is not the novel, but if anything precisely the epic; which specialises in the heterogeneous space of the world-system, and must learn to provide a stage for its many different voices. (pp. 56–7)

This then is Moretti's central objection to Bakhtin; in the modern world at least, the novel is the centripetal form while epic is the centrifugal one. There is a danger of making this into an argument about terms: given that it is an arbitrary decision to describe his list of 'world texts' as epic, it would be futile to argue about whether those characteristic modern texts addressed to the world-system are really epic or not. It is more valuable to engage with Moretti's substantial point: that the nineteenth-century novel homogenises in the way that it encompasses the nation-state, and that it becomes progressively more homogeneous in linguistic and formal terms as the century progresses. By contrast, his world texts, drawn from the beginning of the nineteenth century through to the second third of the twentieth, speak to the world-systems and have to find ways of representing it in all its variety and difference.

It may appear that there is a distinction here without a difference; or rather, Moretti's argument may seem to oppose as a categorical distinction what is in fact the same problem distinguished only by a difference of scale. This is the problem: should we think of the various assimilative strategies of both the nineteenth-century novel and what we can agree with Moretti to call 'world texts' as strategies that homogenise and subordinate, or ones which permit or affirm difference? Two answers, one obvious, and one, I hope, less so. Different novels, one must surely recognise, manage these matters differently; one would respond differently to that question if one was considering *Bleak House* or *Middlemarch* or *The Newcomes* – to restrict oneself solely to the canon of the mid-nineteenth-century English novel. Each of these texts finds differing metaphors to figure the social totality, and diverse narrative strategies for linking together the various localities that they encompass in their efforts to represent the nation. But the less obvious answer is that the forces holding together the nation-state – partially imaginary ones, of course, as Benedict Anderson's famous title 'imagined communities' underlines[5] – are not the same as those that constitute the world-system, where both market and empire bring together in various contested relationships differing nationalities and widely differing social systems. This is why there is a distinction in Moretti's difference after all; that is, we must recognise that 'world texts' and nationally based nineteenth-century novels perform different tasks. While the formal problem remains the same (to find ways of assimilating or juxtaposing different voices, drawn from widely differing social classes or nationalities, such as 'barbarians and lower social strata', to recall Bakhtin), the accomplishment of this task will be very different according to whether the ultimate perspective is that of the nation or the world.

Modern Epic, therefore, mounts a challenge to Bakhtin in wide categorical terms; Moretti appropriates 'epic' and 'novel' to serve an argument about modernity in which the distinguishing feature of the modern world is the global character of the networks of which it consists. However, the argument here, and still more in *Atlas of the European Novel*, has the signal merit of retaining and emphasising the category of nationality; in Moretti's account, the novel is the form *par excellence* which provides the national imaginary. This is his central contradiction of Bakhtin, for whom epic was the form that celebrated and memorialised the national past.

One of the most striking features of Moretti's argument is the way it attempts to provide maps of the nineteenth-century novel – literally – and shows how these maps coincide with (indeed produce and reinforce) the newly stabilising borders of nation-states. There are two phases of his argument which are especially significant here. The first concerns the place of the border in the historical novel. His canonical instance is Walter Scott and the presence of the Highland line in his fiction. Moretti's case is in a sense a classically Lukácsian one, though the Lukács in question is the writer of *The Historical Novel* rather than *The Theory of the Novel*. To cross the border (in Balzac and Pushkin, as much as in Scott) is to cross an historical as much as a spatial boundary; it is to journey back into an earlier historical stage – from a civilised state to a savage state. This is how Moretti summarises his analysis:

Love, between the man from England and the woman from the Lowlands estate: a miniature of a national union based on the agreement, the mutual desire of the more 'civilized' spaces. But war (and no prisoners), against the still 'savage' space, so that the state may finally achieve Weber's 'monopoly of legitimate violence', crushing once and for all Pugacev and Fergus and Bonnie Prince Charlie, don Rodrigo and the Signora and the Unnamed, the Chouans and the Cossacks and the Knights of the Temple. State building requires *streamlining*, historical novels tell us: the blotting out of regional borders (Scott, Balzac, Pushkin), and the submission of the Gothic strongholds of old feudal privilege.[6]

In general terms this is bound to seem averse to Bakhtin's benign description of the novel; to see the form as complicit with the legitimation of state violence is not an insight which will appeal to a Bakhtinian. But Moretti takes his account further and angles it into an explicit disagreement with the Russian thinker. In a so-called 'theoretical interlude' which immediately follows the passage I have just quoted, he analyses a section from *Waverley*, when the hero of the novel approaches the border – not that between England and Scotland, but between the Lowlands and the Highlands (it will be recalled that he makes the crossing in the company of the robber Donald Bean Lean). In Moretti's account, the crossing of the border is accompanied by some stylistic disturbance; the prose becomes more excited, more lurid, until, once the crossing has been safely made, it can revert to its more usual analytical evenness. This is the occasion for Moretti's explicitly anti-Bakhtinian moment; taking objection to the account of the novel as characterised by *polyphony*, he contends, on the contrary, that in the nineteenth century the novel is the form which evens out polyphony and contains different historical experience within the same assimilative purview. In effect, but with the object of his criticism now specifically the historical novel, this is the same objection as he made in *The Modern Epic*: far from celebrating difference or the social periphery (however that is to be understood), the novel is the form that incorporates the non-national other by virtue of an essentially stylistic homogenisation.

If the discussion of the nineteenth-century historical novel provokes Moretti to an explicitly anti-Bakhtinian assertion (or reminds him of his objections as made in *The Modern Epic*), the succeeding discussion of the *Bildungsroman* is equally uncongenial to Bakhtin's whole orientation towards the novel. Moretti provides more maps, this time of the trajectories of the heroes (and heroines) of nineteenth-century *Bildungsromane*. Here, there is another kind of national imaginary to that found in the historical novels, one that is based upon the passage from province to capital, and serves to construct national relations in these terms: youth to age, innocence and experience, provincial narrowness and metropolitan freedom. However the *Bildungsroman* constructs these oppositions and other related ones, the novel is the form above all which provides imaginative substance for the unitary nation-state in the nineteenth century – a role which is quite contradictory to the role proposed for the novel-in-general of Bakhtin's writings.

Well, what are we to make of this large objection to Bakhtin – or shall we say, this flat contradiction of Bakhtin's account of the novel in the nineteenth century, based upon a sophisticated alternative mapping, of a literal kind, of different manifestations of the form in the period? In the first place, it can readily be pointed out that Moretti's argument is based on a particular selection of novels – an impressively international selection, but one which could not possibly be the whole story. We would get a very different picture, even of the English authors he discusses, if we were to take *Bleak House* rather than *David Copperfield*, *The Newcomes* rather than *Pendennis*, and *Daniel Deronda* rather than *Middlemarch*. Take the second of these alternatives. *The Newcomes* combines a very wide variety of narrative material, in the manner of many big mid-nineteenth-century multi-plot novels, but it does so in a way which implicitly rejects the ambitious metaphors of webs or fogs which in Eliot or Dickens seek to give coherence or unity to the novels they inhabit. Thackeray's novel, in fact, organises his diverse material in a way to suggest its random and fissiparous character, where the juxtapositions of the various plot-lines indicate not homogeneity but arbitrariness. In other words, the categorical disagreement between Bakhtin and Moretti can be partially mitigated by attention to an alternative canon of novels; the analysis of specific novels intimates a plurality of ways in which novels seek to assimilate the multiple social and geographical experiences they contain.

The difficulty of this line of argument is that it can appear to dissolve the very necessity of any categorical juxtaposition of epic and novel, and to question whether broad generic definitions can be sustained at all. By an odd argumentative reversal the issue becomes this: not whether the formal properties attributed by Bakhtin to different kinds of writing actually pertain in the nineteenth century, but whether these qualities (of formal decentring, disruption, relativising and so on) actually are to be found in the forms to which he ascribes them. In short, in the nineteenth century, is the novel the form which connotes 'novelness', or is it rather to be found in those 'world texts' which Moretti describes as epics – or indeed in the epic as such? It may be possible to answer this question by saying 'some novels do have the character of novelness, and some don't', without losing the value of Bakhtin's categories.

This possibility is strengthened by the recognition that, if one leaves aside Moretti's claim of epic status for his 'world texts', the material that the novel seeks to assimilate is indeed 'epic' in a more familiar sense. His own account of border crossings from *Atlas of the European Novel* is a case in point. Moretti's analysis of the stylistic disturbance caused by a border crossing suggests that the historical novel's assimilation of its various constitutive sections includes the assimilation of diverse *generic* material (that is, in classically Bakhtinian fashion, the novel swallows up other genres). The historical novel's ambition or capacity to assimilate the historical experience of those on the wrong side of internal borders involves the assimilation of peoples who readily see their own experience in terms of epic, or, if not epic, in other 'archaic' or popular genres. The question, therefore, of whether or not the effect is one of 'streamlining' or wholesale historical elision (as Moretti suggests) is in fact an open one.

Again, the canonical example is Walter Scott, and among his novels the canonical case is *Waverley*. The hero's bewitchment by Flora is as much generic as personal. When he accompanies her up the romantic glen to hear her sing her ballad, he is entering a different generic universe to the one that he inhabits either in England or on the Lowland side of the Highland line. Flora has learnt the use of the harp from 'Rory Dall, one of the last harpers of the Western Highlands'. 'The seat of the Celtic muse,' she tells him, 'is in the mist of the secret and solitary hill, and her voice in the murmur of the mountain stream.'[7] When she gets to sing her song, it is in English – she has translated it for Waverley's benefit. But the idiom, an elevated dactylic version of the heroic ballad, sufficiently evokes the world of epic:

> 'Tis the summons of heroes for conquest or death,
> When the banners are blazing on mountains or heath:
> They call to the dirk, the claymore, and the targe,
> To the march and the muster, the line and the charge.
>
> (p. 180)

Waverley has crossed the internal border, as Moretti suggests, but we need to add that in doing so the novel's hero has entered a different generic zone also.

Behind Flora's heroic call to arms, and behind Scott's association of the heroic virtues with clan society, lies half a century of controversy over *Ossian*, and indeed the whole Scottish Enlightenment with its various versions of the 'stages' of human progress from savagery to civilisation. But I wish to conclude my discussion of Moretti and Bakhtin by simply pointing out that what Moretti's maps fail to include is any sense of ambivalence, or any sense that the passage from one generic world to another might be an emotionally charged one. Indeed, it is almost a commonplace to say that Waverley's passage from youth to experience is one that involves loss as well as gain – loss *more* than gain, perhaps. So the metaphor of 'streamlining' won't do; the historical novel does indeed assimilate other generic material, but it can do so in a way that is rhetorically unstable and conducive to radical reversals of the evaluations and shapings that seek to enforce it.

CONCLUSION

Lukács's account of epic and novel in *The Theory of the Novel* is an overwhelmingly temporal one, though there are some incipiently spatial aspects to it. But it is also Hegelian, and in asserting that the novel is the form for modernity, he acknowledges that the transition from antiquity to modernity, where it is a transition that can be made in space rather than in time, is one which will be a generic shift. Bakhtin's models of epic and novel are much more obviously spatial, and link the question of nationality to the genres, such that the national imaginary is to be understood as connected to their formal dispositions. But his particular valuations in this respect are explicitly contradicted by Moretti, at least as far as the nineteenth and twentieth centuries are concerned. For the latter, the novel is the form that homogenises and streamlines, assimilating all to the confines of the nation-state. The differences between the two thinkers turns on the different ways that one can understand the formal ambitions or capacities of the novel to hold together the diverse material which it includes, and in the case of Scott's *Waverley* and other nineteenth-century novels these ambitions are more fragile or rhetorically unstable than Moretti contends.

The case of Scott is absolutely crucial for the nineteenth-century novel in English, as it seeks to assimilate the historical experience of the 'northern and western extremities' (to recall Jane Austen's formulation), and, later in the century, as it seeks to assimilate the colonial extremities also. Let me put the matter this way. I agree with Bakhtin that the novel is a form which sucks in and recycles other generic material. For the Lukács of *The Historical Novel*, the manner in which Scott assimilates the experience of gentile society (the society of the *gens*) is by a process of Hegelian *Aufhebung*, an essentially temporal supersession in which the historical experience of a whole social order is transformed, assimilated and surpassed by the order that succeeds it. But this account needs to be supplemented by the recognition that this is a spatial as much as a temporal phenomenon, and that the resulting synthesis is always an unstable one. The modern world may get the assent and cooperation of the hero, but the gentile world gets the glamour. In many cases, this is the glamour of epic. This whole pattern we could describe as a structure of feeling which informs Scott's successors especially in the adventure novels of the late nineteenth century.

These debates imply a further way of describing epic and novel in the nineteenth century: they may be seen as elements of a complex generic repertoire, among which writers could choose as they sought to shape or make sense of the world which confronted them. It is true that 'repertoire' suggests too simple or value-free a choice; we can nevertheless supplement the notion by recognising that the elements in the repertoire of genres come laden with their own histories and their own historically charged meanings. While the novel is a capacious genre which can assimilate other genres, the allusion to epic within the form of the novel need not be overwhelmed by the ironies and provisionalities characteristic of 'novelness', but can instead act as the disruptive force which transcends the novelistic bracket which seeks to contain it. A further paradox therefore: if according to Moretti it may not be the novel in the nineteenth century which is the characteristic carrier of novelness, equally it may be epic, carrying with it all the socio-historical associations of barbaric alterity, that is the best form to speak to 'barbarians and other lower social strata', and thus best placed to disrupt the assimilations of a homogenising novel form.

These are all phenomena that can be grouped under the heading of 'uneven development', the simultaneous co-existence of social strata at widely differing stages of social evolution. In the late nineteenth century, European, and especially British, imperialism meant that 'uneven development' was a global phenomenon productive of some spectacular juxtapositions, as the developed capitalist societies of Europe and America confronted multiple social groups at extraordinarily varied moments in their history. Uneven development is a phenomenon vividly evoked by Hilaire Belloc: 'Whatever happens, we have got / The Maxim gun and they have not'. Scott's novels early in the century laid out the template by which this imperialist uneven development could be mapped, the assimilation of 'peripheral' peoples within these islands being the model for the assimilation of the peoples encountered on the imperial border. In the chapters that follow the implications of this generic mapping are pursued in relation to a range of late nineteenth-century poems and novels.

CHAPTER 7

Epic and the Imperial Theme

EMPIRE AND ATAVISM

'Uneven development': the term works especially well in relation to the remarkable juxtapositions and conflicts of the late nineteenth-century world, when the sophisticated products of advanced capitalist society were brought into contact, in myriad ways, with traditional societies at widely differing stages of development. But it might be used also to describe the cultural landscape within those advanced capitalist societies themselves: a diverse repertoire of genres, each of them bearing within themselves implications or ideological connotations drawn from socially diverse histories. Epic and novel in competition: but also, across a range of different media, new technologies of production and reproduction in conflict and collaboration with ancient forms. The late nineteenth century had its own word for the pleasure people might take in those traditional forms, such as epic, which appeared to speak to the older, less advanced, or barbaric propensities in human nature: atavism. This chapter seeks to describe how a theory of atavism linked epic and its cousin ballad to the history of the empire at the end of the late nineteenth century and the beginning of the twentieth.

I introduce this topic by way of Joseph Conrad's *Victory*, completed just before the outbreak of the First World War. Conrad speaks, in his 'Note to the First Edition', of 'that pagan residuum of awe and wonder which still lurks at the bottom of our old humanity'; and Heyst, meditating on his unusual energy in the course of the narrative, reflects that '"There must be a lot of the original Adam in me, after all."'[1] In both these passing quotations, the resurgent residuum is associated, not with the primitive other of empire, but with the 'civilised' protagonist of the tale. In the first quotation in particular, the aesthetic foundation of the story, its capacity to produce 'awe and wonder', is associated with a 'pagan residuum' that the civility of the nineteenth century has failed to suppress.

This is to touch a note upon which Conrad played more fully else-where. For example, in a 1906 review of John Galsworthy's *A Man of Property*, he praises the novelist – the very antithesis of the adventure writer – for writing in an especially contemporary manner. To be con-temporary, in this account, is to have moved beyond the simple pleasures of what Conrad calls 'fairy tale':

> In the essential of matter and treatment it is a book of to-day. Its critical spirit and its impartial method are meant for a humanity which has outgrown the stage of fairy tales, realistic, romantic, or even epic. For the fairy tale, be it not ungratefully said, has walked the earth in many unchallenged disguises, and lingers amongst us to this day wearing, sometimes, amazingly heavy clothes. It lingers; and even it lingers with some assurance. Mankind has come of age, but the successive generations still demand artlessly to be amazed, moved and amused. Certain forms of innocent fun will never grow old, I suppose.[2]

As with the previous two brief quotations I don't want to bear too heavily upon this, but the scope of what Conrad describes as 'fairy tale' deserves attention. Subsumed under it, in addition to 'realistic fairy tales', are romance and epic – forms which, in a way with which we are now familiar, are to be thought of as archaic, or at least as 'lingering' from an earlier stage of humanity. For Conrad this is absolutely not a matter of regret; on the contrary, it is the fact upon which his own fictions are built, however complicated may be the reflections constructed around the fairy stories that he tells. That is to say, at the heart of Conrad's stories is an atavistic residuum of archaic narrative material.

Conrad was not alone in the late nineteenth century in assigning a kind of evolutionary or developmental dating to the forms of fiction. Some twenty years before he wrote that review of *The Man of Property*, Andrew Lang was writing in a similar vein. The context in this case is an article defending the fictions of Stevenson and Rider Haggard, who were pro-ducing, in the 1880s, a series of adventure stories for which Lang sought to provide the appropriate critical defence:

> Are we to be told that we love the 'Odyssey' because the barbaric element has not died out of our blood, and because we have a childish love of marvels, miracles, man-eating giants, women who never die, 'murders grim and great', and Homer's other materials? Very well. 'Public opinion', in Boston, may condemn us, but we will get all the fun we can out of the ancestral barbarism of our natures. I only wish we had more of it. The Coming Man may be bald, toothless, highly 'cultured', and addicted to tales of introspective analysis. I don't envy him when he has got rid of that relic of the ape, his hair; those relics of the age of combat, his teeth and

nails; that survival of barbarism, his delight in the last battles of Odysseus, Laertes' son ... Not for nothing did Nature leave us all savages under our white skins; she has wrought thus that we might have many delights, among others 'the joy of adventurous living', and of reading about adventurous living ... The advantage of our mixed condition, civilised at top with the old barbarian under our clothes, is just this, that we can enjoy all sorts of things.[3]

In this passage, what appears as little more than a passing remark in Conrad's review takes on the status of a full-blown and complex mapping of the forms of fiction. To begin with, there is a presumed transition here from barbarism (or savagery) to civilisation, though Lang does not spell out this term directly. At all events, 'we' are in a state of transition from one to the other, though at the moment we are in a mixed condition. Future man, in this account, will have evolved further away from the animal than present humanity has done – with a possible dig at Henry James, he [future man] will be more like the products of the salons of contemporary Boston. Secondly, the delight in adventure stories, typified above all by pleasure in *The Odyssey*, is a product of this earlier, barbarian (and more animal) past – and this is a pleasure that Lang would not wish to forego. This pleasure, after all, is innocent – 'fun', to use a term that Lang shares with Conrad. Finally, there is a racial mapping at work in this passage also, for 'we', who are white, derive this pleasure from the savage beneath our skin. Epic, and the cognate form of adventure fiction, are atavistic survivals of a primitive, childish, savage, barbaric and racially other past.

Such defences of the adventure story have been the occasion, a hundred years later, of a particular strain in postcolonial criticism which has aligned it, rather too simply, with the rebarbative politics of empire. The starting-point for this line of critique begins with a fine book that was published in 1980 by Martin Green, called *Dreams of Adventure, Deeds of Empire*. Green's principal thesis is that 'the adventure tales that formed the light reading of Englishmen for two hundred years and more after *Robinson Crusoe* were, in fact, the energizing myth of English imperialism'.[4] In this general account, it is the presence of a tradition of adventure writing outside the compromises and moral complexities of canonical domestic realism which provided imaginative sustenance for British imperialism. Furthermore, this tradition took a particular twist in the nineteenth century, further simplifying what was already a moderately simple tradition of writing:

The middle of the nineteenth century saw a very striking and very significant change in the culture's idea of children. Their literature was in effect captured by the aristomilitary caste. Adventure took the place of fable; and the adventure took on the characteristics of romance. Children's literature became boys' literature; it focused its attention on the Empire and the Frontier; and the virtues it taught were dash, pluck, and lion-heartedness, not obedience, duty, and piety. (p. 220)

This is the context in which to put the adventure novels of Stevenson, Haggard and Henty – they all get bracketed together in this account. These novels represent a resurgence of the atavistic form of the romance; elsewhere Green argues that other atavistic forms, such as the epic and saga-literature, make a comparable comeback in the nineteenth century. Green's general account, then, is that the ethically and politically simplifying forms of romance, as they provide the material for adventure stories, also provide the imaginative shape of, and sustenance for, the politics of empire.

Cognate with this, Patrick Brantlinger, in his 1988 book *Rule of Darkness: British Literature and Imperialism, 1830–1914*, argues that

Heroes (and imperialist writing often translates experience into epic terms) are made 'to strive, to seek, to find, and not to yield' to the blandishments of home ... Against these complexities [of the domestic social and political world], which often call for submission to social norms treated as 'laws' of evolution, imperialism offers a swashbuckling politics and a world in which neither epic heroism nor chivalry is dead. Both are to be rediscovered in crusading and conquering abroad.[5]

Like Green, Brantlinger too argues a strong case for epic providing the appropriate model for imperialist adventuring, perhaps even serving in the acculturation of the imperialists themselves. Similar to Green's argument, also, is his strong contrast between the complexities of the domestic world and the cultural forms associated with it (the realist novel, *par excellence*) – and the simplifying world of epic.

There is a further aspect to this account, to be observed in the long quotation from Green above – that there is a gendered aspect to this process: 'Children's literature became boys' literature'. This aspect of Green's case has been especially developed by Joseph Bristow in his book *Empire Boys: Adventures in a Man's World*, where he argues that the adventure stories of the late nineteenth century provide an education into a certain kind of masculinity; there is, moreover, a continuity between this kind of masculinity and imperialism. In this account, less generous and inclusive than Green's, in my view, but with this important emphasis on masculinity, adventure fiction stands arraigned as a form in which boys learn to be imperialist men.[6]

This is how Brantlinger characterises in general terms the shifts in British culture at the end of the nineteenth century and the beginning of the twentieth:

Although the equation is far from exact, imperialism as an element in British culture grew increasingly noisy, racist, and self-conscious as faith in free trade and liberal reformism declined. The militant imperialism of the late Victorian and Edwardian years thus represents a national (indeed, international) political and cultural regression, a social atavism to use Joseph Schumpeter's term, but an atavism with more dimensions, both economic and cultural, than Schumpeter recognized. (p. 33)

The terms and dimensions of this 'cultural regression' and 'social atavism' have been amply filled out by recent scholarship.[7] Two books in particular have painted a picture of the late nineteenth century and early twentieth century suffused to saturation point with martial and xenophobic sentiments, in which atavistic forms including epic poetry played a crucial role. Robert MacDonald, for example, insists on the importance of poetry in inculcating an heroic version of 'the island story' as a buttress to imperialist sentiment; in doing so he provides a useful list to make up a canon of heroic patriotic verse:

Poetry especially had the ability to dignify and make memorable the historical moment; patriotic verse was frequently anthologised, its presence together compounding the effect. Thomas Campbell's 'The Battle of the Baltic' was a favourite piece. Macaulay's 'Horatius at the bridge' and his 'Armada' became Victorian classics, as popular as Tennyson's 'The *Revenge*', and 'The Charge of the Light Brigade'. Elizabeth's defeat of the Spanish, or the failure of the Crimean war, were now 'read' through the language of verse, rhythm and rhyme adding their own rhetorical weight to an historically 'unimportant' incident, creating for the auditor a particular reality of war, in which (as in Tennyson's 'Lucknow' or 'The Charge of the Light Brigade') a handful of heroes faced fearful odds. 'Into the Valley of Death / Rode the Six Hundred'. Other verses swelled the imperial canon: Felicia Hemans's 'England's Dead' was a favourite, to be joined in the anthologies by Henry Newbolt's 'Drake's Drum' and W. E. Henley's 'England, my England'. Poetry kept up with the progress of the Empire: Alfred Austin composed an ode on the Jameson Raid, Conan Doyle wrote 'The Song of the Bow', and A. C. Benson 'Land of Hope and Glory'. C. R. Low, a prolific writer of patriotic history, attempted a single-handed monument to the nation, publishing in 1892 *Cressy to Tel-el-Kebîr*, a poem that took over three hundred pages to describe the battle scenes of five and a half centuries. He followed this with *Britannia's Bulwarks* (1895), a tribute to the Royal Navy. At the height of imperial enthusiasm dozens of patriotic anthologies were published, from *Ballads of the Brave* (1890) to *Lyra Heroica* (1891) to *Deeds of Glory* (1901) to *War Songs of Britain* (1903). Poetry transformed the everyday: a journalistic account of the bombardment of Alexandria (1882) could be heightened and given a patriotic context by a verse from Campbell. (pp. 59–60)

None of this is specifically epic poetry, though as we shall see there were a variety of attempts in the nineteenth century to write imperial history in epic terms. Many of the poetic examples cited were, however, written as ballads, and to that extent sought to use a native heroic idiom in the manner we have already extensively observed; indeed, the comparative success of ballad over epic has some suggestive implications, as we shall see later in this chapter and in discussing Kipling's poetry.

An important aspect of these late-twentieth-century accounts of the late nineteenth century is that they seek to provide, with more or less sophistication, an account of the formation of an ideology or a mentality. Crucial to all these critics, Green, Bristow and Brantlinger as much as MacDonald and Eby, is the belief that the saturation of young men in heroic literature contributed to their willingness to believe in their own destiny as servants of the empire. Thus MacDonald argues that:

Generations of public school boys, taught little but the classical authors, were trained in Greek and Roman ideas of patriotism and the glory of death in battle; by 1885, in the climate of the New Imperial age, the image of the warrior-patriot was quite consciously cultivated at Eton, Haileybury and Cheltenham. (p. 89)

while Eby asserts that

The youthful reader [of Langbridge's anthology *Ballads of the Brave*] would presumably be uplifted and toughened by exposure to the Arming of Achilles, the Destruction of Sennacherib, the Battle of Marathon, the Death of Roland, the Fight at Maldon, the Burial of William the Conqueror, the Last of the Redmen, and so on. (p. 6)

Eby adds a telling anecdote of Henry Newbolt learning the *Aeneid* by heart while at preparatory school, and being thrilled as his teacher alternated accounts of the then-current Ashanti war with quotations of the deeds done below the walls of Ilium. The picture that emerges from this scholarship, then, is one of an educational system (especially that provided for the elite) successfully transmitting a set of martial and patriotic values to its children; selecting and creating a canon of heroic poetry to aid it in the effort; and – though this is my gloss, rather than an explicit aspect of these accounts – interpreting the epic tradition as a useful means in this task.

This programme of scholarship has a clear sense of the terminus to which this set of values was leading: August 1914 and the slaughter of the First World War. The writing of Bertrand Russell furnishes the most powerful testimony to this prescription. In his famous letter to *The Nation* in August 1914 protesting against the outbreak of war, he provided an analysis of war-fever which combines the diagnosis of atavism with a particular take on heroic literature. First the account of the pro-war crowds:

Those who saw the London crowds, during the nights leading up to the Declaration of War, saw a whole population, hitherto peaceable and humane, precipitated in a few days down the steep slope to primitive barbarism, letting loose, in a moment, the instincts of hatred and blood lust against which the whole fabric of society has been raised.

And then the indictment of the literature which has contributed to this reversion to barbarism:

And behind the diplomatists, dimly heard in the official documents, stand vast forces of national greed and national hatred – atavistic instincts, harmful to mankind at its present level, but transmitted from savage and half-animal ancestors, concentrated and directed by Governments and the Press, fostered by the upper class as a distraction from social discontent, artificially nourished by the sinister influence of the makers of armaments, encouraged by a whole foul literature of 'glory', and by every text-book of history with which the minds of children are polluted.[8]

'This whole foul literature of "glory"': the phrase appears to dispatch for ever the heroic view of the martial virtues celebrated in epic. Scholarship on late nineteenth-century imperialism can thus join hands with the scholarship of the First World War which, after Paul Fussell, we have come to see as putting the definitive *quietus* to the literature of glory.

Yet the presence of Bertrand Russell in this account should alert us to the fact that late-nineteenth-century and early-twentieth-century imperialism was never as monolithic as most of this recent scholarship suggests. In fact, Russell was himself reproducing, with exceptional courage and verve, what was in effect the standard liberal critique of imperialism and jingoism in the first years of the twentieth century. The arguments of Brantlinger and others, in effect, are doing no more than repeating these liberal arguments from ninety years previously. These arguments can be found, for example, in the great anti-imperialist writer of the beginning of the century, J. A. Hobson. In his book of 1901, *The Psychology of Jingoism* – written in a state of shock at the jingoistic support for the Boer War – Hobson sought to explain the cultural and psychological sources of jingoism. What he produces is a full-scale account of atavism, where the jingo spirit is to be explained, very explicitly, by a resurgence of an otherwise suppressed savagery or animality – the two terms become more or less interchangeable for Hobson. He is careful to insist that jingoism is distinctly a product of *civilisation* – that is, it is a spectator-spirit, different from a desire to participate directly in combat: 'I have distinguished the spectatorial passion of Jingoism from the cruder craving for personal participation in bloodshed which seizes most savage peoples when the war-spirit is in the air. Jingoism is essentially a product of "civilized" communities, though deriving its necessary food from the survival of savage nature.'[9] But it is the 'survival of savage nature' that Hobson wishes to emphasise:

Whether it be that the idiosyncrasies in a crowd cancel one another, and so the operative character is composed of common fundamental or race factors, or whether the superstructure which centuries of civilization have imposed upon the ordinary mind and conduct of the individual gives way before some sudden wave of ancient savage nature roused from its sub-conscious depths, need not concern us here ... For purposes of the present study, however, the hypotheses of reversion to a savage type of nature is distinctly profitable. The war-spirit, as displayed in the non-combatant mass-mind, is composed of just those qualities which differentiate savage from civilized man. (pp. 19–20)

If this is the main point to Hobson's account of jingoism – and who can blame him for reaching out for some all-encompassing explanation of this kind when faced with the organised bullying of the pro-war campaign and the extravagances of Mafeking night – there is also an important cultural aspect to his account. 'If we would know the real ideals which represent the best standard of conduct for the nation,' he writes, 'we must turn not to works of piety, but to the life of the nation as mirrored in its literature and history' (p. 45) – and he adduces Spenser and Malory as truly representative of the English nature, exhibiting a more aggressive type of manliness that more accurately suggests the truth of England than other, gentler, cultural forms.

The general context for Hobson's more specific arguments about jingoism can be estimated from the work of the radical and free-thinking Scottish journalist John Robertson, who published a powerful critique of patriotic sentiments in 1899, *Patriotism and Empire*. Like Hobson, Robertson insists on the essentially atavistic character of inflamed patriotic feeling:

Scratch thus the patriot, and you find the pirate; test the devotee of freedom, and you find the insolent oppressor. And to no one who has much meditated on the normal moralities of men is the upshot disconcerting. What other outcome should there be from the self-glorifying parade of a primeval instinct, taken without purification by man from beast? If the braggart among men be an offence to the civilized moral sense, how shall nations satisfy the first principles of civilized ethics when they set to themselves the pose and the phrase of the braggart as a discipline and an ideal? Not from the thistles of the savage prime shall be gathered the fruits of international civility. If men, as constituents of nations, will not consent to think and reason for the whole as they do for themselves and each other singly, they must fatally, as nations, remain at the moral level of the human animal, scientific only for the work of mischief, licensing itself to be brutal and irrational in mass while claiming to denounce brutality and eliminate unreason in the individual. And the individual will all the while assuredly reflect the ideals of the mass.[10]

This indeed is a radical repudiation of patriotic sentiment altogether; Robertson extends it swiftly to imperialist feeling also: 'To put the case shortly, if nationalism is bad, imperialism is worse. If to intoxicate one's self on fatherland be unwholesome, to grow drunken on empire is pestilent' (p. 52). However, he takes his analysis further than those of his fellow-liberals, by stretching to a critique of the uses of epic in creating these mistaken patriotic and imperialist sentiments. But where Hobson was simply to assimilate a liking for Malory and Spenser as telling a militarist truth about the English, Robertson both denies that epic poems represent the essence of the nations that produce them, and also is prepared to see epic poetry as itself repudiating simple martial or patriotic feeling:

The Homeric epics, fruits of a life that was hardly even an embryo of the Greece of the world's memory, no more speak for civilized Greece than does the *Chanson de Roland* for France, or the *Nibelungenlied* for Germany; and Hawthorne already has 'spoken for America,' in so far as that may be, much more truly than Homer could possibly do for the Greece of Pericles, or Shakespeare for modern England. (p. 64)

This is an argument that neatly concedes the antiquity of epic poetry (and Shakespeare too, for that matter), and uses it to repudiate the supposedly national qualities of those so-called national epics. But Homer in particular has been traduced in aligning him with an uncomplicated patriotism:

It is indeed an express dishonour to literature to define it as being at its best an utterance or outcome of that one of all the animal instincts which has been the least sublimated in civilized life. In contrast with the passion of love, the passion of hate, on all its lines, remains nudely barbarian; and the false fraternity that grafts on it is ethically the very lowest form of the spirit of union. Not by voicing such elementary emotions has literature come to be a spring of moral sustenance and joy to men. In the oldest of the great epopées known to us, the highest moments are manifestly those in which the singer transcends the blinder passions of the earlier prime, and looks from the height of grave compassion on the clashing destinies of men. Not the rage and triumph of Achilles but the trouble and the doom of Hector, Andromache's penalty and Priam's pain, make noble for all time the poems we call by the name of Homer. (pp 67–8)

Whether or not this is true of *The Iliad*, it certainly permits Robertson to absolve the poem – and epic poetry more generally – of complicity in the patriotism, imperialism and militarism he denounces with such gusto.

Comparable themes can also be found in the writings of the Liberal journalist and politician C. F. G. Masterman, who in *In Peril of Change* (1909) contrasted the literature of the late nineteenth century with an earlier period in the following terms:

The contrast was glaring between the literature of the earlier Victorian era and the literature of the closing days. The old had been cosmopolitan. The new was Imperial. The old had proclaimed the glory of the 'one imperishable cause', allied through all the lands; the struggle for liberty against the accumulated atheisms of a dozen centuries. The new was frankly Tory; with the Tory scoffing at the futilities of freedom, described now as a squalid uprising of the discontented against their masters. The old had been 'Liberal'; in that wide definition including such extremes as a Browning and a Tennyson. The new branded Liberalism as but a gigantic fraud by which the weak deluded the strong into an abnegation of their natural domination. The old had been humanitarian; preaching, if with a somewhat thick voice, yet with a sanguine air, the coming of the golden age. War would be abandoned as irrational. A free and universal trade would bind the nations into one brotherhood. The sweet reasonableness of the English character would shine forth its radiance through all the envious nations of the world. The new had no such hopes or dreams. It revolted always against the domination of the bourgeois. It estimated commerce as a means of conflict and a weapon of offence. It clamoured for the ancient Barbarism; and delighted in war; and would spread an English civilisation, not by the diffusion of its ideas but by the destruction of its enemies. It was a message of vigour and revolt congruous to a nation wearied of the drabness of its uniform successes; with the dissatisfaction and vague restlessness which come to both individuals and communities after long period of order and tranquillity."

Here Masterman anticipates precisely Brantlinger's account of the appeal of a 'swashbuckling' politics in contrast to the drabness of domestic conflicts, and he couples it with a diagnosis of this new Tory politics as a return to an 'ancient Barbarism'. It should be recalled, against any too-ready assumption of the pervasiveness of imperialist ideas, that Masterman was soon to become a member of the Liberal cabinet.

So it is possible to find very readily in early-twentieth-century Britain a powerful and articulate critique of imperialist ideology, which anticipates closely the denunciatory 'postcolonial' criticism of the last twenty years. This critique makes prominent use of the notion of atavism: imperialism is to be understood as an atavistic return to the barbaric residuum in human nature. Given what we have learnt about the dependence of notions of 'progress' upon the assignment of epic to a barbaric past, it is no surprise to find that in several cases this denunciation of atavism is coupled with some repudiation of heroic literature, be it the 'whole foul literature of glory', or Hobson's belief in the essential Englishness that emerges in the writings of Malory and Spenser. This residuum emerges in dangerous form in the more advanced conditions of contemporary commercial civilisation.

Theories of atavism, therefore, could be made to serve surprising political ends. John Robertson could make such a theory anticipate Belloc's sharp couplet on the Maxim gun:

The story of a manufacturer who ruins a hundred poorer producers by temporarily underselling them is still unpleasant to the ear of the smoking-room; it is only when the principle is applied to warfare, and the dangerously courageous inferior races are mowed down with machine-guns, that we thrill with entire satisfaction. (p. 123)

The irony of this assertion lies in the use of the phrase 'dangerously courageous inferior races'; a theory of atavism which is applied to the imperialist countries necessarily leaves intact the very structure of thought upon which it is itself built.

IN SEARCH OF THE IMPERIAL EPIC

Chris Brooks's and Peter Faulkner's anthology of British poetry of the empire, *The White Man's Burden*, serves as a convenient starting-point in a search for the imperial epic.[12] The anthology is, perhaps, the contemporary counterpart of those many late-nineteenth-century anthologies of heroic verse castigated by writers like MacDonald, which I will be discussing more fully shortly. Poems which for Langbridge (*Ballads of the Brave*) and Henley (*Lyra Heroica*) would have been inspiriting and uplifting, reappear in this late-twentieth-century context as the exhibits in a black museum, held up for mournful examination as exemplary of a set of attitudes now irretrievably past – were it not for the new imperialism which has seized our ruling elites in the early twenty-first century.

Introducing Gerald Massey's 1860 poem about the Indian Mutiny, 'Havelock's March', Brooks and Faulkner write that 'it was one of the few poems contemporary to the Mutiny that attempted to give it an epic dimension' (p. 193). In general, indeed – extending this remark from the Indian Mutiny to the empire at large – the epic of empire existed more in the idea than in the execution; despite the assertions of Green and Brantlinger ('imperialist writing often translates experience into epic terms', supra p. 130), the *translation* of the category of epic into the modern world proved difficult, as we have seen in other contexts. In particular, the problem of epic pastiche, which afflicted nineteenth-century attempts at epic, applied with just as much force to the imperialist efforts we are about to consider. The anachronism of epic, and the possibility of overcoming this via the national ballad metre, appear both as a problem and a solution for the epic of empire also.

There were nevertheless many efforts, of the kind suggested by Brantlinger and others, to write the history of the nation, and of the empire in particular, in epic terms. One of MacDonald's examples, Charles Rathbone Low's *Cressy to Tel-el-Kebîr* (1892), is especially naive and explicit:

> I sing of arms, and of a race,
> Who yield to none the pride of place
> In deeds of gallantry.[13]

But this turns out to be no more than a versified patriotic history, whose epic invocation is all there is to indicate any epic achievements. Far more interesting is the project of W. C. Bennett, whose effort to write a 'Ballad history of England' was initiated in the early 1880s. Bennett, unlike Low, had a developed and explicit sense of the relationship of epic to ballad in the context of a national history, and this version of epic primitivism frames and explains his project.

Bennett wrote the *Contributions to a Ballad History of England* probably in 1880; his ambitions for the project were not small.[14] He dedicated the volume to Gladstone, wishing 'to make the glories of our history "Household Words" on the lips of the people'. The importance of this as a ballad history is central to the plan, because Bennett knows about the relationship of ballad to epic:

> Our history must reach the people now as it reached them of old. They are to be moved by the same means which have moved them through all ages – as the universal mind of the Greek races was kindled and ennobled by the thunder-march of the Ballad-epics of Homer; as the imagination of the Teutonic nations was swept along by the gloomy torrent of the Nibelungenlied; as the Spaniard was fired and nationalised by the battle-music of the Cid. And how much our national life needs the delight and the forgetfulness of self which the Ballad and Song can give! (p. x)

So the ballads that follow in the collection are to have this explicitly inspiring and heroising function. Bennett is conscious of the limitations of his own powers; the words above come in an introductory essay which is an appeal to the poets of Britain and America to join him in the production of these national-heroic ballads, and thus to produce a corpus of work which will be to the British and the Americans what Homer was to the Greeks:

> I ask the English poets of our time – and in that word English I include rejoicingly those of the mighty States beyond the Atlantic – to aid me in giving to the English-speaking peoples of to-day and of the future the blessing and treasure of such a National Ballad and Song literature as shall make the great deeds of their fathers a daily part of their thoughts and feelings, as shall weld together, in common pride and life for a common greatness, the scattered commonwealths of our kindred. In the lapse of but a few ages – but days in the lives of nations – our tongue will become the almost universal speech, and our race the all-ruling one. Already we add yearly to the Anglo-Saxon races ringing the world, more than the entire population of some of the secondary States of Europe; nor is it difficult to approach a calculation of that period when English will bear that relation to the most important Continental tongues which it now bears to the local dialects of our native soil. (p. xi)

This grand imperial vision, accommodating the English-speaking Americas, needs as its initial step and necessary foundation the treasure of a 'National Ballad and Song'. Bennett's hopes for his ballads are not therefore modest: 'as in every Norwegian farmer's house the Heimskringla lies beside the Bible, so will this work lie, if it be worthily completed, a treasury of elevating enjoyment and of noble feelings, in all the homes of our country' (p. xiv). The absurdity of this ambition should not distract us from the aptness with which it fits the liberal critique of empire as cultural atavism.

Yet even here the dedication of Bennett's volume to Gladstone – hate-figure for late-nineteenth-century imperialists – should make us pause. Perhaps surprisingly, Bennett's 'Ballad History' turns out to be a liberal, not to say a radical project. He sought to provide a popular history, not a top-down one; and there are strong elements present in it of 'the Norman Yoke' in the notion of the Anglo-Saxon races. Indeed, the ballad set after the Norman Conquest, 'The Hunt of the Saxon Swine', is a bloody and explicit version of the Norman Yoke. In addition, some of this verse is overtly nationalist and republican: a poem called 'The Tricolour' (1855) is a clarion call for all the subject peoples of Europe to cast off their royal and imperial masters and to rally under the tricolour instead. This can go side by side with a poem like 'Our Great England over the Water' (about America), or one called 'Our Glory Roll' ('Oh my land, thou land of heroes!'). There are several poems about the Crimean War but none about the Indian Mutiny – the sentiments are predominantly anti-Cossack (thus anti-Russian and anti-imperial) rather than imperialist.

This impression of the liberal character of these would-be national ballads is confirmed by Bennett's subsequent periodical, *The Lark*, in which he sought to further his attempts to provide a popular and heroic national poetry. The periodical, which only lasted for four numbers, was openly linked to official Liberalism, contained poems written in praise of Gladstone and Bright, attacked the Tories and attempted to link contemporary Liberal battles to the Good Old Cause. One poem even went so far as to offer the Rebecca Riots of the 1840s as a model of popular political action. So at the very least it is important to recognise how an attachment to a national-popular poetic can combine radical (or at least Liberal) politics at home with imperial sentiments abroad.

A similar ambivalence encompasses even a poem like Massey's 'Havelock's March', anthologised by Brooks and Faulkner, as I have noted, as one of the few poems about the Indian Mutiny with genuinely epic ambitions. The poem recounts, in epic terms, Havelock's march to relieve Cawnpore and Lucknow during the Indian Mutiny of 1857. Its diction is broadly neoclassical and its conception of heroism is unproblematic, as in the following passage describing the British advance to the relief of Lucknow:

> The masked artillery raked the road, and ploughed them front and flank;
> Some gallant fellow every step was stricken from the rank;
> But, as he staggered, in his place another sternly stepped;
> And, firing fast as they could load, their onward way they kept.
> Now, give them the good bayonet! with England's sternest foes,
> Strong arm, cold steel has done it, in the wildest, bloodiest close:
> And now their Bayonets flash in forks of Lightning up the ridge,
> And with a cheer they take the guns, another, clear the bridge.
> One good home-thrust! and surely, as the dead in doom are sure,
> They send them where that British cheer can trouble them no more.[15]

Notably the hero of the poem – in this extract, at any rate – is the ordinary British soldier ('some gallant fellow'); while I would not hesitate to describe this as a poem with epic ambitions, one concession to modernity appears in the popular character of the epic hero. This is a poem which combines a popular-national history with celebration of the martial virtues as they manifest themselves in the mass battles of modernity rather than the individual conflicts of the Homeric epic.

This points to a persistent problem that accompanies the attempt to write the epic of empire in an age of democratic imperialism – a problem explored more fully in the following chapter on Kipling. But the popular character of Massey's verse is not an accident, for Gerald Massey was an old Chartist of working-class origins and radical sympathies – however much later clouded by aristocratic patronage and mystical speculations. Accompanying 'Havelock's March' in its original volume were poems in praise of Garibaldi, and an alternative and more democratic national anthem. As the later case of Bennett suggests, the liberal association of imperialism with conservative politics – witnessed by Masterman above – too readily excludes the popular and even democratic sentiments that could find expression in imperialism; more pertinently for the present argument, these popular-national sentiments found their natural expression in a version of epic which sought to heroise the common soldier along with his commander.

So it is certainly possible to find attempts at an imperial epic, whether they persist in a broadly neoclassical diction like Massey's or try for the national-ballad metre like Bennett's later in the age of more explicit imperialism. These epics nevertheless have their own complicating liberal allegiances which should qualify any too ready assimilation of them to postcolonial critiques or their early twentieth-century forerunners. Other complications beset the effort at a full-scale national-imperial epic in the later nineteenth and early twentieth century, as the case of Charles Doughty's prodigious epic, *The Dawn in Britain*, amply demonstrates. Principal among these is the problem of epic pastiche bestowed upon the form by the understanding of it as essentially archaic.

Doughty originally published his poem in 1906–7, in six volumes. It is an extraordinary achievement: twenty-four books, each with its argument, recounting the exploits of the ancient Gauls as they fought with and for the Roman empire over a period of approximately 450 years. But the oddest aspect of the poem is its diction: Doughty set himself the task of writing the whole poem in Spenserian English, since he felt that all English since Elizabethan times had been corrupted. So the poem is an epic poem of ancient Britain written in Elizabethan English at the end of the nineteenth century.

Doughty was fully conscious of the national element of his design. The 1943 edition is prefaced by an Introduction by Ruth Robbins in which she sets out his conception of the poem quite fully:

To prove to his countrymen that their language was not 'outworn', he would 'find the new Anglicism': 'I seek my desire to lead the Anglicism into a good channel.' The channel he chose was a 'norm of language as that used in the days of 8th Henry and Elizabeth.' He would write in the vigour of the early English Renaissance, not only (not even chiefly) by reviving 'words of an honest ancestry', but by using all words stripped of associations, as if they were being used for the first time, in the freshness of the prime of the Mother Tongue. To inspire his countrymen to a new vision of national greatness, he would create an epic poem in which he would sing of the heroic beginnings of the nation. The twofold approach to the past, through the language of the Renaissance and the matter of antiquity, presented no difficulties to Doughty's imagination.[16]

To achieve this, Doughty immersed himself in sixteenth-century prose; he even adopted the abbreviations of black-letter type in his handwriting. So Doughty could only write a national poem by obliterating the contemporary world, and adopting the language of an age more properly heroic. The resulting poetry reads like this:

> Loud shout the dukes. Resounds the lofty night,
> With smitten shields, and cries of mortal wights.
> Brunt upon brunt, and new and new alarms:
> Now Brennus; now, uneath, stout Heremod,
> The poise of war sustain. Like sudden wind,

In that, come scour to them of Britain warhounds;
Whereby they know, that Belin's army approach.
Hark a far-sounding of iron-throated war-horns!
Amazed, the battle press of enemies,
Convert their warlike face. Gauls, whom leads Belin,
Have fired yon harvest fields. Before them, goes
Red flame, as billows wild, in wild night wid.
Of feeble corn stalks, is that fearful light;
Whereby yet-shimmering night of stars is quenched.
Day springs: like to swift storm, comes the *trimarch*!
With levelled spears, they smite a confused press.
Then shrink, twixt double army of the Gauls,
Iberians. And when now the dawn unfolds,
Is seen that hostile nation of the hills,
Well-nigh consumed; strewn with their carcases,
Strange blackened field and trampled shield and arms!
Being thus the Aquitanian Gauls avenged;
In the next days, divide the island kings,
To them much cattle, and more, to store their farms,
Than ere had crude Iberians from them reaved.

(Book I, p. 42)

Such poetry was never going to be popular. The problem that besets it, in fact, resembles that which bedevils William Morris's *Sigurd the Volsung*: the intense effort to purge the language of distracting and unheroic modernisms, and to recreate an antique and more properly heroic idiom suited to its subject matter, is exactly what prevents the poem from achieving the popular appeal to its contemporary audience that the project of writing the national epic should logically encompass. In the extract given, for example, the poetry suffers from two considerable difficulties. There is first the diction itself: the use of archaisms such as 'uneath', 'twixt', 'yon' and 'ere', threatens not merely to archaise the poem but to make it incomprehensible. More damagingly, the persistent, almost obsessive, use of poetic inversion makes the simple reading of the poem a constant challenge. While these are difficulties that the reader can eventually overcome as s/he simply gets used to them, the ultimate perversity of the aesthetic choices – a heroic poem about the ancient Britons in pastiched Elizabethan English – constantly threaten to scupper it. I do not think it special pleading on behalf of Morris's poem to say that at least the idiom of *Sigurd the Volsung* could be justified as in some sense an approximation of a poetic idiom contemporaneous with the subject matter itself.

So our search for the imperialist epic has led us at this point to three aesthetic and popular dead-ends, each of which attempts a different strategy to circumvent the fundamental inhospitability of the modern world to the traditional epic. W. C. Bennett attempted to write ballad epics of national history equivalent to the poetry of Homer; for whatever reason – perhaps simply because they were so feeble or perhaps because of their too-explicit links with official Liberalism – these poems absolutely failed to capture the national readership that Bennett envisaged for them. The second strategy, adopted by Gerald Massey, persisted in a broadly neoclassical idiom and used it for an epic on the topic of an imperial incident; while Massey did achieve a small-scale success in terms of readership, the poem certainly never entered the canon of popular heroic verse. Finally, adopting the most eccentric approach to the problem of anachronism, Doughty attempted a full-scale epic of national origins in an archaic heroic idiom; while the poem aquired some admirers, notably T. E. Lawrence, it too has entered the archive never to be retrieved. What, then, are we to make of the assertion that imperialism understood itself in the atavistic terms of epic?

Of these three strategies, it was actually Bennett's – the ballad-epics of national history – which came nearest to providing a national epic for an imperial age, though Bennett's own efforts did not enter the national anthology. It is worth re-examining MacDonald's list, quoted earlier, to get a sense of what that heroic anthology consisted of: Thomas Campbell's 'The Battle of the Baltic'; Macaulay's 'Horatius' and his 'Armada'; Tennyson's 'The *Revenge*' and 'The Charge of the Light Brigade'; Felicia Hemans's 'England's Dead'; Henry Newbolt's 'Drake's Drum'; and W. E. Henley's 'England, my England'. The predominance of ballad forms in this list is notable; in fact *all* the narrative poems use ballad forms of one kind or another. Though the problem of pastiche is less apparent, therefore, than in the attempts at outright epic, it is still a problem that bedevils these poems, as we saw when discussing Macaulay's poetry earlier, and as we will see in considering Tennyson's 'The *Revenge*: A Ballad of the Fleet'.

It is not difficult to recognise how this poem accords with a dominant version of the patriotic national story. Not only does it tell a narrative of English heroism in the face of overwhelming odds, it is also told as a specifically Protestant story – for the *Revenge* engages in battle with Catholic Spaniards, and behind them, as Tennyson explicitly indicates, lies the threat of the Inquisition and torture. However, these evident aspects of the content of the poem are in some ways less important than the poem's manner; Tennyson has attempted the ballad mode in a way which deliberately mimics the inclusiveness of the authentic popularly composed form:

> But anon the great San Philip, she bethought herself and went
> Having that within her womb that had left her ill content;
> And the rest they came aboard us, and they fought us hand to hand,
> For a dozen times they came with their pikes and musketeers,
> And a dozen times we shook 'em off as a dog that shakes his ears
> When he leaps from the water to the land.[17]

This is basically a simple four-beat ballad metre, which Tennyson varies in places for emphasis – like the three-beat anapaestic last line of this stanza. The poem's subtitle, 'A Ballad of the Fleet', indicates this element of pastiche; the conception is carried through also in the use of the first-person plural narration. Indeed the great looseness which Tennyson permits himself in the use of the metre contributes strongly to the effect of a popular speaking voice that the poem creates, even without the occasional elision (as in the fifth line quoted) to reinforce this effect. Ballad-like also is the abrupt narrative opening of the poem: 'At Flores in the Azores Sir Richard Grenville lay'; while the various speeches of the protagonists and seamen are also presented with a ballad-like directness and simplicity.

All of which is not to say that this *is* a ballad; it inevitably diverges from its model, if only in the very freedom which Tennyson has allowed himself in following the form. Moreover, while there is no doubt that the poem does overwhelmingly endorse the heroics which it sings, there is even here the suggestion that Sir Richard Grenville's desire to continue the fight verges on the pathological:

> But Sir Richard cried in his English pride,
> 'We have fought such a fight for a day and a night
> As may never be fought again!
> We have won great glory, my men!
> And a day less or more
> At sea or ashore,
> We die – does it matter when?
> Sink me the ship, Master Gunner – sink her, split her in twain!
> Fall into the hands of God, not into the hands of Spain!'
>
> (p. 1243, ll. 83–90)

From this order the seamen unsurprisingly demur. However, I am not seeking to rescue or recuperate the poem, rather to point to its success as an heroic poem, and to how that depends upon Tennyson's creative use of the ballad form. This is the condition of the subsequent popularity of the poem in the national anthology, and its prolonged after-life as a recitation piece and school room classic.

Christopher Ricks suggests Campbell's 'Battle of the Baltic' and Macaulay's 'The Armada' as analogues for the 'spirit' of the poem, and it is significant that these two should also be nautical poems.[18] Perhaps the wealth of vernacular nautical ballads made these imitations especially tempting to poets wishing to write heroic national poetry. Macaulay's poetic fragment of 1832 also harks back to the heroic national moment of the war against Spain; for him too the battle against the Armada has a liberal-Protestant meaning, though it is only implicit in the opening of the poem:

> Attend, all ye who list to hear our noble England's praise;
> I tell of the thrice famous deeds she wrought in ancient days,
> When that great fleet invincible against her bore in vain
> The richest spoils of Mexico, the stoutest hearts of Spain.[19]

This is closer to direct imitation of the ballad form than Tennyson's poem, since this is straightforward ballad metre; but it too seeks to include its readers in an unproblematic community of sympathy and interests via pastiche of the national ballad form. The pastiche is therefore less artificial than that in Macaulay's Roman poems; the presumed audience for this recital ('Attend all ye who list . . .') is a national English one with a history in common with the ballad's speaker.

Campbell's poem similarly alludes to ballad form, though there is no assumption of the first person:

> Of Nelson and the North
> Sing the glorious day's renown,
> When to battle fierce came forth
> All the might of Denmark's crown,
> And her arms along the deep proudly shone, –
> By each gun the lighted brand
> In a bold determined hand;
> And the Prince of all the land
> Led them on.[20]

The swinging and emphatic iambic rhythm of Campbell's verse lends itself to recitation; though this is not a ballad form, it is an emphatically verbal one. Like Macaulay's poem, this is from the early nineteenth century; Campbell, however, was less historically aware than Macaulay and his poem is nearer to neoclassical models of heroic verse than would become normal later in the century.

These poems all have their specific qualities, then, though their particular success in entering the national anthology was their reliance on ballad or near-ballad forms; in effect, the rightness of those advocates of the national ballad metre as the appropriate form for a heroic national poetry was proved by the success of these poems and others like them. I wish to conclude this chapter, however, by considering not the notional anthology to which these poems contributed, but the actual collections of heroic poetry assembled at the end of the century with the specific purpose of forming and bolstering national and imperial sentiments.

The two most successful anthologies of this kind were Frederick Langbridge's *Ballads of the Brave: Poems of Chivalry, Enterprise, Courage and Constancy* (1890), and W. E. Henley's *Lyra Heroica: A Book of Verse for Boys* (1891).[21] Although only the second of these volumes makes its presumed readership explicit in the title, Langbridge's volume too is aimed at boys, as his preface makes clear:

This volume is the outcome of an opinion – recently expressed to me by an experienced schoolmaster, but long latent in my own mind – that, in spite of the existence of a vast number of books of good poetry for boys, a good Boys'-Poetry-Book is still very hard to find. In other words, it appears to me that, while there are many collections of poems which we should like boys to like, there are very few collections of poems which they do like. In making this compilation, therefore, I have held a brief for high-spirited lads, and have fixed as a poem's primary qualification for admission either the spirit of courage or adventure, or else a happy narrative style. (p. vi)

The very explicitness of this gendering is striking and provides strong evidence for the kind of argument that I set out in the first half of this chapter – that heroic poetry was co-opted (or indeed was already predisposed) to serve in the acculturation of boys in the service of a heroic national and imperial ideal.

One element of Langbridge's remarks in his Preface, however, points to a perhaps insuperable difficulty in this project: boys' resistance to many forms of official indoctrination. There is no evidence that his own anthology – no matter how widely reproduced, used as a school text-book, or awarded as a school or church prize – ever overcame the very resistance that he noticed, among boys, to the previous anthologies that he wished to improve upon. Kipling writes especially well about this resistance in *Stalky & Co.* We might call this the paradox of the

impossibility of official indoctrination, though it may well be, as *Stalky &
Co* also suggests, that the unofficial curriculum of an educational system,
to which boys are perhaps more susceptible, is every bit as rebarbative in
its attitudes as the official one. At all events, the pervasiveness of these
anthologies in schools – my own 1940 edition of *Lyra Heroica* once
belonged to Henriques in 6d – is no proof of their success in the
indoctrination of children.

While registering this caveat, it is still evident that Langbridge and
Henley, and others like them, are intent on reordering and reconstituting
the national poetic corpus into a coherent national story, in which the
martial values are predominant. Henley is perhaps more successful in this
than Langbridge, who takes a wider compass and is prepared to include
translations in his work. Henley, by contrast, begins with Shakespeare and
Agincourt, and runs through British poetic history up to his own 'Pro Rege
Nostro' and 'Last Post'. He includes a generous selection of the Border
Ballads, the usual suspects that we have been discussing (Macaulay, 'The
Battle of the Baltic', Tennyson's '*Revenge*'), and includes also some recent
poetry by Kipling and Stevenson. It is a surprise to find a generous
selection also from William Morris – *Sigurd the Volsung* figures prominently, and is the only genuinely epic poem in the anthology. But altogether, both anthologies provide versions of heroic poetry which interpret
heroism overwhelmingly in martial and patriotic terms, and which
assimilate all the diverse examples that they provide to this framework.

Langbridge is conscious of this; after the passage that I have already
quoted, his preface continues:

However, I did not want my book to be a mere accumulation of fighting pieces –
I did not want 'heads to be broke' all over every page – and I have included in my
definition of courage, the courage which bears as well as that which dares; the
courage which knows how to be beaten as well as that which does not know when
it is beaten; the courage of the Quaker as well as that of the Crusader. (p. vi)

Nevertheless, this moderating or tempering impulse is effectively overwhelmed in the actual anthology that follows. Martin Green could certainly quote Langbridge's anthology, despite this disclaimer, as evidence
of his assertion that 'children's literature became boys' literature; it
focused its attention on the empire and the frontier; and the virtues it
taught were dash, pluck and lion-heartedness, not obedience, duty, and
piety' (see above, p. 130). Or rather, it is possible to see in Langbridge's
anxieties the persistence, even into a project such as his own, of earlier

nineteenth-century pedagogic ideals only partially displaced by the newer (that is to say: older, more 'primitive') ideals of heroism and the heroic national story.

It is important not to overstress these complications. While it is undoubtedly the case that these anthologies are not ultimately coherent; that boys could take from them meanings quite outside the boundaries suggested by the anthologies themselves; and that their effectiveness as official ideology is hard to calculate – there is no denying their attempted reconstitution of the national poetic inheritance in an effort to inculcate the heroic virtues among boys. In addition, their most successful entries are not the explicit epics they include – and anyway Milton is represented in Henley's anthology by 'Lycidas' and some of the sonnets, not by *Paradise Lost* – but the ballads or ballad imitations. If the nineteenth century did eventually produce a national-heroic corpus to match the 'ballad-epics of Homer', it was overwhelmingly in ballad metre or close approximations to it.

So where does this search for an imperial epic leave us? The nineteenth century witnessed many efforts to cast English or British national history in epic terms. However, the full-scale attempts in this genre, notably Doughty's *Dawn in Britain*, absolutely failed to find the readership that their project in some sense demanded. The same can be said, still more strongly, of the innumerable scraps and fragments of epic verse devoted to various episodes of the national story. Far more successful, and more unequivocally entering into a genuine national anthology, were the many ballads and ballad-like poems that did become part of a national repertoire, with Macaulay, Mrs Hemans, and the Tennyson of 'The *Revenge*' especially prominent. It was this repertoire that formed the backbone of those actual efforts to inculcate the heroic virtues among the impressionable young.

These various failures and successes all revolve around the problem of the anachronism of both epic and ballad in the nineteenth century. In fact, the comparative success of ballads and ballad forms suggests the correctness of the advocates of the national ballad metre earlier in the century: that the condition for a genuinely popular national-heroic poetry was the use of popular poetic forms, and that only in this way could any kind of equivalence to the role of epic in more primitive societies be found. These considerations weighed very strongly on the most successful of all the imperialist poets, Rudyard Kipling. In the following chapter we shall see how his verse also constructs and reconstructs itself in accordance with the problems of epic primitivism and its relationship to native heroic forms.

CHAPTER 8

Kipling, Bard of Empire

KIPLING THE MODERN BARD

The notion of Kipling as the 'bard of empire' is now such a cliché as scarcely to invite commentary. I hope that the preceding chapters will have alerted readers to the realisation that behind the familiar phrase lies a submerged problematic, that of epic primitivism, which emerges into partial view in the contemporary reception of Kipling's poetry, in its subsequent criticism and indeed in Kipling's own conception of himself as a poet. This chapter explores the implications of a bardic notion of poetry at the end of the nineteenth century, when the empire in question was in no sense equivalent to the empire sought by Agamemnon and very different also to that sought by Aeneas. Marx's questions, with which I began this book, asked, 'Is Achilles possible with powder and lead? Or the *Iliad* with the printing press, not to mention the printing machine? Do not the song and the saga and the muse necessarily come to an end with the printer's bar, hence do not the necessary conditions for epic poetry vanish?' Kipling's poetry, if genuinely bardic, would seem to suggest that the 'song and the saga and the muse' could indeed co-exist with the printing machine – could indeed thrive only on condition that the printing press provided it with publicity. If Kipling in any sense wrote epic poetry, it was under conditions of modernity that radically trans-posed both its form and its content. But it is nevertheless in Kipling's verse, rather than in the pastiches of Doughty or even Morris, that a genuinely popular heroic aesthetic is to be found.

This matter of the popular character of Kipling's poetry was one of the grounds of dispute in the relatively acrimonious debates which it pro-voked in the 1890s. The widespread sense that his poetry, particularly the 'Barrack-Room Ballads', marked an unprecedented kind of verse, char-acteristically linked this observation, for good or ill, to a sense of its popular appeal. Indeed, Ann Parry has argued it was precisely this popularity of the poems that made Kipling an object of suspicion to a portion at least of the literary reviewers.[1] They were undoubtedly split in interesting ways. It may be that the following opinion of Lafcadio Hearn, expressed in a private letter in 1897, was an eccentric one:

I have no more qualified ideas about Kipling. He is to my fixed conviction the greatest of living English poets, and greater than all before him in the line he has taken. As for England, he is her modern Saga-man – skald, scôp, whatever you like; lineal descendants of those fellows to whom the Berserker used to say: 'Now you just stand right here, and see us fight so that you can make a song about it'.[2]

But even those sympathetic reviewers who praised Kipling's verse, while they may not have considered him explicitly as a modern 'Saga-man', nevertheless typically praised him as a popular poet, as J. H. Millar did in a highly partisan review in 1898:

It is surely no vain imagination to suppose that the Jubilee rejoicings of last year possessed a deeper significance and were informed with a more exalted spirit than those of ten years before. The soul of the nation seemed to be more profoundly stirred. Ideas and aspirations of a loftier order seemed to have taken root in the nation's heart. And if such indeed were the case, it was to Rudyard Kipling more than to any other writer that the change was due, just as it was he who seized upon the unspoken national thought and enshrined it in imperishable verse.[3]

In this view, Kipling has become the utterer of the national *geist*, indeed one of the principal influences forming it. But equally those who attacked Kipling linked their attack to the appeal that he appeared to make to a popular audience or readership. Thus F. Adams, writing in the *Fortnightly Review* in 1893, deplored the fact that the poems were devoid of the 'deeper note'; they were rather 'a feast of patter songs, dispensed to the twang of the contemporary banjo in the bibulous atmosphere of the post-prandial smoke concert'. And Robert Buchanan's famous 1899 assault on Kipling as 'the voice of the hooligan' equally stressed his dangerously popular character, using the trope of atavism with exactly the opposite valuation to that of Lafcadio Hearn:

The Hooligan Imperialism of the present is a relapse back to barbarism of our public life, our society, our literature ... As for our popular literature, it has been in many of its manifestations long past praying for; it has run to seed in fiction of the baser sort, seldom or never, with all its cleverness, touching the quick of human conscience; but its most extraordinary feature at this moment is the exaltation to a position of almost unexampled popularity of a writer who in his single person adumbrates, I think, all that is most deplorable, all that is most retrograde and savage, in the restless and uninstructed Hooliganism of the time.[4]

Here the combination of apparent anti-imperialist sentiment with class snobbery is hard to disentangle. Nevertheless all these reviews revolve around the popularity of Kipling's poetry and refer this to older models of what should constitute the popular poet.

Further to this lies the evident opposition, in the 1890s, between Kipling as *popular* poet and the coterie poets of the time. One possible way of understanding this opposition was to invoke the ballad tradition, as in the following review by Neil Munro in 1899:

A brain-weary people, sick of abstruse sermons played upon dulcimers, have hailed with gladness a song and chorus accompanied by the banjo. Some of the strenuous young gentlemen who sing in pestilently unmusical and jerky measure of life, time, and early demise have an equipment Mr Kipling cannot or does not boast of. They rejoice in vocabularies extensive and precious; they have a fastidiousness that keeps them clear of the cheap tune, the vulgar hero, the sentiment of the *Lion Comique*, the dialect that is unheard in drawing-rooms. They can write much that Mr Kipling could not write to save his soul, but they cannot write so as to be read or listened to, which, cant aside, has been the first ambition of every ballad-maker since the days when Homer smote his lyre.[5]

As the final phrase suggests, with its allusion to Kipling's poem 'When 'Omer Smote 'Is Bloomin' Lyre', the analogy between Kipling's own poetry and the ballad tradition from Homer onwards was one with which Kipling himself was familiar. It has been taken up in recent criticism and indeed forms the principal plank in Peter Keating's defence of Kipling's poetry. He argues that the ancient ballad-maker provides the most important model for Kipling's own practice as a poet:

In conscious opposition to the modern Aesthete, Kipling placed the ancient singer of tribal lays, the troubadour, minstrel and scop. Poetry, for Kipling, was a public activity, a communal rite; and the Poet, a seer or *vates*, whose power with words should be directed outwards, and not simply back into the work itself.[6]

So while these have not been the predominant terms in which Kipling's poetry has been criticised, there is for all that a substantial strand of critical thought which has either defended or attacked his poetry by reference to its popular character, has set this against the self-consciously aesthetic character of the poets contemporary to him and has invoked the popular-balladic tradition as the appropriate analogue for understanding the poetry.

This would be less significant were it not that it drew upon an important element of Kipling's own self-understanding, as Munro's allusion to his poem 'When 'Omer Smote 'Is Bloomin' Lyre' suggests. Indeed, there are a number of poems by Kipling which reflect upon his own role as a poet, though characteristically by allegory or historical analogy. The lyric about Homer is a case in point; it was first published in *The Seven Seas* (1896) as the introductory poem to the eighteen 'Barrack-Room Ballads' that formed the last section of that volume (*Barrack-Room Ballads and Other Verses* was earlier published as a separate volume in 1892). It thus serves as an explicit defence of Kipling's own practice as a poet:

> When 'Omer smote 'is bloomin' lyre,
> He'd 'eard men sing by land an' sea;
> An' what he thought 'e might require,
> 'E went an' took – the same as me!
>
> The market-girls an' fishermen,
> The shepherds an' the sailors, too,
> They 'eard old songs turn up again,
> But kep' it quiet – same as you!
>
> They knew 'e stole; 'e knew they knowed.
> They didn't tell, nor make a fuss,
> But winked at 'Omer down the road,
> An' 'e winked back – the same as us![7]

This is, in the first instance, a comic defence of plagiarism. Homer stole – I steal – we both know it and collude. The context in which Homer's thefts occur is that of the bardic notion of epic origins; the Greek poet is here to be understood as one who incorporated the popular songs that surrounded him by 'land an' sea', a process of incorporation comically understood as theft. The comic nature of the poem, its deliberate and self-conscious self-depreciation and invitation to the readership to collude, should not conceal the equivalence that is nevertheless being asserted between Homer and the poet speaking here.

Part of the comedy, however, lies in the demotic accents in which this claim for equivalence is being asserted. The assertion is not the grand or absurd claim of Frederick Rowbotham that he is the 'English Homer'; on the contrary, there is an element of comic debunking, so that Homer becomes "Omer". This is not quite a parodic or carnivalesque degrading of epic in the Bakhtinian sense; it rather amounts to the assertion that the best way of thinking about Homer is to see him as resembling more a contemporary popular entertainer or music-hall singer than an exalted poet. The equivalence between 'Omer and the writer of these verses (and the Barrack-Room Ballads that follow) thus cuts both ways. It asserts, in a movement of comic bravado, the claim to bardic status in the present; but it also implies the popular and demotic nature of Homer in the past. Epic, in a manner scarcely anticipated by Bakhtin, is to become bathed in the heteroglot accents of contemporaneity.

Another poem published in the same collection, though this time in the 'Seven Seas' part of the volume rather than as a Barrack-Room Ballad, is 'The Song of the Banjo', which takes up some of the same themes as 'When 'Omer Smote 'Is Bloomin' Lyre' and extends them into a fuller and altogether more politically contentious set of assertions about popular poetry, music, empire and race. The poem is written in a set of eight strophes and antistrophes, each of which announces a different role for the banjo as it is carried around the world by the pioneers of empire. In its own way, it is yet another of Kipling's attempts to imagine the empire in its full geographical extent. But it is also a comic poem, which playfully imitates the sound of the banjo in its insistent iambic and trochaic rhythms, and in its pleasantly absurd nonsense-choruses which imitate the plinkety-plink of the instrument more directly. It is the fullest poetic statement of Kipling's aesthetic ideals which connect his kind of popular poetry to the popular-balladic notion of epic.

The very choice of the banjo as the instrument to carry these aesthetic ideals is itself contentious. As we saw when considering the reviews of the poetry, the banjo was a frequent analogy that reviewers drew upon to give a sense of its popular appeal. 'The Song of the Banjo' can thus be seen as a direct rebuke to F. Adams's review, quoted above, which considered the poems to be like 'the twang of the contemporary banjo in the bibulous atmosphere of the post-prandial smoke concert'. Equally, Neil Munro would take up the instrument, metaphorically, after Kipling's poem had been published, to defend his verse: while the aesthetic poet played upon dulcimers, a 'brain-weary' people was happy to hear these tunes twanged upon the banjo. Behind these contentions over the way to describe the poetry lies a presumed social history of the banjo as the instrument of choice for popular music. Interestingly, in the light of Kipling's assertion in the poem that the banjo is 'the war-drum of the White Man round the world', that social history included the origin of the instrument in Africa, from where it was carried to America by black slaves; in the course of the nineteenth century the banjo became strongly associated with black-faced minstrel performances. Kipling's poem thus inevitably bears within itself a trace of the very history that it seeks to overlook.

The poem deals in turn with these following aspects of imperial expansion, to each of which the banjo ministers in its own particular way. The instrument can be packed conveniently in the baggage-train of an army so that it can serve as a useful morale booster for weary troops; it can serve to spur them on to battle in impossible-seeming situations; it can remind the afflicted Younger Son (archetypal pioneer of empire for Kipling) of memories of home; it can accompany and revive the sailor as he takes ship again; it helps to move the pioneer over the canyons of the West; it can act as a plangent and sentimental reminder of your deeper emotional life; it can encourage men to face their own death in battle; and its long history linking it back to the lyre makes it a reminder of the continuities of human history. At several places in the poem Kipling makes explicit the banjo's equivalence to the heroic songs of the ancient past, as in these two consecutive sets of strophe and antistrophe from the middle of the poem:

> In desire of many marvels over sea,
>> Where the new-raised tropic city sweats and roars,
> I have sailed with Young Ulysses from the quay
>> Till the anchor rumbled down on stranger shores.
> He is blooded to the open and the sky,
>> He is taken in a snare that shall not fail,
> He shall hear me singing strongly, till he die,
>> Like the shouting of a backstay in a gale.
>
> With my '*Hya! Heeya! Heeya! Hullah! Haul!*'
>> [O the green that thunders aft along the deck!]
> Are you sick o' towns and men? You must sign and sail again,
>> For it's 'Johnny Bowlegs, pack your kit and trek!'
>
> Through the gorge that gives the stars at noon-day clear –
>> Up the pass that packs the scud beneath our wheel –
> Round the bluff that sinks her thousand fathom sheer –
>> Down the valley with our guttering brakes asqueal:
> Where the trestle groans and quivers in the snow,
>> Where the many-shedded levels loop and twine,
> So I lead my reckless children from below
>> Till we sing the Song of Roland to the pine.
>
> With my '*Tinka-tinka-tinka-tinka-tink*'
>> [And the axe has cleared the mountain, croup and crest!]

> So we ride the iron stallions down to drink,
> Through the cañons to the waters of the West!
>
> (pp. 81–2)

Part of the impulse behind this verse is the same as Elizabeth Barrett Browning's in writing *Aurora Leigh*: Kipling wishes to assert the epic grandeur of contemporary history, so that the travels of Johnny Bowlegs as he embarks on yet another voyage can be considered equivalent to those of Ulysses, and the construction of a railway through the canyons of the West can claim comparison to the heroism celebrated in the *Song of Roland*. Yet the aesthetic that governs the poetry, and which it so brashly announces, is very different from that of E. B. Browning's; while it certainly attempts its own moments of grandeur, as in lines such as 'So we ride the iron stallions down to drink', these coexist with the comic and deflationary imitations of the sound of the banjo, which aggressively asserts the popular character of the achievements celebrated. Again the equivalence between an epic past and a heroic present cuts both ways; the present moment can certainly claim some of the elevation that attaches to the past, but equally that epic past is to be reinterpreted in the light of the *tinka-tinka-tink* of the banjo. The effect is the opposite of mock-heroic bathos; where the early eighteenth century had measured the present against the past and found it wanting, moving from 'dire offences' to 'trivial things', here the poem moves from the trivial sound of the banjo to the uplift of the final two lines of the antistrophe. Epic grandeur is reinterpreted as including the comic and the insistently modern, in accents that are themselves proof of this act of reinterpretation and reclamation.

These themes are made explicit in the concluding strophic/antistrophic set of the poem, which insists on the continuity of the Homeric past to the present:

> The grandam of my grandam was the Lyre –
> [O the blue below the little fisher huts!]
> That the Stealer stooping beachward filled with fire,
> Till she bore my iron head and ringing guts!
> By the wisdom of the centuries I speak –
> To the tune of yestermorn I set the truth –
> I, the joy of life unquestioned – I, the Greek –
> I, the everlasting Wonder Song of Youth!
>
> With my '*Tinka-tinka-tinka-tinka-tink!*'
> [What d'ye lack, my noble masters? What d'ye lack?]

So I draw the world together link by link:
Yea from Delos up to Limerick and back!

(pp. 83–4)

The direct descent of the banjo from the lyre, unequivocally asserted
here, becomes the occasion for an assertion of continuities which belie
historical distance. The banjo in its final manifestation is the voice of 'the
everlasting Wonder Song of Youth'; the celebration of the ancient Greek
joy of life is continued in the present in the tune of a banal-seeming popular
instrument. The diversity of voices in the poem, indicated by the bracketed
insertions, can interestingly move from a lyrical expressiveness – '[O the
blue below the little fisher huts!]' – to the assumed voice of the antique
serving-man – '[What d'ye lack, my noble masters? What d'ye lack?]' –
indicating perhaps the deferential status of the banjo, for all its grand
claims, in the wider scheme of things.

The cultural combativeness of this in the 1890s should not be underestimated; Kipling has annexed a characteristic topic of the aesthetes, the
Greek joy of life, for popular culture. And this indeed is a wider conclusion that one might draw from this poem, that Kipling was a self-
conscious and combative poet with a developed aesthetic sense which he
advanced in opposition to some at least of the current fashions of the day
in these matters. 'The Song of the Banjo' announces this aesthetic in
serio-comic terms; 'In the Neolithic Age' and 'The Story of Ung' both
assert something similar in less uncomplicatedly comic accents. The
former poem imagines the strife between poets as a savage struggle
between tribal bards, settled by tomahawk; the more pacific conclusion is
announced by the Totem of the tribe:

'There are nine and sixty ways of constructing tribal lays,
And every single one of them is right!'

(p. 125)

This rather moderates the cultural combativeness of 'The Song of the
Banjo'. On the other hand, 'The Story of Ung' is an unequivocal allegory
on the importance of the artist pleasing his audience and swallowing any
of their criticisms. Ung is a creator of pictures in prehistoric times; he
resents criticism of them by his fellow tribesmen until his father points
out that it is these people who provide him with food in return for his
pictures. Clearly these are comic poems, and their restaging of the scenes
of epic primitivism should not be taken too seriously; yet they too in their

own way testify to the importance of that set of notions for Kipling's self-understanding as a poet.

This problematic, and Kipling's particular inflection of it, was a constant theme of his in the poetry of the nineties and the first years of the twentieth century. When he was preparing *The Five Nations* (1903) he thought of adding a sixth – the United States – and speculated on the possibility of a popular heroic song that would combine the histories of Britain and America. According to Robin Gilmour, '[he] had playfully suggested that someone should combine "The British Grenadiers", "Marching through Georgia" and other songs to "create the greatest song of all – The Saga of the Anglo-Saxon all round the earth"'.[8] The contemporary bard or 'Saga-man' would write, not in elevated accents, but in popular forms, and be accompanied not by the lyre but by a brass band playing a march by Sousa.

KIPLING AND THE BALLAD

These poems of Kipling, and the reviews that he received in the 1890s, revolve around his status as a poet: how might a popular poet be conceived in the modern world? What seriousness should one attach to the analogy with the ancient bard or epic poet? Is his popularity itself a sign of an atavistic survival? As we have seen, different writers, and above all Kipling himself, produced different answers to these questions. He was in fact a frequent poet on the topic of art and his own conception of the artist; but while the poems that we have discussed to some extent reproduce the aesthetic that they announce, a number of his other poems work more simply without that self-referential or self-positioning gesture. In particular, there are a number of poems which come close to the mode of pastiche in their effort to reproduce the manner of the Border Ballads. These poems include 'The Last Rhyme of True Thomas', 'The Ballad of East and West' and 'The Lament of the Border Cattle Thief'. The two latter are especially interesting in transposing the Border of Scott and the national ballad metre to the North-west Frontier, while the former turns out to be yet another meditation by Kipling on his own position as a poet, this time in relation to secular power.

'The Last Rhyme of True Thomas' is one of the few poems by the adult Kipling which is an outright pastiche, though his adolescent verse contained a very large number of parodies.[9] Kipling has taken the form of the Border Ballad and imitated it to produce another account of the role of the poet. Its nearest analogue as a poem is perhaps Scott's 'Thomas the

Rhymer' in *The Minstrelsy of the Scottish Border*, which similarly mimicked the antique ballad form in order to meditate on the nature of the poetic role and to make implicit connections between the ancient bard and the modern poet. In Kipling's poem, the King has decided to honour the poet by conferring a knighthood on him, but Thomas rejects the honour and instead demonstrates that his powers as a poet are of a higher and stronger nature than any that might be conferred by secular power. The poem provides another version of the scene of recitation:

> True Thomas played upon his harp,
>   The fairy harp that couldna lee,
> And the first least word the proud King heard,
>   It harpit the salt tear o' his e'e.
>
> 'Oh, I see the love that I lost long syne,
>   I touch the hope that I may not see,
> And all that I did o' hidden shame,
>   Like little snakes they hiss at me.
>
> (p. 119)

In this instance, Thomas demonstrates to the King the power of poetry to act upon the memory and conscience; he later indicates its capacity to summon up the martial spirit, and to make memory a Paradisal rather than a Hellish matter. Thomas is described as living by the 'milk-white thorn / That guards the gates o' Faerie'; the power of the poet, we are to understand, is other-worldly and not commensurate with the merely secular rewards within the gift of the King.

This is to read the poem allegorically, in a similar manner to 'The Story of Ung' or 'In the Neolithic Age'. However, the density of the imitation, its immersion in the linguistic and social details of the Border Ballad, invites another reading also, in which the ballad form itself is enjoyed for its own sake, or, at least, the complex interpretative process, set in play by pastiched forms, is triggered. As the reader encounters this poem, s/he knows that it is not 'really' an old ballad; but s/he also knows that the poem is seeking to provide some sort of equivalence to the characteristic effects of the imitated form. What we have, in short, is a knowing simulacrum of the ballad, which both entertains and elides the distance between the past and the present.

Comparably complex games of similarity and difference are put into motion by those ballads of Kipling which use the manner of the ballad to tell stories of the Indian Border. Some of the poems in *Barrack-Room Ballads* do this, the most famous of which is 'The Ballad of East and

West'. Discussion of the poem has been too much taken up with the question of its racial politics, above all on the strength of its opening line: 'Oh, East is East, and West is West, and never the twain shall meet'; the importance of lines 3 and 4 as a correction to this assertion has not been overlooked, but is perhaps not widely remembered:

> But there is neither East nor West, Border, nor Breed, nor Birth,
> When two strong men stand face to face, tho' they come from the
> ends of the earth!'[10]

However, one context for the poem does seem to me not to have been sufficiently understood: its use of the ballad form, specifically the Border Ballad, so that it reproduces the structure of feeling about the Border which Scott had encoded a hundred years previously. The opening of the narrative evokes this context explicitly:

> Kamal is out with twenty men to raise the Border-side
> And he has lifted the Colonel's mare that is the Colonel's pride
> (p. 75)

Were it not for the Indian name, this could be the opening of one of the 'muckle sangs', a resemblance to which is reinforced by the use of a regular ballad metre throughout, and by traditional-sounding formulations: 'Then up and spoke the Colonel's son'. There may even be a submerged reference to Scott in the name of Fort Bukloh that features in the poem. At all events, the story is told in a manner which overwhelmingly echoes that of the Border Ballads.

This immediately suggests an equivalence between the tribes of the North-west Frontier and the clans of the Scottish Border. The narrative of the poem, in addition, reinforces the equivalence; it recounts how the Colonel's son chases after Kamal, defies him when at his mercy, but so impresses him with his courage that Kamal sends his own son to serve in the Guides. This is indeed, as the quoted introductory couplet asserts, a story of 'two strong men stand[ing] face to face'; but the egalitarianism of this is sharply undercut by the incorporative logic of the story, which sends Kamal's son to serve in a lowly capacity in a British regiment. The poem thus reproduces Scott's way of understanding the Border families, and the martial virtues which characterise them and some stages of the pre-modern world; they are admirable, and their heroism and honour can be suitably incorporated in a subordinate capacity in the fighting machines of a superior modernity.

This is one resolution to the equivalence suggested by Kipling's Ballads of the Afghan Frontier between this frontier and the Scottish Border. Other ballads resolve the equivalence in different ways, but all suggest that the particular virtues found by Scott and others in the Border families – the pre-modern values of honour, heroism and clan-loyalty – are to be rediscovered on the Frontier. A poem which resolves these matters differently is 'The Lament of the Border Cattle Thief'. This too makes the equivalence explicit, partly by the title, partly by the ballad metre employed and partly by the use of such vocabulary as 'byre', 'kine' and 'reive'. But in this case the poem presents a more unregenerate picture of the Border cattle thief than the heroic tribesman Kamal in 'The Ballad of East and West' (the speaker is the cattle thief who has been captured and branded):

> But for the sorrow and the shame,
>   The brand on me and mine,
> I'll pay you back in leaping flame,
>   And loss of the butchered kine.
>
> For every cow I spared before
>   In charity set free,
> If I may reach my hold one more
>   I'll reive an honest three.
>
> For every time I raised the lowe
>   That scared the dusty plain,
> By cord and sword, by torch and tow
>   I'll light the land with twain.
>
>   (p. 126)

The poem therefore confronts us with an unrepentant cattle thief whose punishment has only served to reinforce his determination to avenge what he sees as his dishonouring. But it also has another function than that of warning, as though it said 'this is the kind of people that we are dealing with'. Partly by virtue of his association with the Border, the cattle thief of this 'Lament' enjoys a real glamour; his assertion of his honour, however rebarbative, still extorts admiration from the reader. We are confronted with an exemplary figure of the pre-modern world, imbued with some at least of the heroic virtues, and invited to recognize both his danger and his attraction. This is not far indeed from the representations of Rob Roy and Vich Iain Vhor.

Other poems in this group – all published as 'Other Verses' along with the Barrack-Room Ballads in 1892 – similarly construct the Frontier as cognate in some way with the Border of the ballads. The group includes the Ballads of Boh Da Thone, of the King's Jest and the King's Mercy. As readers we are led to confront a pre-modern world in which the heroic virtues have persisted; this is not always an attractive spectacle, and it doubtless presents some severe policing problems, but it undoubtedly retains some glamour also. These poems are related to others which also deal with Eastern material in an heroic or unironic way, but do not mediate this via an explicit equivalence with the Border Ballads: poems such as 'With Scindia to Delhi' and 'The Sacrifice of Er-Heb'.

The first of these, written in a form of ballad metre, recounts an heroic exploit from the Indian Wars of the eighteenth century, but in this instance all the combatants are Indian. In fact, the poem is rather densely stuffed with local proper names, so that the English reader is confronted with a thick and almost impenetrable texture of exotic locality:

> Thrice thirty thousand men were we to force the Jumna fords –
>   The hawk-winged horse of Damajee, mailed squadrons of the Bhao,
> Stark levies of the southern hills, the Deccan's sharpest swords,
>   And he the harlot traitor's son the goatherd Mulhar Rao!
>
> (pp. 103–4)

The experience of reading the poem is thus one in which the central incident upon which it is based only gradually emerges into view beyond this veil of insistent local colour. Kipling is partly mimicking the ballad form here, which characteristically assumes an acquaintance on the reader's or listener's part with particular local details. However, to use such a technique in this instance is to require the reader to reconstruct a relatively alien world and then to see emerging from it a more familiar romance: the rescue of a beggar-girl by Scindia, and his desperate and ultimately futile flight with her pursued by an enemy bent upon rape. The heroic world of the ballad, with its moral simplicities and tribal loyalties and hatreds, has been rediscovered in the insistently alien and pre-modern world of the sub-continent. The whole poem thus has the force of an exemplary fragment, in which the reader can glimpse an instant of recognizable heroism and despair across geographical, social and historical distances:

> Our Gods were kind. Before he heard the maiden's piteous scream
>   A log upon the Delhi road, beneath the mare he lay –
> Lost mistress and lost battle passed before him like a dream;
>   The darkness closed above his eyes. I bore my King away
>
> (p. 111)

So while the comparison to the Border Ballads is in this case less insistently signaled than in the poems discussed earlier, this poem too mediates the experience of the subject-peoples of empire via categories that permit them the ambiguous glamour of the heroic ballad tradition.

'The Sacrifice of Er-Heb' is similarly resistant to immediate recognition of locale and character by the reader; in fact it is quite insistent upon the exotic otherness of the poem's setting, since it is set in an imaginary Himalayan valley with a theology and nomenclature of its own. Unlike 'The Story of Ung' or 'In the Neolithic Age', however, this poem cannot simply be read off as allegory; the poem attempts some genuine heroic elevation and endows the topography and theology of its imaginary valley with convincing circumstantial detail:

> Taman is One and greater than us all.
> Taman is One and greater than all Gods:
> Taman is Two in One and rides the sky,
> Curved like a stallion's croup, from dusk to dawn,
> And drums upon it with his heels, by which
> Is bred the neighing thunder in the hills.
>
> (p. 146)

So like 'With Scindia to Delhi' this has the force of a mysterious fragment, which recounts an heroic tale in an exotic and extraordinary land; however, this is not the recent history of India, but an impossibly distant and remote history that is now being recounted as the locus for an heroic story.

These poems by Kipling thus form a set of variations upon the heroic ballad, mediating their subject matter via different resolutions of the play of resemblance and difference to and from a British history that the use of the ballad sets in play. In the case of 'The Ballad of East and West' Kipling suggests quite a close resemblance between its subject matter and that of the Scottish Border; in 'The Sacrifice of Er-Heb', an almost impenetrable distance is evident.

THE BARRACK-ROOM BALLADS

The poems just discussed represent one way in which Kipling carries forward and transforms the problematic which links heroic verse, ballad and the pre-modern world: a problematic which he inherits specifically from Scott and, behind him, the Enlightenment account of epic. Though they are striking in their way, and original in locating this problematic on the Indian Border rather than the Scottish, they do not have the originality that characterises the Barrack-Room Ballads themselves. Both *Barrack-Room Ballads and Other Verses* and *The Seven Seas* contain sections wholly devoted to poems under this heading, and it is to these in particular that we now turn. These are the poems which struck Kipling's contemporaries especially strongly, and it is these which manage to assert the heroic in demotic and contemporary terms, in a wholly unprecedented way.

Kipling's originality, in effectively inventing a new poetic idiom, was fully recognised by his contemporaries, though they tended to understand it above all in terms of his being the poet of the army and the common soldier, a field for poetry hitherto unexplored. Lionel Johnson struck the typical attitude in his review of *Barrack-Room Ballads and Other Verses*:

What Smollett in prose, and Dibdin in verse, did for the Navy, no one has yet done for the Army. Famous achievements and signal successes of armies, or of regiments, or of individual men, have been sung. Agincourt, Flodden, Blenheim, Waterloo, the Crimea, the Mutiny, have inspired praises, not always stilted and official; but the personal sentiments of the British soldier have not been the theme of any British poet worth naming.[11]

However, the manner of Kipling's achievement is not sufficiently acknowledged in simply asserting the originality of his subject matter. It is not only that the 'personal sentiments of the British soldier' have now become the topic for poetry; more importantly, the Barrack-Room Ballads present these personal sentiments in an idiom which seeks to reproduce, in some manner, their characteristic dialect. Kipling's ability to offer these sentiments, and their actions, as genuinely heroic, while at the same time preserving their demotic accents, makes the poetry of the Barrack-Room Ballads an original resolution of the problems that beset the writing of heroic poetry in the modern world.

A characteristic poem in this context is 'Route Marchin', which takes as its topic the army on the march: a topos of the epic, here transformed into serio-comic terms:

> We're marchin' on relief over Injia's sunny plains,
> A little front o' Christmas-time an' just be'ind the Rains;
> Ho! Get away you bullock-man, you've 'eard the bugle blowed,
> There's a regiment a-comin' down the Grand Trunk Road;
>> With its best foot first
>> And the road a-sliding past,
>> An' every bloomin' campin'-ground exactly like the last;
>> While the Big Drum says,

With 'is '*rowdy-dowdy-dow!*' –
'*Kiko kissywarsti* don't you *hamsher argy jow?*'

(p. 66)

The comedy is partly at the poem's speaker's expense: Tommy has some grand ideas about the importance of his regiment. Moreover, the presumed reader of the poem is invited to collude in this humour at the speaker's expense; a later footnote to the poem informs us on the topic of 'language' that 'Tommy's first and firmest conviction is that he is a profound Orientalist and a fluent speaker of Hindustani. As a matter of fact, he depends largely on the sign language' (p. 67). So readers are positioned to see Tommy's pretensions and recognise the irony. On the other hand, this ironic frame is not sufficient to undercut completely the grandeur of the scene, which retains a strong character of excitement and even elevation. The rhythm of the Big Drum may be comically conveyed, like the strumming of the banjo, yet it still manages to thump its way through the poem to martial effect.

A striking feature of this poem is its linguistic diversity – not only the imitation of working-class speech, but a further imitation of cocknified Hindustani (the italicised phrase in the quotation is translated in a footnote as 'Why don't you get on?'). Kipling, it seems, has taken the diametrically opposite approach to diction to that adopted by Morris or Doughty: he has sought to assert his heroic sentiments in the most degraded of contemporary vocabularies. Far from seeking the specialised and elevated dialect of epic, separated off from the accents of everyday speech by a 'zone of epic distance', to use a phrase of Bakhtin's, his poetry is bathed in the language of the market place. Equally it deploys a heteroglot diversity that shuns the purifying and simplifying dictions of the mode of epic pastiche. The condition for a popular heroic poetry in the linguistically stratified and diverse world of the late nineteenth century would appear to be that the heroic should immerse itself in the demotic, not seek to distance itself from it.

It should be said that the heroic is itself transformed in this immersion. Few of the Barrack-Room Ballads retail militarily exciting events. One poem that comes close to an account of a heroic military exploit is 'Ford o' Kabul River':

> Kabul town's by Kabul river –
> Blow the bugle, draw the sword –
> There I lef' my mate for ever,
> Wet an' dripping by the ford.

> Ford, ford, ford o' Kabul river
>   Ford o' Kabul river in the dark!
> There's the river up and brimming, an' there's 'arf a squadron
>   swimming
>   'Cross the ford o' Kabul river in the dark.

(p. 60)

There is undoubtedly some excitement here, and the poet does not baulk at the suggestion of the heroic in that interpolation in the second line: 'Blow the bugle, draw the sword'. Yet such an interruption to the pre-dominant tone of the poem can only be temporary; in mimicking the accents of the common soldier, Kipling has caught something also of his self-deprecation and anti-heroic attitude. Like the majority of the Bar-rack-Room Ballads, this poem asserts the heroic not in grandiloquent language but as a consequence of bloody-minded persistence.

This is largely to be explained by the peculiar rhetorical stance adopted by Kipling, or perhaps one should say the particular way that he seeks to negotiate the rhetorical situation of the late nineteenth century, a period bounded by class in an insurmountable way. Let us describe Kipling's project in the 'Barrack-Room Ballads' in the simplest manner: he seeks to bespeak sympathy for the common soldier. Questions of address are therefore important; despite the dedication of the 'Barrack-Room Ballads' section of the volume to 'T. A.' (Tommy Atkins), the latter is not often even the presumed addressee of many of the poems – which, like 'Shillin' a Day', the last poem in the section, are explicitly aimed at a middle-class reader capable of charity towards the old soldier. And more generally, the book, like any book of poems, must presume a readership distinct from the common soldier. Yet Kipling chose to address this readership, and to seek a charitable attitude towards the lowest ranks of the imperial army, not by softening or sentimentalising soldiers, but by presenting them in their most rebarbative aspects: as drunks, rioters, even as looters. It is at the very least a bold strategy: to confront the reader of the volume with some of the harsh, even shocking, truths about soldierly life, and still to insist upon both the necessity of such people (the empire depends upon them) and also upon the fact that such people deserve unconditional respect.

Moreover, as we have seen, these poems are written in a language which draws upon the heteroglot diversity of the late nineteenth-century empire, incorporating not only the urban demotics that striate the metropolitan centre (notably Cockney and working-class Irish) but also the jargon of the Indian barrack-room. This is, after all, why they are called 'Barrack-Room Ballads'. Rhetorically, therefore, the poems challenge the reader to recognise the heroic and the respectable even in situations where the presumed speaker of the poem (many are dramatic monologues) speaks in an unfamiliar dialect about matters which are deeply uncomfortable.

The most extreme poem of this kind, and one which still has very considerable power to provoke (still *more* power to provoke, one should say, in an age which can only practice its imperialism clothed in sanctimonious liberal accents), is 'Loot':

> Now remember when you're 'acking round a gilded Burma god
>   That 'is eyes is very often precious stones;
> An' if you treat a nigger to a dose o' cleanin'-rod
>   'E's like to show you everything 'e owns.
> When 'e won't produce no more, pour some water on the floor
>   Where you 'ear it answer hollow to the boot (*Cornet:* Toot! Toot!) –
> When the ground begins to sink, shove your baynick down the chink,
>   An' you're sure to touch the – (*Chorus*) Loo! Loo! Lulu! Loot! loot!
>   loot! Ow the loot! . . .
>
>   (pp. 32–3)

This indeed is a dramatic monologue – the speaker is a presumed old hand giving advice to a younger soldier. However, the poem cannot be sanitised by suggesting that it is ironic; though the form does create a distance between poet and speaker, it is not a distance which simply undercuts what the speaker says. The poem is nevertheless unstable; it allows Kipling to make the reader confront the realities of imperial soldiering without either condoning or condemning the actual soldiers. On the other hand, the jaunty demotic accents, with the serio-comic chorus, certainly don't bracket the shocking action portrayed in this stanza with anything one could describe as moral or political seriousness.

Nor is it appropriate to say that the strident racism of this poem is balanced by other 'Barrack-Room Ballads', most famously 'Gunga Din', which appear to offer positive representations of native people. 'Gunga Din' and 'Fuzzy Wuzzy', two poems in this vein, indicate the respect of the common soldier for the native imperial servant and the colonial enemy respectively. While these are indeed magnanimous gestures on Kipling's part, the point about magnanimity is that it is exercised *de haut en bas*; there is no sense at all either that the racial hierarchy of colonial India should be overturned in the light of the recognition that Gunga Din is a 'better man', or that the expedition to the Sudan should be stopped because the Fuzzy Wuzzy is an exceptionally brave foe. In short, the 'Barrack-Room Ballads' negotiate the rhetorical situation of late nineteenth-century Britain in an especially uncompromising way.

All of which amounts to saying that these are not epic poems. As we have seen, they seek to write heroic poetry in a manner which exactly contradicts the generic prescriptions for epic suggested by Bakhtin and followed in their own peculiar ways by Morris and Doughty. Even their description as 'ballads' alludes more to their broadly demotic character rather than evoking the particular popular-balladic tradition drawn upon in such poems as 'The Ballad of East and West'. They remain uncomfortable reading; perhaps the ultimate source of this discomfort is exactly the way that the poems abolish the zone of epic distance: here, the poems say, in insistent contemporary accents, is the true character of imperialism, and these men are its typical servants. Perhaps the realities of imperialism in the modern world do not permit epic poetry after all.

HIGH-MINDED KIPLING

Kipling writes poetry in a variety of styles and manners. I have been arguing that the Barrack-Room Ballads represent a distinctive resolution to the problematic explicated and discussed in this book: how to write heroic poetry in the modern world. Elsewhere, however, and especially after the publication of *Barrack-Room Ballads* and *The Seven Seas*, he was increasingly to write in an idiom that resolved these possibilities in yet another direction. When he sought for elevation, the register that he chose most naturally was not epic diction but the dialect of the hymnal. 'Hymn Before Action' and, famously, 'Recessional' indicate how Kipling sought to achieve elevated effects (what J. H. Millar called 'a more exalted spirit') by means of a vocabulary and sentiments derived not from Milton or the heroic ballad tradition, but from *Hymns Ancient and Modern*.

'Hymn Before Action' is particularly interesting in this context, precisely because its supposed situation is that which the epic tradition exalts in quite other ways. In this tradition, it is not humility but heroic memory that is enjoined upon the warrior on the eve of battle. Not so for Kipling in this instance:

> The earth is full of anger,
>   The seas are dark with wrath.
> The Nations in their harness
>   Go up against our path:

Ere yet we loose the legions –
   Ere yet we draw the blade,
Jehovah of the Thunders,
   Lord God of Battles, aid!

High lust and froward bearing,
   Proud heart, rebellious brow –
Deaf ear and soul uncaring,
   We seek Thy mercy now!
The sinner that forswore Thee,
   The fool that passed Thee by,
Our times are known before Thee –
   Lord, grant us strength to die![12]

This too is not without its own problems of pastiche; 'The Church's One Foundation' acts here both as model and as possible rebuke. Where Kipling does invoke a martial language ('loose the legions', 'draw the blade'), however, he does successfully counter it with a religious language that he just about sustains in good faith (though it is worth noting that Lionel Johnson, while impressed as we have seen by the Barrack-Room Ballads, was appalled by the 'hollow insincerity of this rhetoric' as it was deployed in the 'Other Poems'). In short, the characteristic register deployed by Kipling when seeking for unambiguous and unironic elevated effects was not that of epic but that of the hymnal.

Having said as much, however, there remains one further relevant group of poems to discuss, namely those in which Kipling rehearsed and celebrated a heroic national history. In fact, this was a project to which he was drawn repeatedly over the twenty years between the publication of *Barrack-Room Ballads and Other Verses* and the outbreak of the First World War; the first and very striking example of the genre is 'A Song of the English' in *The Seven Seas*. As we saw in the previous chapter, in many ways the most ready channel for heroic verse on English history was provided by naval heroism; in a sense the whole volume *The Seven Seas* can be seen as an example of a familiar genre, in which Britain's maritime past was to be celebrated in heroic terms. Kipling's entry into this genre is nevertheless oblique.

'A Song of the English', the first poem in *The Seven Seas*, attempts to combine a grand overview of the empire with an heroic version of English history, though this heroism is presented in tragic terms. The poem thus begins with a hymn-like invocation in the manner of 'Hymn before Action', moves to 'The Coastwise Lights', which evokes the coastal waters of England as the meeting-place of shipping that comes from the ends of

the empire; continues with 'The Song of the Dead', which invokes all
those who have died in the various outposts of the empire but who are
conceived as paving the way for the multitudes to follow; has a section on
'The Deep-Sea Cables', which now disturb the drowned with whispers
that nevertheless unite the empire; persists with 'The Song of the Sons'
and 'The Song of the Cities', which both imagine the voices of the
imperial children scattered around the earth and the voices of the great
imperial cities; and concludes with 'England's Answer', which reasserts
England's imperial mission and function as mother of an imperial race.
Described in this way, it is a provocative poem, a highly self-conscious
effort to succour the imperial imagination. It is moreover fiercely directed
at its immediate political moment; in 'The Song of the Cities', Quebec
and Montreal sing this:

> Peace is our portion. Yet a whisper rose,
>   Foolish and causeless, half in jest, half hate.
> Now wake we and remember mighty blows,
>   And, fearing no man, wait!
>
> (p. 13)

This is a reference to the recent (1895) Venezuela crisis between Britain
and the United States which had briefly threatened war between the two
countries and would have involved Canada.[13] Equally, Capetown's song
reads thus:

> Hail! Snatched and bartered oft from hand to hand,
> I dream my dream, by rock and heath and pine,
> Of Empire to the northward. Ay, one land,
> From Lion's Head to Line!
>
> (p. 14)

This is not an empire recollected in tranquility, but one imagined as
dynamic and expanding.

The strength of Kipling's imagination should not be underestimated. It
is nowise to gainsay the imperialism of the poem to notice how it
manages to combine the synoptic view of empire with minute evocation
of its details. The section on 'The Coastwise Lights', for example,
manages to envisage the action of the coastal lights that surround the
country in attractive specificity and to combine this with a sense of the sea
lanes being the 'shuttle' of empire. Indeed, we could advance this as a
characteristic of Kipling's imperial vision: his repeated effort to find a

perspective that can combine the synoptic overview, the grand panoramic sweep of empire in all its historical and geographical extent, with an insistence upon the granular and irreducibly material particularity of its multiple instances.

This can result in an unexpected and often sardonic slant on England's national history, an attitude which is certainly heroic but pervaded with surprising ways of imagining that heroism. This is true of both the poem sequences that Kipling wrote before the First World War to accompany accounts of English history: for *Puck of Pook's Hill* (1906), and for C. R. L. Fletcher's *A History of England* (1911), a fiercely conservative and partisan history for which the poet provided a set of occasional poems. Here is a poem from the former volume that imagines England's history in terms of a history of its trees:

> Of all the trees that grow so fair,
>   Old England to adorn,
> Greater are none beneath the Sun,
>   Than Oak, and Ash, and Thorn.
> Sing Oak, and Ash, and Thorn, good Sirs
>   (All of a Midsummer morn)!
> Surely we sing no little thing,
>   In Oak, and Ash, and Thorn!
> Oak of the Clay lived many a day,
>   Or ever Æneas began;
> Ash of the Loam was a lady at home,
>   When Brut was an outlaw man;
> Thorn of the Down saw New Troy Town
>   (From which was London born);
> Witness hereby the ancientry
>   Of Oak and Ash and Thorn![14]

The matter of Britain, specifically invoked here, is pleasantly reimagined as subordinate to an older arboreal history. *Puck of Pook's Hill* is part of a cultural battle in the first decade or so of the twentieth century, a contest over the English landscape and the meanings that are to be found there. Where Edward Thomas, or, in another register, E. M. Forster, were to seek to inscribe national but not imperial meanings to that landscape, Kipling in a poem like this certainly seeks to insist on its attractiveness but to attach it to an imperial history.

This is a relatively straightforward and moderately attractive example. More rebarbative are the poems that accompany Fletcher's history, many of which draw direct example from the history recounted, to offer morals on the necessity of rearmament in the present, in poems such as 'The Dutch in the Medway'. A similar imperative perhaps governs 'Brown Bess', a celebration of the musket that was the principal arm of the British army in the eighteenth and early nineteenth centuries:

> In the days of lace-ruffles, perukes and brocade
>   Brown Bess was a partner whom none could despise –
> An out-spoken, flinty-lipped, brazen-faced jade,
>   With a habit of looking men straight in the eyes –
> At Blenheim and Ramillies fops would confess
> They were pierced to the heart by the charms of Brown Bess.
>
> Though her sight was not long and weight was not small,
>   Yet her actions were winning, her language was clear;
> And everyone bowed as she opened the ball,
>   On the arm of some high-gaitered, grim grenadier.
> Half Europe admitted the striking success
> Of the dances and routs that were given by Brown Bess.[15]

This is an accomplished poem, which sustains the grim analogy between Brown Bess and an eighteenth-century lady with remarkable success. The poem, in these and succeeding stanzas, takes the reader through a history of British military success from Marlborough to Wellington; but yet it does so in words that are not 'stilted and official', to use Lionel Johnson's phrase, but sardonically humorous. To describe the musket as 'An out-spoken, flinty-lipped, brazen-faced jade' is at once to insist on its insuperable materiality, and to recast a national heroic history in terms of grim comedy. Is Achilles possible with powder and lead? Clearly not in any unambiguously unironic sense: but perhaps he does reappear serio-comically as that 'high-gaitered, grim grenadier'.

Poems of this kind, and indeed the Barrack-Room Ballads, are grounds for the assertion that Kipling did not romanticise war in his poetry. Robin Gilmour has made this case by comparing him with the nineteenth-century tradition of heroic military poetry that has appeared intermittently in this book:

The charge that Kipling's view of war was romantic can be judged by comparing him with figures such as Macaulay, Tennyson or Chesterton, poets who romanticized fighting men because they did not know them. Mulvaney and his friends are not heroes; they do not fight Homeric encounters against great odds. In Kipling's work there is no Roman leaping into the Tiber after holding a bridge against an entire army, no undismayed man riding into 'the jaws of death' without reasoning why, no lunatic 'at Flores in the Azores' taking on fifty-three

Spanish ships with his solitary vessel – not even a 'last and lingering troubadour' buckling on his sword and confounding the Turks at Lepanto.[16]

This is an argument which is true as far as it goes. But it actually confuses two different assertions: that war in Kipling's poetry is not romantic, and that Kipling's soldiers are not heroes. I take the first assertion to be true, while the latter is false. It is perfectly possible – and Kipling does it – to assert that war is not romantic yet equally to assert the heroism of those who fight it. In fact, this might be thought to be a characteristic twentieth-century response to warfare, if Paul Fussell is at all to be believed. But Gilmour's argument does require us to consider in what ways Kipling writes heroic poetry – to ask, in conclusion, what might be the modes of heroic poetry under the conditions of modernity that Kipling recognises.

As we have seen, except when he ventures upon the Border Ballad, Kipling largely avoids the temptations of epic pastiche. But this is not because he managed to invent an idiom for the heroic which allowed him to write in an elevated manner without resorting to the antique. On the contrary, it would appear that the condition for a genuinely popular heroic poetry in the late nineteenth and the early twentieth centuries was that the heroic should abandon its claims to be the highest of the genres and instead bathe itself in the demotic accents of the market-place. This gives a particular twist to the relation between epic and empire. Far from having an unequivocal descent from Virgil by which each supports the other, in an age of democratic imperialism empire can only gain poetic support if poetry loses its elevated character. As we have seen, when Kipling sought for an uplifting idiom he found it not in any neoclassical idiom, nor in the imitated language of primitive epics or sagas, but in the cadences of the hymnal.

Kipling provides one terminus, then, for the problematic of epic primitivism in the nineteenth century. Not that he ceased writing poetry in the twentieth – many of his most famous poems, including 'If—', belong to a later phase in his career than most of the poems discussed here. But it is above all in the poems published in *Barrack-Room Ballads and Other Verses* and *The Seven Seas* that his most innovative experiments were carried out, in ways that ran through the formal possibilities created by the heroic ballad tradition as he understood it, and the demands of the popular poet. Perhaps ultimately they are not epic poems at all, and that to find the genuine article in a poet contemporary with Kipling one should look to Charles Doughty. However, even to invoke this name is to demonstrate the validity of Kipling's aesthetic choices. He was an unconscionable man, who professed some ferocious and insupportable political views, which were at the heart of his poetry. But he nevertheless solved some artistic problems which defeated most of his contemporaries.

CHAPTER 9

Epic and the Subject Peoples of Empire

Among the tribe of balladeers and inditers of would-be heroic verse, for all their variety and mixed achievements, the alignment of epic and empire appears ultimately straightforward and bears out in broad terms the analysis of postcolonial critics like Patrick Brantlinger and Martin Green that 'imperialist writing often translates experience into epic terms' (see above, p. 130). Kipling's writing indicates a much more complex realisation of the heroic in relation to empire, and in some of his ballads at least it intimates that the heroic virtues are to be found on the other side of the frontier. This chapter enlarges upon this possibility; it is devoted to that entailment of the problematic of epic primitivism which suggests that it is the subject peoples of empire, rather than the imperialists themselves, whose experience and self-understanding is best understood in epic terms. In both poetry and prose, the nineteenth century saw a variety of attempts to write epics placed historically and geographically outside Britain and to represent those in conflict with imperial authority as peoples characterised by a heroic mentality. As a result, the ready alignment of epic and empire is reversed.

IRISH AND INDIAN EPIC REVIVED

Some of the paradoxes and complexities of the relationship of national poetic revivals and imperial history in the nineteenth century can be reckoned from the fact that two authors of such epics – Edwin Arnold and Samuel Ferguson – were both loyal servants of the empire and were indeed both knighted for their services to the British state. Both, however, were the authors of epic poems which drew upon ancient material; Ferguson offered his poetry explicitly as part of an Irish literary revival, while Arnold saw his poetic efforts as a contribution to assisting the understanding of 'East and West'.[1]

Ferguson's poetry, which predominantly revived early Irish stories and recast them in an attempted contemporary epic idiom, is kin to a more widespread nineteenth-century European phenomenon, in which the epic and national traditions of the subaltern peoples of the European empires were rediscovered, invented and reinvented. In this respect, he can be put alongside Elias Lönnrot in Finland, who created *The Kalevala* out of oral materials, or Adam Mickiewicz in Poland, who created a national poetry as part of a specifically nationalist project. Ferguson's most fully realised epic is the poem *Congal* (1872), inspired by the Irish bardic romance called *Cath Muighe Rath*, or 'the Battle of Moyra'; it is not a translation, but a version which draws out what the poet took to be the epic possibilities implicit in the romance.

Ferguson in fact had a considerable wealth of old Irish material available to him, much of it being published in scholarly editions in the nineteenth century; these efforts of a cultural-nationalist kind had a similar inspiration to his own, though Ferguson himself never learnt Gaelic. Some of these narratives were closely related to the Ossianic corpus that had been the subject of such controversy in eighteenth- and early nineteenth-century Scotland; *Ossian* indeed remains one of the models for Ferguson's poetry. The poetry certainly reproduces bardic notions of epic as heroic national song, and like Walter Scott in his poems, repeatedly dramatises the original scene of bardic recitation. *Congal*, in fact, could scarcely be more bardic – Congal, on his way to celebrate a reconcilement feast with Domnal, is side-tracked into a bardic haven where at a feast three successive Bards get up and recite relevant and inspiriting lays. On the other hand, the poem as a whole recounts the end of bardery and the triumph of Christianity: Congal is the last of the warrior-kings of Ulster and is eventually defeated by the overall King of Ireland, Donmal, with his Christian bishops. Congal on his death-bed is partially reconciled to Christianity and recants his martial life. However, since the whole of Book IV (the final and culminating book) is given over to a very bloody account of a battle, Ferguson has his cake and eats it too: he both revels in the possibilities of epic battle-scenes, and can eventually repudiate them as part of Ireland's pre-Christian and pre-modern past.

Ferguson overcomes the problems of epic pastiche in *Congal* by forging an idiom partly Ossianic and partly Miltonic, held together by loose rhyming fourteeners, as in this description of the climactic battle of the poem:

> But as a pack of curled waves clamouring on
> Divide and ride to either side, resurging, round a stone

That makes the tide-mark; or as storms, rebounding from the breast
Of some impassive mountain huge, go raving forth in quest
Of things prehensible, broad oaks, or wide-eaved homes of men,
To wreak their wrath on; bellowing forth from every hollow glen
That girds the mighty mountain foot, they on the open vale
Issue tremendous; groan the woods: the trembling mothers pale
Beneath their straining rafters crouch, or, driven from hut and hall,
Hie to the covert of some rock or rock-built castle wall:
So Brasil's battle, burst in twain against the steadfast face
Of Kinel-Conail, still pursued, oblique, its headlong race
Past the impenetrable ranks; and, swift as winter wind,
Fell thundering down the lanes of death, on Orgiall's host behind.
Clan-Colla split before the shock: Clan-Brassilagh poured in;
And dire confusion filled the plain, and dreadful grew the din.[2]

This manages its epic elevation with some success; the sustained epic similes of the first ten lines of this extract justify the grand Miltonic diction, and though there is some bathos in the last line with 'dire confusion filled the plain', the broadly neoclassical diction and long lines of the verse sustain the narrative excitement across the flow of the verse.

Ferguson's poetry, I have intimated, was part of a wider cultural-nationalist project which gathered force in mid-century Ireland; in fact it was a precursor of the Celtic revival more commonly dated at the end of the nineteenth century. Yet Ferguson could combine this genuine nationalism with a fervent pro-imperial sentiment, expressed in *Congal* when the poet steps back from the action to anticipate, in appropriate epic fashion, the future descendants of one of the participants in the battle:

And therefore so it was
That Freckled Domnal, set at large, for the abovesaid cause,
Which neither Prince might contravene, though for the issue loth,
In equal single combat had the conquest of them both;
Yet neither slew; but gave their lives in barter of his own:
Which Freckled Domnal afterwards sat on the Alban throne,
A famous sovereign: and his race in Yellow Eochaid's hall
Reigned after him; till Selvach, son of Fercar, named the Tall,
To proud Dunolly's new-built burg transferred the royal chair.
('Twas in his time Columba's Clerks, because they would not bare
The head-top to the tonsuring shears of Ceolfrid, neither count
Their Easters by the Roman moons, were sent beyond the Mount
By Necton and his Fortren Picts; when, in the Gael's despite,
His Saxon builders, from the Tyne, brought North the general rite.)
And after Selvach, once again to shift the wandering throne,

Came conquering Kenneth Alpinson, the first who sat at Scone,
Full King of Scotland, Gael and Pict; whose seat to-day we see
A third time moved, there permanent and glorious to be,
Where, in Westminster's sacred aisles, the Three-Joined-Realm
    awards
Its meed of solemn sepulture to Captains and to Bards;
And to the hands pre-designate of awful right, confides
The Sceptre that confers the sway o'er half of Ocean's sides.
But Domnal's brothers in one grave on Irish Moyra lie;
And to this day the place from them is called Cairn-Albany.
The hardy Saxon little recks what bones beneath decay,
But sees the cross-signed pillar-stone, and turns his plough away.

(pp. 106–7)

Despite the highly bardic nature of this poem, its inspiration here is neoclassical; Ferguson's model is more that of secondary than primary epic. This permits his unembarrassed reference to Britain's imperial future ('The Sceptre that confers the Sway o'er half of Ocean's sides'); there is no effort to disguise the modernity of the poem, even as it treats of a very distant past. In a naive gesture, Ferguson seeks to create an epic national past for Ireland within the confines of the British imperial state.

In fact, despite the immersion of the poetry in bardic conceptions, Ferguson shows himself to be somewhat suspicious of the bards, who are aligned with the pre-Christian past of Ireland. This suspicion emerges most strongly in 'The Tain-Quest', the last of the poems included in the posthumous 1897 volume *The Lays of the Red Branch*.[3] In this poem, a bard is shamed at a feast because he cannot reproduce the heroic tale *Tain-Bo-Cuailgne*. His son Murgen barters his soul to recover a copy of the poem; at the subsequent feast the spirit of Fergus Son of Roy reappears during its recital and claims his part of the bargain. This is Ferguson's version of 'The Lay of the Last Minstrel'; it too is a poem concerned with the loss of the heroic bardic tradition. What is lost in this case is the greatest of the epic poems of old Ireland: the *Tain* which Ferguson himself was never to attempt to translate or imitate. Like Scott's poem, too, there is a striking connection between the Bard within the poem and the poet telling it – a connection remarkably emphasised in 'The Tain-Quest' because the spirit of the old bards, when he does arrive to terrify the guests and claim the bard's son, is himself called 'Fergus Son'. The modern poet's verses thus dramatise the costs and indeed the potentially destructive force of a recovered bardic tradition; the poem concludes with a verse lamenting the corrupted state of the current (nineteenth-century) state of the *Tain*, explained by a curse put upon it by Murgen's beloved:

> So it comes, the lay, recover'd once at such a deadly cost,
> Ere one full recital suffer'd, once again is all but lost:
> For, the maiden's malediction still with many a blemish-stain
> Clings in coarser garb of fiction round the fragments that remain.
>   (p. 160)

The recovery of this poem *now* would appear to be the culmination of Ferguson's efforts at creating an epic national tradition for Ireland, but that is precisely the task most fraught with danger.

One of the admirers of Ferguson's poetry was W. B. Yeats; a descendant of his verse is thus the unequivocal nationalism of the Celtic revival and poetry such as 'The Wanderings of Oisin'. The different national context of India presented Edwin Arnold with quite other problems when he sought to write an epic poem on the life of Buddha – *The Light of Asia*, published in 1871. Clearly, Arnold was not himself Indian, nor a Buddhist; his explicit project was to assist in the mutual understanding of East and West, as he put it in his Preface to the poem:

It has been composed in the brief intervals of days without leisure, but is inspired by an abiding desire to aid in the better mutual knowledge of East and West. The time may come, I hope, when this book and my 'Indian Song of Songs' will preserve the memory of one who loved India and the Indian peoples.[4]

This therefore is a very different project from that of Ferguson; Arnold seeks to provide, in a suitable poetic form, the story of Buddhism, as part of an effort to make accessible to a Western audience the nature of Buddhist beliefs. Arnold thus casts himself as the mediator between one part of the empire and its imperial centre; to write the poem, he adopts the role of Buddhist believer.

Arnold resembles Ferguson in this, that he writes in a broadly neo-classical manner:

> But lo! Siddârtha turned
> Eyes gleaming with divine tears to the sky,
> Eyes lit with heavenly pity to the earth;
> From sky to earth he looked, from earth to sky,
> As if his spirit sought in lonely flight
> Some far-off vision, linking this and that,
> Lost – past – but searchable, but seen, but known.

> Then cried he, while his lifted countenance
> Glowed with the burning passion of a love
> Unspeakable, the ardor of a hope
> Boundless, insatiate ...
>
>   (p. 78)

and the poem continues with one of Gautama's visions. Even from this brief passage it can be seen that Arnold has sought an idiom of unimpeachable poetic dignity, suitable to his project of cultural mediation: Buddhism is to come clothed in the accents of the highest cultural prestige among the metropolitan audience to whom the poem is aimed. This cannot of course be a martial epic, given the nature of the subject; and while Arnold may have avoided the perils of epic pastiche by adopting a grand-sounding neoclassical idiom, he has perhaps achieved this at the cost of a culturally unspecific dignity that finally sounds simply pompous. Nevertheless, *The Light of Asia* does provide unequivocal and extensive evidence, to those who may have doubted it, of an epic history in India which long predates European contact.

Ferguson and Arnold, for all their differences, were writing from national situations in which there was a substantial literary and epic past, albeit in both cases a past which was the subject of considerable contestation. While neither writer was a nationalist, both were writing in contexts which were undeniably national – or, at least, where matters of national self-understanding and prestige were at issue in the reproduction of epics from the distant past. The antiquity of this epic material, however, and the fact that both India and Ireland were evidently not *barbarous* (even if, to use another vocabulary, they might be construed as backward), meant that the epics which both poets produced could be assimilated to acts of national recovery. Elsewhere on the margins of empire, the contact with peoples who might more persuasively be thought of as *barbarous* implied that the attribution of epic status to their histories presented a range of different aesthetic and political problems.

HOMER ANTHROPOLOGISED

In tracing what I have described as a generic map of the world in the nineteenth century, there is no doubt that the template was first laid down most clearly in the novels of Scott. *Waverley* is the paradigmatic instance: the Highland line which the young Waverley crosses is at once a geographical and generic border, and beyond it lies the pre-modern world of the clans, but also the world of romance. This pattern will be repeated across Europe and America, naturally with varieties of emphasis and inflection, as Fenimore Cooper and Manzoni and Pushkin and Tolstoy map the borders and histories which surround and precede modern nation-states. The predominant generic vocabulary for this tradition is that of romance, though as we have seen in the case of Scott himself, the relationship between epic and romance is a close one. Now, however, I wish to consider a range of late-nineteenth-century stories and novels where *epic* is explicitly drawn upon to mark the boundaries of the modern world. In this area the central novelistic figure is that of Rider Haggard, though Robert Louis Stevenson and Joseph Conrad also make significant use of the problematic of epic primitivism in their novels.

An important precursor of the novelistic appropriation of epic in the work of this group of novelists, especially Haggard, was the understanding of the mode in anthropological terms. This development was undoubtedly implicit in the problematic of epic primitivism in the first place. Ever since Robert Wood set the Homeric controversy in motion in the eighteenth century, a cornerstone of the arguments of primitivising critics had been the analogy between the world to be found in epic and that found by travellers among non-modern peoples. To the extent that any theory of the progress of civilisation depended upon the transition from savage to barbaric to civilised society (theories in which epic played a central role), then the accounts of epic produced in these theories were already anthropological. However, it was the rise of anthropological science properly understood in the mid-nineteenth century which sealed and made explicit this 'anthropologisation' of epic.

More radically, since anthropology was itself the inheritor of the three-stage theory of civilisation of the Scottish Enlightenment, the anthropologisation of epic is in a sense a large tautology: a hundred years after Wood and Ferguson had used Homer to create a sense of the primitive world, the primitive world was deployed to help in the understanding of Homer. Edward Tylor, for example, in *Primitive Culture* (1871), based his whole system upon the transition from Savage to Barbaric to Civilised stages of society and used occasional analogies drawn from Homer to prove his points. He precisely reproduced the nexus of ideas discussed throughout this book, insofar as he combined a sense both of inevitable progress from the barbaric world and of nostalgia for it:

The onward movement from barbarism has dropped behind it more than one quality of barbaric character, which cultured modern men look back on with regret, and will even strive to regain by futile attempts to stop the course of history, and restore the past in the midst of the present.[5]

Tylor's anthropology like that of Andrew Lang and (especially) James Frazer, was overwhelmingly literary and started from an immersion in the culture of the classical world.

Indeed, it is the figure of Andrew Lang who provides a remarkable link between the worlds of Homeric scholarship, anthropology and popular reviewing and story-telling. He was the author of three books on Homer as well as a substantial, two-volume, book of anthropology called *Myth, Ritual and Religion* (1887), in addition to innumerable edited books and collections of journalism. His Homeric and anthropological theories do not at first appear to coincide. Lang was a convinced unitarian and anti-Wolfian in his Homeric criticism, seeing the poems as the product of a single poet from a particular stage in Grecian history: a conception far from the notion of a congeries of older material postulated by the Wolfians. In his anthropology, by contrast, he was an advocate of the three-stage theory of human progress and saw most of the mythological material so widespread in all societies as being produced in the savage stage; the absurdities of mythologies are thus the survivals, in later stages of human progress, of older, savage, explanations of human and natural phenomena. Lang thus believes at once in the greatness and even uniqueness of Homer, and the pervasiveness throughout human life of savage and barbaric material preserved in folkloric and mythological stories.

These two positions are readily reconciled, however, when it is accepted that not all races have made the transition to the civilised, or indeed even to the barbaric, stage of progress. Those that have made the transition, like the Greeks, can preserve in their mythological stories innumerable savage survivals, while at the same time producing a poet like Homer who can write poetry of a remarkable level which is yet quite consistent with his particular phase of society. Lang is thus capable of a real universalism, even if it is tempered by talk of the 'higher races':

Many peoples have passsed through a stage of culture closely analogous to that of Achæan society as described in the *Iliad* and *Odyssey*. Every society of this kind has had its ruling military class, its ancient legends, and its minstrels who on these legends have based their songs. The similarity of human nature under similar conditions makes it certain that comparison will discover useful parallels between the poetry of societies separated in time and place but practically identical in culture.[6]

And indeed Lang's criticism of Homer is full of such parallels. He was particularly taken by similarities between Homeric Greece and the 'Germanic aristocracy, "the Franks of France", in the eleventh, twelfth, and early thirteenth centuries of our era' (p. 297); but elsewhere he is happy to draw analogies, particularly on the technological level, between the ancient Greeks and the Algonquin Indians and the Zulus.

Lang thus provides an example of a writer who understands Homer historically and even anthropologically, and yet who preserves the highest possible respect for the poet as a creative individual. It is not this aspect of his thought that makes him so relevant to my argument, however, even though it provides evidence of the potentially anthropological understanding of epic being available in the late nineteenth century. In addition to this, he was also a popular reviewer, mentor of Rider Haggard and collaborator with him of a continuation of the *Odyssey*. It was Lang above all, as we saw in the quotation above (p. 128), who made the connection between the appeal of epic and the appeal of contemporary adventure stories; it was an anthropological understanding of epic which enabled Haggard to write both *King Solomon's Mines* and *Nada the Lily* in ways that incorporated epic into his account of the Zulus.

In fact, Haggard wrote the former novel in 1885 before he came into contact with Lang; but it nevertheless gives an understanding of Zulu life and prehistory which is exactly cognate with Lang's notions. *King Solomon's Mines* was the first of Haggard's attempts at adventure novels, which he embarked upon partly in admiration of Stevenson's success in the form. It concerns the journey of three white men into the land of the Kukuanas, near relations and possibly the ancestors of the modern Zulus. The Kukuanas are treated with very considerable respect by Haggard, and are indeed associated with the heroic and the barbaric virtues in a way that precisely expresses that generic mapping that I have been attempting to articulate. This is most evident towards the end of the novel, after the culminating battle of the book ends in victory for the good Ignosi, the undiscovered Prince of the Kukuanas who has returned with the white men to reclaim his inheritance. Following the battle, the narrator of the novel, the old hunter Quatermain, describes the victory-song thus:

Ignosi bound the diadem upon his brows. Then advancing, he placed his foot upon the broad chest of his headless foe and broke out into a chant, or rather a pæan of triumph, so beautiful, and yet so utterly savage, that I despair of being able to give an adequate version of his words. Once I heard a scholar with a fine voice read aloud from the Greek poet Homer, and I remember that the sound of the rolling lines seemed to make my blood stand still. Ignosi's chant, uttered as it was in a language as beautiful and sonorous as the old Greek, produced exactly the same effect on me, although I was exhausted with toil and many emotions.[7]

Although he 'despairs of giving an adequate version' of the chant, Quatermain/Haggard does actually attempt a sample of an Homeric, that is a Kukuana, that is a Zulu, victory-chant – from which the following is drawn:

'Then breathed I on them, and my breath was as the breath of a wind, and lo! they were not.
   My lightnings pierced them; I licked up my strength with the lightning of my spears; I shook them to the ground with the thunder of my shoutings.
   They broke – they scattered – they were gone as the mists of the morning.
   They are food for the kites and the foxes, and the place of battle is fat with their blood.' (p. 189)

We get here the full panoply of epic diction – elevated language, inversion, periphrasis and epic simile. The association of Ignosi and the Kukuanas with the Homeric virtues and qualities is complete. Indeed, it is more than an 'association' – these people embody the heroic virtues, so that they are a contemporary version of the Greeks of Homer's time.

It is not just at this moment, moreover, that the connection between this contemporary barbaric people and archaic cultural forms is established. It is a feature of the whole book, informing above all the translation conventions which govern the novel's prose. Thus the vernacular of the white heroes is almost invariably treated jokily and non-heroically; it's *low*. The speech which is presumed to be translated from Kukuana (an archaic dialect of Zulu) is dignified, rhetorical, *high*: it uses 'thee' and 'thou', repetition, epic similes. This is the speech on ordinary occasions, not just at moments of grand celebration which provoke the chant that I have quoted. This characteristic of the discursive hierarchy of *King Solomon's Mines* is one that it shares with Conrad's fiction above all, and is an especially important indicator of the generic mapping that underlies all these late nineteenth-century adventure novels.

Another moment of atavism occurs in the novel when the barbaric Northern ancestry of Sir Henry Curtis resurfaces. Sir Henry is a magnificent physical specimen, explicitly compared to Ignosi; he dons native dress for the battles, upon which Quatermain comments that 'the dress was no doubt a savage one, but I am bound to say that I seldom saw a finer sight than Sir Henry Curtis presented in this guise. It showed off his magnificent physique to the greatest advantage' (p. 159). At one point he is compared to the old Northern Berserkers: Kukuanaland – the margin of empire – not only itself manifests the heroic mentality, it also permits atavistic survivals within the civilised world to resurface and flourish.

Nevertheless, the epic here attaches to the Kukuanas not the Zulus – which is to say that Haggard stops short of an outright attribution of epic qualities to actually existing Zulus. This is in keeping with his accounts of the Zulus to be found elsewhere in his writings, starting with his historical account of Zululand in *Cetywayo and his White Neighbours; or, Remarks on Recent Events in Zululand, Natal, and the Transvaal*, first published in 1882, and continuing right through to the end of his career with the Zulu trilogy *Marie* (1912), *Child of Storm* (1913) and *Finished* (1917). In these texts, though there is undoubtedly a real admiration for their life and virtues, the Zulus are unequivocally *savages*; which does not preclude some attribution of heroic qualities to them. A characteristic instance occurs in *Cetywayo and his White Neighbours*:

> No wonder that we find him [*Cetywayo*] in despair renewing his prayer that Sampson will allow him to make 'one little raid only, one small swoop,' and saying that 'it is the custom of the country, when a new king is placed over the nation, to wash their spears, and it has been done in the case of all former kings of Zululand. I am no king, but sit in a heap. I cannot be a king till I have washed my assegais.' All of which is doubtless very savage and very wrong, but such is the depravity of human nature, that there is something taking about it for all that.[8]

This is the voice of the conservative cynic impatient of the platitudes of liberalism and nostalgic for the simpler brutalities of savage life. Even savagery can have its attractions.

King Solomon's Mines, therefore, reproduces the problematic of epic primitivism in relation to native African life, but it does so in a mediated form by which the Zulus cannot quite appear *in propria persona*. However, the novels which include the character of Umslopogaas – *Allan Quatermain* (1887) and *Nada the Lily* (1992) – do permit Zulus to enjoy epic status in more unqualified ways.

It is the earlier of these two novels which recounts the death of Umslopogaas. It is prefaced by an elegy for his death written by Andrew Lang in Greek and English:

> Lament, ye birds, the battle's fallen star,
> But you, sweet nightingales, forbear to sing,
> Ye vultures only, floating from afar,
> Shriek o'er the sepulchre on shadowy wing

Of him that fed you full with spoils of war
While through the smitten fields his axe would ring.[9]

This is in itself a strange production – a lament written in all seriousness
for the death of a fictional character. The use of Greek also manages to
continue the association, begun in *King Solomon's Mines*, between Zulu
heroism and the Homeric heroic virtues. The little poem is not without
its pathos, and its concluding line with its emphatic iambic rhythm
manages a moment of genuine elevation.

The novel repeats the basic narrative device of the preceding book, as
Quatermain and his white companions, with Umslopogaas, set out in
search of a lost African kingdom, this time with a white population. The
Zulu warrior accompanies them also, and his characterisation is a full
account of the martial virtues: his courage, naturally, but also his stoicism,
his patience and his loyalty. In addition he speaks in a heroic diction
which the white characters find at times to be embarrassing, because it is
too close to boasting. Early in the novel Quatermain, the narrator,
explicitly remarks that 'there is nothing I hate so much as this Zulu
system of extravagant praising – "bongering" as they call it' (p. 23). At
this stage, the novelistic values of irony and plain speech are dominant. At
the climax of the book, however, in which Umslopogaas holds the pass
single-handedly against the heroes' enemies, 'bongering' re-emerges in an
unironic context as the old Zulu asserts his triumphant heroic status:

'Ow! For the man who can die like a man; ow! For the death grip and the ringing
of steel. Ow! We are ready. We wet our beaks like eagles, our spears flash in the
sun; we shake our assegais, and are hungry to fight. Who comes to give greeting
to the Chieftaness [Inkosi-kaas]? Who would taste her kiss, whereof the fruit is
death? I, the Woodpecker, I, the slaughterer, I the Swiftfooted! I, Umslopogaas,
of the tribe of the Maquilisini, of the people of the Amazulu, a captain of the
regiment of the Nkomabakosi: I, Umslopogaas, the son of Indabazimbi, the son
of Arpi the son of Mosislikaatze, I of the royal blood of T'Chaka, I of the King's
House, I the Ringed Man, I the Induna, I call to them as a buck calls, I challenge
them, I await them. Ow! It is thou, it is thou!' (pp. 258–9)

This heroic litany is granted to Umslopogaas as he embarks upon his
bloody last battle. His death, and Lang's lament for it, make the novel re-
enact the pattern which descends from Scott, by which epic heroism is
celebrated and regretted in the same moment. This diction, artificial and
invented as it is, is expected by Haggard to carry real power, and it
exceeds the novelistic ironies which surround it earlier in the book.

However, perhaps the most remarkable of these variations on the theme of Zulu society and epic primitivism is the 1892 novel *Nada the Lily*, which recounts the prehistory of Umslopogaas, and indeed aspires to provide an epic of Zulu life. There is a minor framing device which permits the story to be told by an ancient Zulu who has survived from the time of Chaka; the novel is thus written in the heroic mode in a language which attempts to reproduce Zulu heroic idioms, and the story told is almost exclusively a Zulu one, avoiding the introduction of white society altogether – with the exception of a minor confrontation with the Boers. *Nada the Lily* therefore seeks to reproduce the putative values of Zulu society, and does so without the narrative intervention of Allan Quatermain as in *King Solomon's Mines*. A battle scene occurs in *Nada the Lily* which invites comparison with the scene from the earlier novel. On this occasion, the battle purports to be a historic confrontation between Chaka's army and the forces of another African chieftan:

Up over the shoulder of the hill came the sun of Slaughter; it glowed red upon the red shields; red grew the place of killing; the white plumes of chiefs were dipped in the blood of heaven. They knew it; they saw the omen of death. And, ah! They laughed in the joy of the waking of battle. What was death? Was it not well to die on the spear? What was death? Was it not well to die for the king? Death was the arms of Victory. Victory should be their bride that night, and oh! Her breast is fair.

Hark! the war-song, the *Ingomo*, the music of which has the power to drive men mad, rose far away to the left, and was thrown along from regiment to regiment – a rolling ball of sound –

We are the king's kine, bred to be butchered,
  You, too, are one of us!
We are the Zulus, children of the Lion,
  What! did you tremble?

Suddenly Chaka was seen stalking through the ranks, followed by his captains, his indunas, and by me. He walked along like a great buck; death was in his eyes, and like a buck he sniffed the air, scenting the air of slaughter. He lifted his assegai, and a silence fell; only the sound of chanting still rolled along the hills.[10]

Because there is no intervention here of a novelistic narrator, this reads more like epic pastiche than the comparable passage from *King Solomon's Mines*. Or at least, both passages are caught in the difficulties of pastiche: in the earlier novel Haggard has to reproduce a sample of Kukuana epic poetry, framed by explanatory commentary; here, in the later book, both the fragment of heroic verse and the surrounding narration are seeking to reproduce an epic idiom, albeit largely in prose.

Haggard's aspiration is to write a novel of Zulu life in which epic elevation, and the mentality from which epic emerges, are made visible to the reader. Epic is thus inevitably framed by 'novel', for this is undoubtedly novelised speech – surrounding all these lines are invisible quotation marks indicating that this is the characteristic diction and mentality of a man such as the narrator. Insofar, then, as this speech is offered as exemplary of a way of life and an attitude of mind, it cannot attain the simplicity and directness of the primary epic to which it aspires. This is the sophisticated product of a novelised society which has absorbed epic and cannot sound the epic note unproblematically.

This problem can be seen especially clearly in a long and strange central section of the novel when its two heroes, Umslopogaas and Galazi, take on wolf-like characteristics and go on hunting expeditions with a pack of wolves. This is by far the wildest and strangest section of the book, and invites comparison with the lycanthropic sections of the *Volsungasaga*. Haggard has effectively mimicked the pattern of those primary epics which retain a large element of 'savage' material as a survival from an earlier stage of society. Indeed, he is explicit about this in his preface:

As for the wilder and more romantic incidents of this story, such as the hunting of Umslopogaas and Galazi with the wolves, or rather with the hyaenas – for there are not true wolves in Zululand, – the author can only say that they seem to him of a sort that might well have been mythically connected with the names of those heroes. Similar beliefs and traditions are common in the records of primitive peoples. (p. xi)

In short, Haggard has sought to manufacture the kind of epic that might have been written by a people like the Zulus – this is Zulu story mediated by the anthropological understanding of Lang. The result is a genuinely powerful novel, but one which is produced via a sophisticated novelistic mentality and which seeks to predispose the reader to understand it in a comparably sophisticated way. However hard Haggard strives for epic elevation, his words remain resolutely novelistic.

Nada the Lily is exceptional among Haggard's Zulu fiction in largely excluding any white perspective, thus providing a heroic account of Zulu life as it might have been told by a Zulu himself. His late Zulu trilogy is not constructed formally in this way, though it too precisely repeats the pattern inherited from Scott: a recognition that the pre-modern world of the clans cannot survive into modernity, at the same time both cele-brating and mourning the terrible passage from the past to the future. This is how Haggard articulates that ambivalence in the dedication to *Child of Storm*:

To serve their Country in arms, to die for it and for the King; such was their primitive ideal. If they were fierce they were loyal, and feared neither wounds nor doom; if they listened to the dark redes of the witch-doctor, the trumpet-call of duty sounded still louder in their ears; if, chanting their terrible 'Ingoma,' at the King's bidding they went forth to slay unsparingly, at least they were not mean or vulgar. From those who must continually face the last great issues of life or death meanness and vulgarity are far removed. These qualities belong to the safe and crowded haunts of civilised men, not to the kraals of Bantu savages, where, at any rate of old, they might be sought in vain.

Now everything is changed, or so I hear, and doubtless in the balance this is best. Still we may wonder what are the thoughts that pass through the mind of some ancient warrior of Chaka's or Dingaan's time, as he suns himself crouched on the ground, for example, where once stood the royal kraal, Duguza, and watches men and women of the Zulu blood passing homeward from the cities or the mines, bemused, some of them, with the white man's smuggled liquor, grotesque with the white man's cast-off garments, hiding, perhaps, in their blankets examples of the white man's doubtful photographs – and then shuts his sunken eyes and remembers the plumed and kilted regiments making that same ground shake as, with a thunder of salute, line upon line, company upon company, they rushed out to battle.[11]

'Doubtless in the balance this is best': this is actually the most positive that Haggard can manage to be when imagining the martial past and degraded present of Zulu society. His imaginative excitement and com-mitment remain unequivocally attached to the 'plumed and kilted regi-ments' evoked here in elevated style.

Haggard was actually obsessed with epic and wrote two other attempts at epic stories. In collaboration with Lang, he wrote in 1890 a continuation of the *Odyssey*, called *The World's Desire*: Odysseus sets off from a plague-ravaged Ithaca in search of Helen and finds her in Egypt. This is a story closer to *She* than to *King Solomon's Mines*. And in 1891, he published *Eric Brighteyes*, an attempt to recreate an Icelandic saga. These were not con-temptible experiments; the requirements of epic pastiche, especially in *Eric Brighteyes*, meant that Haggard produced a sparer and much less moralistic prose than that of the Allan Quatermain novels. In neither of them, how-ever, was he required to engage with the subject peoples and pre-modern antagonists of empire as he had been in his African novels.

THE ADVENTURE NOVEL

Haggard's fiction, even in the context of Lang's criticism and anthropology, remains relatively simple. Though he is capable of powerful effects, and though epic in his fiction has been thoroughly novelised, no matter how straightforwardly he attempts narrative excitement, he remains ultimately a naive writer. This is evidently not the case with Joseph Conrad, a highly self-conscious novelist even in his earlier adventure fiction. Yet it is striking that both writers reproduce comparable discursive hierarchies, by which the native peoples of empire are, on occasion, granted epic status, though this perspective is subsumed under the wider narratorial overview in the novel.

We have noticed Haggard's ambivalence with respect to the savage virtues of the Zulus. Conrad's ambivalence with regard to the barbarities of native peoples is still more pronounced. Nevertheless, there is not a straightforward repudiation, as a consideration of the early novel *An Outcast of the Islands* (1896) demonstrates. Here the barbaric virtues are associated with two different non-European elements of the population of Sambir – the settlement in the East Indies, where both this novel and the earlier *Almayer's Folly* are set. The virtues are associated in the first place with the ex-Sulu pirates led by Lakamba; and still more with the Arab pirates, Omar and his former adviser Babalatchi, the latter now the chief adviser to Lakamba. Both parties have appeared in Sambir after lives of piracy – Omar and Babalatchi after being defeated by a Dutch warship. Conrad has no desire to downplay the ferocity of the pirate life that both groups have been living. On the other hand, he associates some of the elevated features of archaic style with the language used by Omar, and indeed some of this archaic language spreads into sections of the narration. There is thus produced a peculiarly complex hybrid style, as in the following passage indicating the events which have led to the Arab pirates' flight to Sambir:

And then began Omar's second flight. It began arms in hand, for the little band had to fight in the night on the beach for the possession of the small canoes in which those that survived got away at last. The story of that escape lives in the hearts of brave men even to this day. They talk of Babalatchi and of the strong woman who carried her blind father through the surf under the fire of the warship from the north. The companions of that piratical and son-less Æneas are dead now, but their ghosts wander over the waters and the islands at night – after the manner of ghosts – and haunt the fires by which sit armed men, as is meet for the spirits of fearless warriors who died in battle. There they may hear the story of their own deeds, of their own courage, suffering and death, on the lips of living men. That story is told in many places. On the cool mats in breezy verandahs of Rajahs' houses it is alluded to disdainfully by impassible statesmen, but amongst armed men that throng the courtyards it is a tale which stills the murmur of voices and the tinkle of anklets; arrests the passage of the siri-vessel, and fixes the eye in absorbed gaze. They talk of the fight, of the fearless woman, of the wise man; of long suffering on the thirsty sea in leaky canoes; of those who died ... Many died. A few survived. The chief, the woman, and another one who became great.[12]

The condensed reference to the *Æneid* allows the reader to begin to assimilate this episode in epic terms, though the blind Omar is both Æneas himself, and Anchises borne on Æneas's shoulders from the flames of burning Troy. More generally, the complex double-voiced discourse of the passage moves in and out of the heroic vocabulary of the 'armed men' who tell and retell the story around their fires. Thus the ghosts 'haunt the fires by which sit armed men, as is meet for the spirits of fearless warriors who died in battle'. Here, the vocabulary and indeed the whole mentality of the subordinate group momentarily achieves narratorial authority, as it does again at the end of the passage. This then is a complex and shifting discursive hierarchy, in which the heroic valuations of the pirates and their sympathisers are by no means simply repudiated. Epic elevation has migrated from Troy and taken up momentary residence around the campfires of East Indian pirates. Conrad's complex experiment in point of view has permitted this eruption from an archaic past. Significantly, the translation conventions of this novel – the ways in which those supposed to be speaking a native language are rendered – resemble those of Rider Haggard, though in a more discreet way. Thus archaic 'high' diction is associated with the Sulus, Malays and Arabs, the latter case being especially interesting because the language of Islam also appears as a language of dignity.

In the earlier *Almayer's Folly* (1895), the barbaric virtues had been less unequivocally repudiated. Almayer's mixed-race daughter is driven to choose between the different parts of her inheritance: between the enfeebled European civilisation of her father and the more savage and piratical inheritance of her mother. The conflict is figured in the book as one of atavism:

And listening to the recital of those savage glories, those barbarous fights and savage feasting, to the stories of deeds valorous, albeit somewhat bloodthirsty, where men of her mother's race shone far above the Orang Blanda, she felt herself irresistibly fascinated, and saw with vague surprise the narrow mantle of civilised morality, in which good-meaning people had wrapped her young soul, fall away and leave her shivering and helpless as if on the edge of some deep and unknown abyss.[13]

This passage, which anticipates the world-view soon to be articulated in *Heart of Darkness* – that civilisation teeters on the brink of an ever-threatening savagery – does so in a manner which is perhaps more interesting. For the line drawn in *Almayer's Folly* between 'civilised morality' and 'savage glories' places on the side of savagery 'stories of deeds valorous'; the heroic virtues briefly appear here, in a moment of ambivalence, across the line from civilisation. In this novel also, as in *An Outcast of the Islands*, matters are complicated by the discursive hierarchy of the prose; the phrase 'deeds valorous' in the passage quoted appears as an echo of Nina's mother's speech, and she is largely portrayed in a hostile fashion. So finally one would say that the passage repudiates savagery, however heroic, more thoroughly than the comparable moment in the later novel; nevertheless, in both these early novels the overall discursive economy allows the ambivalent presence of the martial virtues (at least momentarily configured as epic) to appear as characteristics of native rather than imperial peoples.

As we have seen, one substantial model for this association of the epic virtues with the margins of the modern world was the fiction of Scott, so it is unsurprising that it was Scott's most professed imitator at the end of the century, Robert Louis Stevenson, who also reproduced this pattern most explicitly in his fiction. Contemporaneous with Haggard's, Stevenson's adventure fiction in the 1880s similarly saw itself as offering some uncomplicated narrative excitement to the jaded palates of urban Britain – and was admired by Lang for similar reasons. If, with considerable ambivalence, Conrad associates the heroic or barbaric virtues with the non-white peoples of the imperial margins, Stevenson, in his Scottish stories, associates them above all with the clans and the Highlands.

This is most evidently seen in *Kidnapped* (1886), where the heroic virtues are embodied in the figure of Alan Breck, alias Alan Stewart. Stevenson, too, is ambivalent about the heroic virtues, though perhaps the boyishness of the fiction – its frank escapism – permits him to be less anxious about this than the more portentous concerns of Conrad. At all events, Breck is a compound of braggart and hero who is permitted some at least of the elevation of the heroic, as when he frees himself and the narrator from captivity on board ship; he celebrates by composing and singing a victory song in Gaelic, which is then helpfully translated:

> This is the song of the sword of Alan:
> The smith made it,
> The fire set it;
> Now it shines in the hand of Alan Breck.
> Their eyes were many and bright,
> Swift were they to behold,
> Many the hands they guided:
> The sword was alone.
> The dun deer troop over the hill,
> They are many, the hill is one;
> The dun deer vanish,
> The hill remains.
> Come to me from the hills of heather,
> Come from the isles of the sea.
> O far-beholding eagles,
> Here is your meat.[14]

The model here is ultimately Ossianic rather than Homeric, and is introduced as a prose rather than a verse translation. Nevertheless Stevenson does attempt to convey a kind of heroic elevation. The fact that it is surrounded by some rather prosaic commentary by Davie Balfour (the novel's narrator) partly undercuts this elevation – he both insists on the part he himself played in the fight and refuses heroic status by being violently sick after the brawl. So the novel includes, incorporates and undercuts the epic moments that it reproduces.

If Stevenson is the inheritor of Scott, he is so on a reduced scale. Where Scott dealt with what Lukács called, in his Hegelian idiom, 'world-historical' events, Stevenson's stories are all personal adventures, despite their evocations of the generic mappings of his earlier nineteenth-century predecessor. The same can be said of another of his eighteenth-century novels, the dark story *The Master of Ballantrae* (1889). This briefly invokes the equivalence between Highland and African society in the Master's boasting claim that he was fit to be a king:

'Had I been Alexander –' he began.

'It is so we all dupe ourselves,' I cried. 'Had I been St Paul, it would have been all one; I would have made the same hash of that career that you now see me making of my own.'

'I tell you,' he cried, bearing down my interruption; 'had I been the least petty chieftan in the Highlands, had I been the least king of naked negroes in the African desert, my people would have adored me. A bad man, am I? Ah! But I was born for a good tyrant! Ask Secundra Dass; he will tell you I treat him like a son ... I have a kingly nature: there is my loss!"[15]

Stevenson here appears to be repudiating the whole complex of paternalistic, regal and barbarous virtues which he identifies with the Master. What Scott has appeared as a profound way of understanding his contemporary world and the history which was transforming it in Stevenson reappears as scarcely stated themes which, nevertheless, provide the generic geography of the world in which his stories unfold.

Andrew Lang welcomed the revival of adventure stories in the 1880s as providing a tonic to the otherwise drab world of the contemporary novel; for him, these stories were themselves descendants of epic, and offered excitements of a kind comparable to those provided by Homer. Such a view is at least debatable; the line from the *Iliad* to *King Solomon's Mines*, considered simply as narratives, is surely too tenuous to sustain Lang's assertion other than as a rhetorical move in the arguments over the nature of fiction. On the other hand, it is certainly true, in all the writers commended by Lang, that the narratives gain excitement and interest as the protagonists cross the various borders which divide the modern from the pre-modern world. This is the process so well described by Franco Moretti. I have been arguing in this chapter, however, that the worlds to which the protagonists travel can themselves be seen in epic terms, and that a condition of this ascription is the primitivist understanding of epic.

Furthermore, the discursive hierarchies of the novels of Conrad, Haggard and Stevenson mean that the irruption of epic into their texts has ultimately an ambivalent charge. There is no escaping, to use a Bakhtinian vocabulary, the novelisation of the word of epic – its appearance in various forms of double-voiced discourse, its surrounding by various deflating and ironising contexts. Equally, there is no possibility of these writers producing in their novels an epic voice unconscious of the modern context in which these voices are imagined. To that extent, epic would appear to have been subsumed, as Bakhtin asserts, by the all-engulfing maw of the novel.

Yet I have also suggested how, in the novels of Haggard especially, but also in the details of Conrad's and Stevenson's fictions, an epic perspective is left to stand unhampered by the surrounding novelistic ironies. These matters cannot ultimately be judged at the level of artistic intention – Haggard may have wished for his readers to admire and lament the death of Umslopogaas in the manner of Andrew Lang, but he could not ensure that they did so, and by and large *Allan Quatermain* and

Nada the Lily have not had much currency in the twentieth century, even as members of a residual canon of children's books. Yet the ambivalence of these books, as they react with such admiration and horror to the persistence of the epic virtues, testifies to the continuing ambivalence of the modern world to the barbarous past from which it sees itself as emerging.

It remains to consider the political ambiguities which attach to the ascription of the epic virtues to the subject peoples of empire. On the one hand, the claim to a history understood in epic terms seems to be an unequivocal benefit for such peoples – and the reminder that Ireland and India have ancient epic histories comparable to those of Greece and Rome is an important corrective to the cultural chauvinism of the metropolitan centres of empire. Such a reminder can never be certain of a sympathetic audience: we have seen how Hegel denied any world-historical significance to Indian epic, and Macaulay famously insisted upon the worthlessness of Indian literature by comparison with that of the West. Nevertheless, the claim to the prestige of epic on behalf of subaltern peoples marked a crucial stage in the nineteenth-century coming-to-consciousness of many of them.

And yet, on the other hand, the ascription of an epic history marked these emergent national consciousnesses with the rebarbative and atavistic characteristic that epic carried, almost by definition, in the modern world – and it certainly did not protect many of these subject peoples from the murderous embrace of imperialism. Either – as in the case of the Zulus – such peoples fell victim to the brutal realities of uneven development or their pre-modern martial prestige could make them, like the Black Watch in Scotland, excellent recruits for the imperial armies. At all events, some of the myriad ways in which the problematic of epic primitivism worked itself out in the twentieth century are sketched in, as a coda, in the following and final chapter.

CHAPTER 10

Coda: Some Homeric Futures

We have noted how the First World War provided one significant terminus for what Russell described as the 'whole foul literature of glory'. While it is true that the War made the survival of the epic view of martial and imperial history difficult to sustain, we should not simply accept that the remainder of the twentieth century had no ways of negotiating and carrying forward the generic legacy of epic. In this final chapter, I suggest some of these ways: how the disputes over the understanding of epic in the nineteenth century were renewed and transformed in the twentieth. The problematic of epic primitivism, with all its accompanying themes and aesthetic challenges, has not been superseded: twentieth-century modernity has resolved these challenges in ways which sometimes resemble closely, though they sometimes depart from, their resolutions in the nineteenth century. The following provides hints only, brief discussions of a few exemplary instances where the persistence of that problematic can be seen most clearly.

MILMAN PARRY AND THE RESOLUTION OF THE HOMERIC CONTROVERSY

The major figure in twentieth-century Homeric scholarship was undoubtedly Milman Parry, whose work both carried forward the problematic of epic primitivism and did so in such a way as to resolve many of the outstanding aspects of the Homeric controversy. In particular, Parry transcended the nineteenth-century distinction between analysts and unitarians (those who wished to break down Homer's poems into their constituent lays, and those who emphasised their creative unity) by the notion of a *traditional* and then an *oral* poet: the peculiarities of the Homeric style could all be explained as characteristic of an oral tradition evolved over several generations, marked by repeated formulae and larger narrative themes. This insight precedes Parry's discovery and study of

'Jugoslav' oral poetry conducted in the thirties; but this study led him towards comparative criticism of epic poetry and its presence in contemporary pre-modern societies.

Parry thus at once repeated and transformed the problematic of the Homeric controversy. He repeated it because many of the motifs that were to be found in the course of the controversy are to be found again in his work: the notion of Homer as an oral poet; the comparisons with other epic or bardic traditions; the belief that analogues can be found for the epic mode in other still-extant societies.[1] He transformed it because he could resolve the controversies that marked the Homeric question by the notions of the *tradition* and *oral* poetry: formulaic poetry retained both different dialectal forms and details from different moments of history, so that there was no need to posit different 'layers'. Parry was himself a 'unitarian' because he had such a strong sense of the tradition which made available the diction, manner and essential nobility of the epic style available to the individual poet working within the tradition.

This was a very considerable scholarly achievement, and while it did not resolve all the issues at stake in the Homeric controversy, at least it put their discussion on a wholly new basis. However, it is important to recognise also that some aspects of the old problematic persist, in a transformed idiom, into Parry's scholarship – especially concerning the ideological attraction of the heroic world to a modernity drained of affect. His account of Homeric diction, especially the use of traditional formulaic metaphors, for example, produces his most explicit statement of the attractions of that diction both to its putative original audience and to a modern readership:

As the fixed diction of the Augustan age can only be understood as the expression of a whole way of life which we may call the proper, so Homer's traditional diction is the work of a way of life which we may call the heroic, if one will give that word all the meaning it had for the men of Homer's time. It is a term which can only be understood in the measure that one can think and feel as they did, for the heroic was to them no more or less than the statement of all that they would be or would do if they could. To give form to this heroic cast of thought they had the old tales that had come down in time, and they had a rhythm in which to tell them, and words and phrases with which to tell them. The making of this diction was due to countless poets and to many generations who in time had found the heroic word and phrase for every thought, and every word in it was holy and sweet and wondrous, and no one would think of changing it willfully. The Muses it was truly who gave those poets voices sweeter than honey. And those parts of the diction which did not carry the story itself, since their meaning was not needed for understanding, lost that meaning, but became, as it were, a familiar music of which the mind is pleasantly aware, but which it knows so well that it makes no effort to follow it. Indeed, poetry thus approaches music most closely when the words have rather a mood than a meaning. Nor should one think that since the meaning is largely lost it ceases to matter if the meaning is good. Though the meaning be felt rather than understood it is there, as it matters whether music idly heard be bad or good. Of such a kind is the charm of the fixed metaphor in Homer. It is an incantation of the heroic. (pp. 374–5)

This is a striking passage, which offers to explain the continuing attraction of a traditional diction to an audience who, it was known, had partially lost an understanding of some of the words and phrases in that diction. The explanation is a historical one: this diction was forged over several generations by the oral poets of an heroic society, and continued to have the appeal of the heroic values which that society held dear. However, the condition for Parry to make this argument is that he himself (or the modern scholar that he represents) should himself be open to the glamour of the poetry that he is studying: the heroic 'is a term which can only be understood in the measure that one can think and feel as they did'. Thus when Parry describes the original audience as hearing the poetry as 'holy and sweet and wondrous', he can only do so because it has that value for him also.

Adam Parry recognised an aspect of this in his father's work; he contends in his Preface to Milman Parry's collected papers that

we can see here that the historical scholar is the child of his own age. In a sense Parry is one of the lovers of the exotic of our own century, and his admiration for a language formed by the clear exigencies of singing and directly expressive of heroic ideals reminds us of Hemingway finding courage and beauty in the vision of the Spanish bullfighter, or of T. E. Lawrence (one of Parry's favourite authors) finding a more satisfactory theatre of self-realization in the austere simplicities of Arab life. (p. xxvi)

This is not ultimately a matter for scholarly resolution; what is at stake here is a persistence into the twentieth century of an attitude towards the premodern world by which its glamour is refracted through the spell of epic. T. E. Lawrence's *Seven Pillars of Wisdom*, the most prominent book by a writer offered in this passage as one of those whom Parry admired, provides one of the most explicit and extended statements of this structure of feeling.

PARRY, DOUGHTY, LAWRENCE: THE EPIC OF ARABIA

Another figure links Parry and T. E. Lawrence, however, and that is Charles Doughty, not in his character as the author of *Dawn in Britain*, but in his earlier guise as an Arabian traveller and author of *Travels in Arabia Deserta*, first published in 1888. Lawrence's admiration is clear – he wrote a respectful preface for a new edition of the book in 1921, which also remained in place when the book was again republished in 1936.[2] Lawrence appreciated Doughty's volumes as a guide to the Arabian hinterland and its tribes, but he also admired their author as a stylist; he found in Doughty's prose a model for his own distinctive and slightly archaic writing style. Parry's admiration was of a different kind; he quotes *Arabia Deserta* as providing evidence for the kind of society which produced one characteristic trope at least of epic poetry: the cattle-raid.[3]

In Chapter 2 it was observed how William Maginn, the mid-nineteenth-century poet and translator, had made the connection between the Border Ballads and Homer by referring to 'moss-trooping Nestor'; drawing upon Nestor's account of a cattle-raid into Elis in Book 11 of the *Iliad*, he had seized upon this similarity to make a central primitivist point. Parry, too, probably in ignorance of Maginn, proposes a comparable but wider argument; he makes the historicist point that the reason why cattle-raids feature so widely in epic poetry is not because of any supposed laws in the evolution of poetry, but because epic poetry emerges from societies in which cattle-raiding is normal and frequent. The best guide that Parry can suggest to such a social state is to be found in Doughty's *Arabia Deserta*, where the *ghrazzu* or raid features as a central part of tribal life. Parry, then, and it may be an aspect of that exoticising tendency noted by Adam Parry, finds one good analogue for the world that produced Homer beyond the margins of contemporary civility in the outlands of Arabia. This equivalence, too, is reproduced in Lawrence's writing.

Doughty himself was not keen to understand Arab tribal society in exactly this way. While he certainly considered the tribes among whom he lived on his travels to be archaic survivals, the comparison to which he was drawn was not with the heroic age of epic, but with the age of the Hebrew Patriarchs.[4] Nevertheless, we have here a striking nexus which links together Doughty the traveller and writer of archaic-seeming epic poetry; Parry the Homeric scholar; and Lawrence the adventurer, scholar and writer of an account of his military adventures in Arabia which reproduces the structure of feeling which emerges from nineteenth-century epic primitivism.

The temptation, perhaps, is to see *The Seven Pillars of Wisdom* as telling Lawrence's own story as an epic. That is certainly the route taken by David Lean in the famous film version, and the re-emergence of epic

in the twentieth-century cinema is a very important aspect of the history
of the genre in this period. But in fact the book tells a more complex
story, in which epic is exactly attributed to the Arabs, with Lawrence
acting as guilt-ridden mediating modern consciousness. To this extent,
the memoir can be thought of as reproducing within itself the novelistic
appropriation of epic that descends from epic primitivism and from
Walter Scott.

The Arabs as the heroes of this epic? Consider this passage from early
in the book, when the Arab army has at last gathered sufficient strength to
venture onto the attack:

There came a warning patter from the drums and the poet of the right wing
burst into strident song, a single invented couplet, of Feisal and the pleasure he
would afford us at Wejh. The right wing listened to the verse intently, took it up
and sang it together once, twice and three times, with pride and self-satisfaction
and derision. However, before they could brandish it a fourth time the poet of
the left wing broke out in extempore reply, in the same metre, in answering
rhyme, and capping the sentiment. The left wing cheered it in a roar of triumph,
the drums tapped again, the standard-bearers threw out their great crimson
banners, and the whole guard, right, left and centre, broke together into the
rousing regimental chorus,
    'I've lost Britain, and I've lost Gaul,
    I've lost Rome, and, worst of all,
    I've lost Lalage—'
only it was Nejd they had lost, and the women of the Maabda, and their future
lay from Jidda towards Suez. Yet it was a good song, with a rhythmical beat
which the camels loved, so that they put down their heads, stretched their necks
out far and with lengthened pace shuffled forward musingly while it lasted.[5]

This is characterised by genuine excitement and élan. There is also some
ironic undercutting, particularly if one recognises that the quotation is
from *Puck of Pook's Hill*; this is the song sung by the Roman Centurion
when the children travel back to Roman Britain and Hadrian's Wall.[6] So
the passage mediates this familiar epic trope – the advancing army
encouraged by their traditional poets – via the suggested equivalence of
an invented semi-serious Roman imperial marching song.

To this extent the paragraph enacts the characteristic movement of the
text as a whole, which is to move into and out of an elevated perspective –
one which might genuinely be described as epic in that it recounts matters
of high martial courage in a matchingly high manner. In this extract,
Lawrence first establishes, and then moves out of, this high manner into
the semi-serious (Bakhtin would call it serio-comic) quotation from

Kipling; the claim to elevation in the writing about this cavalry advance briefly dissolves as another demystifying perspective is evoked. Yet the writing does not remain within this debunking moment; the rhythm of the paragraph finally allows the elevated perspective to reassert itself as the camels shuffle forward with 'lengthened pace'.

This oscillation is characteristic of *Seven Pillars of Wisdom* altogether. In the larger text, however, while it is possible to trace an epic outline to Lawrence's narrative of his own exploits, more typically he acts as the anxiously troubled modern consciousness that surrounds the actively epic deeds and consciousness of the Arabs whom he accompanies. The mediating role of Lawrence as narrator is therefore crucial in presenting and bracketing the attribution of epic status to the Arabs throughout the narrative. This structural narrative position is especially visible in relation to one of the key Arab leaders of the revolt, Auda, whose own manner of retelling his adventures is parodied in one of the central scenes of the book.

The scene is this: a pause in one of the many marches of the Arab revolt has left Lawrence with Auda and his fighters; the old chief has jestingly accused one of his chief lieutenants, Mohammed, of being bullied by his wives about a string of pearls which he had bought in the bazaar at Wejh and then not presented to any one of them. He calls upon Lawrence to attest to the truth of this fabrication. Lawrence is thus in an awkward situation, and he extricates himself from it in this manner:

I began with the introducing phrase of a formal tale: 'In the name of God the merciful, the loving-kind. We were six in Wejh. There were Auda, and Mohammed, and Zaal, Gasim el Shimt, Mufaddhi and the poor man (myself); and one night just before dawn, Auda said, "Let us make a raid against the market". And we said, "in the name of God". And we went; Auda in a white robe and a red head-cloth, and Kasim sandals of pieced leather; Mohammed in a silken tunic of "seven kings" and barefoot; Zaal ... I forget Zaal. Gasim wore cotton, and Mufaddhi was in silk of blue stripes with an embroidered head-cloth. Your servant was as your servant.'

My pause was still with astonishment. This was a close parody of Auda's epic style; and I mimicked also his wave of the hand, his round voice, and the rising and dropping tone which emphasised the points, or what he thought were points, of his pointless stories. The Howeitat [Auda's followers] sat silent as death, twisting their full bodies inside their sweat-stiffened shirts for joy, and staring hungrily at Auda; for they all recognised the original, and parody was a new art to them and to him. The coffee man, Mufaddhi, a Shammar refugee from the guilt of blood, himself a character, forgot to pile fresh thorns on his fire for fixity of listening to the tale. (pp. 285–6)

Lawrence continues the parody, and by doing so successfully extricates himself from the awkward position his host has put him in, since Auda too can appreciate his humour. It is possible to read this incident in several ways. From one point of view, this is Lawrence telling the story of his own adroitness at managing a potentially embarrassing situation: he has got himself out of a tight spot without offending either Auda or Mohammed, and has even raised the morale of the whole group. This is, in effect, a 'little touch of Harry in the night', the politic leader of men encouraging them before battle by humorous means. But in a wider sense, this incident reveals the structural relations of epic within *Seven Pillars of Wisdom*; while the Arabs themselves see their own experience in epic terms, the modern consciousness of Lawrence as narrator of their story, and participator in it, is inevitably bound to other ways of seeing and understanding their enterprise. In this instance, this other consciousness issues itself in parody; throughout the book, however, it is present as an agonised awareness of inhabiting a different world-view from that of the Arab actors in the story, and in some sense of being in a relation of bad faith in respect to them and their enterprise because of it.

Thus the book is punctuated by a series of moments when Lawrence detaches himself from the narrative of events to reflect on his own position within them. In these moments, he is aware both that the Arabs have been led to their revolt against the Turks by active encouragement from the British, including himself, and that the enterprise is an heroic one. Yet he is also aware that he cannot himself participate with an undivided mind in just the heroic endeavours that he has encouraged the Arabs to believe in. He has effectively projected an epic status upon Arab society, encouraged the Arabs to act upon this projection, and failed to follow them in their self-belief. A typical moment of such self-doubt occurs towards the end of Chapter XCIX, when he is reflecting on the ideological inducements which he has bought to bear on the Arabs to get them to join the revolt, recognising that simple bribery will not be sufficient to sustain them in their commitment to it:

We made the Arabs strain on tip-toe to reach our creed, for it led to works, a dangerous country where men might take the deed for the will. My fault, my blindness of leadership (eager to find a quick means to conversion) allowed them this finite image of our end, which properly existed only in unending effort towards unattainable imagined light. Our crowd seeking light in things were like pathetic dogs snuffling round the shank of a lamp-post. It was only myself who valeted the abstract, whose duty took him beyond the shrine.

The irony was in my loving objects before life or ideas; the incongruity in my answering the infectious call of action, which had laid weight on the diversity of things. It was a hard task for me to straddle feeling and action. I had had one craving all my life – for the power of self-expression in some imaginative form – but had been too diffuse ever to acquire a technique. At last accident, with perverted humour, in casting me as a man of action had given me a place in the Arab Revolt, a theme ready and epic to a direct eye and hand, thus offering me an outlet in literature, the technique-less art. Whereupon I became excited only over mechanism. The epic mode was alien to me, as to my generation. Memory gave me no clue to the heroic, so that I could not feel such men as Auda in myself. He seemed fantastic as the hills of Rumm, old as Malory. (p. 565)

Lawrence's interconnections of thought and feeling are complex here, to be sure. In the second paragraph of this extract, he is concerned with the ironies which prevented him from subscribing himself with an undivided mind to the enterprise upon which he had embarked. This inability is fundamentally historic: 'the epic mode was alien to me, as to my generation'. Yet this incongruity of historical moment is overdetermined by peculiarly personal ironies, principally that which had cast the would-be writer into a position of literary seriousness of which he was temperamentally (and historically) incapable of taking advantage.

The preceding paragraph ('We made the Arabs strain . . .') alludes to an equivalent difficulty in Lawrence's situation: his sense of continuous bad faith in relation to his Arab co-actors. His sense of the project on which they were all jointly engaged was necessarily distinct from that of the Arabs themselves. This is in part to do with the fact, explored in the second paragraph, that Lawrence inhabits the modern world while those Arabs inhabit, in his construction of them, a world of epic or as 'old as Malory'. But it is also a function of that modernity that it gives him access to a strategic sense of the place of the Arab conflict as part of the wider World War. At intervals Lawrence withdraws from Arabia to Egypt or Palestine, where, in conjunction with other British Staff Officers, he can weigh and balance the place of the Arab revolt in the wider conduct of the war. Lawrence's narratorial stance is fundamentally premised upon this social, geographical and cultural difference from the Arabs about whom he is writing.

It is therefore possible to think of *Seven Pillars of Wisdom* as one of the places that epic can be found in the twentieth century – but this is necessarily an equivocal place where epic is hedged around by an agonised sense of its misfit in the modern world. This does not make the texture of the prose novelistic, though in places it undoubtedly is so; elevated perspectives are often allowed to stand unchallenged by serio-comic or parodic intentions, though these are to be found in the text also. The conditions of the survival of epic in this text, however, are twofold – or perhaps this is the same condition stated in two different ways. First, epic must be situated beyond the borders of modernity, in those pre-modern spaces where the heroic mode of life still persists. And second, insofar as this is a war memoir, its capacity to understand warfare in epic terms is clearly related to the kind of war that was fought in the Arabian penin- sula, as opposed to the Western Front.[7] 'Is Achilles possible with powder and lead?' Marx asked. Perhaps not. But while the Arab Revolt produced no Achilles, it did occur in a situation where the heroic virtues could still flourish, because the mode of warfare in which it was conducted was a development of a social world which might still plausibly be described as epic. Parry, relying on Doughty, and after them Lawrence, certainly thought so. The strength of *Seven Pillars of Wisdom* is not that it reproduced this perception unequivocally, but that it did so via an equivocal and self-consciously modern narration only too aware of the futility of its epic gestures.

There are other continuities from the nineteenth century which tie Lawrence in with the epic tradition. We have seen that he mentioned Malory as providing one analogue for his understanding of the Arab world. In fact he kept a copy of Malory in his saddle-bag – and in doing so joins a line of notorious military adventurers, starting with Alexander the Great, who travelled with the *Iliad*, and including Napoleon, who was always accompanied by a copy of *Ossian*. Perhaps it is fair to him to record that he used his epic (if Malory can be so described) to understand the world he encountered beyond Europe, and not as a model for his own behaviour in conquering it. Yet the element of willful self-deception in all this is well captured by Robert Graves:

Lawrence so logically pursued his romantic career, which began by putting his nose between the pages of Scott and Tennyson, and then between those of Morris and Malory, and then between those of the original mediæval French and Latin romances, that at last he forced his whole head and shoulders between the pages of an epic in the making, and in the first book met Feisal, and in the second Auda.[8]

This perhaps overstates the element of self-delusion – or at least, the truth that Graves states here about the descent of Lawrence's ideas is doubtless valid, and equally plausible is the picture this paints of his state of mind. But what Graves's account ignores, and what makes Lawrence's writing interesting, is that this romantic delusion about himself, and projection of epic upon the Arabs, is realised in a text that sharply dramatises its sense of its own disjunction from these delusions and projections.

T. E. Lawrence's writing emerges from the metropolitan centre of empire, and the negotiation with epic in *Seven Pillars of Wisdom* involves the writer in projecting himself across physical and cultural barriers. But the nineteenth century bequeathed another model of national epic to the twentieth, which sees it as serving directly the project of nation-building. If the complex national struggles of Europe saw the emergence of rediscovered or rewritten epics from Ossian onwards, so the colonised peoples of the European empires in the twentieth century also produced their primary heroic songs.

So: another continent, another national liberation struggle. South Africa in the 1970s, still in the grip of Apartheid: where better to look for the emergence of a national epic suited to the needs of nation-building? But in the case of Mazisi Kunene's *Emperor Shaka the Great*, this is an epic told without irony; it emerges from native Zulu traditions and is not hedged around with the modernist ironies that characterise *Seven Pillars of Wisdom*. Kunene is not the Zulu Lawrence, but the Zulu Lönnrot who had fashioned the *Kalevala* out of fragments of heroic ballads. So this is another place where epic emerges in the twentieth century, directly analogous to one of its occasions in the nineteenth: an epic is to be constructed out of the oral heroic traditions of a subject people as part of its struggle to build a nation. This is perhaps the one possibility that Rider Haggard did not foresee: that the descendants of Umslopogaas or of that saddened Zulu warrior who prefaces *The Child of Storm* (see above, p. 189) would write their own epic instead of relying on their colonial masters to do it for them.

The analogy with the *Kalevala* can be pursued; *Emperor Shaka the Great*, like the Finnish national epic, is composed out of the fragments of native epic poems run together to make a single narrative. Both poems are part of the effort to create a national consciousness out of the epic materials available to them. But the differences are important also. Kunene's poem is concerned with historical rather than mythical events; he includes fragments of Zulu praise poems as explicit quotations within the text; and the relationship between the poem and the contemporary national liberation struggle is a prominent feature, not so much of the narrative itself, as of the epic 'arguments' which precede each chapter.

Perhaps most importantly, the poem was first published (in 1979) in the author's own translation into English; the peculiar circumstances of the Apartheid state and the author's relationship to the ANC made first publication in the original Zulu impossible. To that extent, since the poem is only available to me in English, some of the stylistic questions which have featured so prominently in this book cannot be addressed in the following discussion of it.

Nevertheless, we can see that the poem reproduces, or rediscovers for itself in the particular circumstances of Zulu national history, many of the tropes that characterise the rediscovered or invented primary epics of the nineteenth century. The place of epic poetry itself in a warrior society is a prominent theme of the poem, as in the following scene, when two Zulu armies are about to meet in combat, and their poets encourage them on the eve of battle:

> As he sung these epics the poet
> Leapt to the sky as if to unhinge the sun.
> The magic powers of war spread like wild fire.
> Shields of the war-hungry warriors thundered from a distance.
> The hills resounded with battle songs in the lands of Malandela.
> In the lands of Langa battle songs echoed in response.
> Women shouted their songs of anger;
> They entered the dark lands of the Ancestors.
> They touched their feet; and shook them from sleep.
> The Ancestors walked on earth, hugging their children.
> The two armies faced each other across the mountains.
> People killed the black bulls for the Forefathers.
> They burnt the aromatic fat for the Ancestors.
> The sweet smell spread with lightness to the Forefathers.
> The voices of war echoed all night through.
> From the crimson flames shot clusters of weapons.
> Old men and women and children sang the songs of past heroes.[9]

There is no question here of imitation; this has its own authenticity which derives from the particular beliefs and traditions of the society from which it emerges. It can, however, be observed that this is a familiar trope – the armies before battle encouraged by heroic songs of past heroes. Perhaps the same point should be made about this that Milman Parry made about the prominence of the cattle-raid in primary epics from across the world; they are a prominent feature of such poetry not because of any laws of poetry but because of the similarities of the societies from which they spring. In the same way, we can see the recurrence of the scene represented in this extract – with features special to it – as a product of a social world which can legitimately be compared with that of Homer.

Kunene is very conscious of, indeed insistent upon, the part that heroic songs have to play in the growth of national consciousness. Throughout the poem, he includes scenes in which epic songs are sung, and their part in inculcating a proper sense of an heroic national past is emphasised. In one scene, for example, Shaka's aunt, Princess Mkhabayi, tells an old legend which clearly points to Shaka as the fulfilment of a national prophecy; at the end of her tale Zunene makes the following comment on the relationship between heroic stories and contemporary nations:

> The wily Princess knew no great history is without heroes:
> Great countries are those that boast a great Ancestry.
> Indeed, artists embellish their past to inspire their children.
> For this she sang the song of Zulu and broke into tears.
>
> (p. 166)

And just to be absolutely clear on this point, after the next story that the Princess tells, Zunene says it again:

> Kingdoms and states and empires are kept intact by their poets –
> It is they who embellish their tales, making the future desirable.
>
> (p. 168)

The poem thus grows out of a very specific belief in the importance of heroic songs in the sustenance of national consciousness in the society about which it writes. Indeed, at times this becomes an exalted commitment to the value of epic poetry:

> Other poets inspired by the same madness followed suit.
> The great Nomnxamama joined him.
> He declared his poem of excellence.
> From all sides came the roar of voices in ecstasy:
> Voices echoed, nourishing each other with great episodes.
> The utterances of poets are like prayers to the Ancestors.
> The era of greatness flourishes with the epics of nations.
>
> (p. 246)

Here, in this especially strongly stated assertion, national greatness is dependent upon the presence of a national epic.

So *Emperor Shaka the Great* is written out of a conscious desire both to reproduce within a wider narrative framework the function and manner of the old heroic praise songs of Zulu society and also to act itself as just such a song on a wider scale. This is just the set of aesthetic and political notions that we have seen operating in relation, for example, to Morris's *Sigurd the Volsung* or Doughty's *Dawn in Britain*. Naturally the ways in which this interrelated set of ideas comes to be realised in the very differing national situations of late nineteenth-century Britain and late twentieth-century South Africa vary widely. The fact that the poem had first to be published in English is symptomatic of one principal difference: that the linguistic and educational system of South Africa was one where no national language could be unproblematically preferred, quite apart from the political difficulties surrounding the publication of the poem in Zulu. But another difference is still more evident in the poem; it is clear that Kunene wishes to promote a direct political relevance for the poem beyond that more general problem of nation building to which the epic is a direct contribution. Shaka is indeed offered as a political model for the contemporary South African struggle in two ways. First, he offers a model of successful military leadership, which is inspired by a grand vision of a united Zulu nation bought together under one polity. Secondly, his success as a military leader is described as being dependent upon an absolute military egalitarianism; Shaka is presented as a rigid opponent of aristocratic privilege, and as a promoter of the *carrière ouverte aux talents*. He thus can act as a beacon in the struggle against Apartheid, in a way which at least divests him of some of the aristocratic military values that habitually accompany epic poetry.

Here, then, is one opportunity for epic poetry in the twentieth century. In a manner which recalls the great rediscovered or invented national epics of nineteenth-century Europe, national epics may be written which emerge from and seek to speak to the national liberation struggles of the formerly subject peoples of empire.

EPIC, NOVEL AND FANTASY

The examples of T. E. Lawrence and Mazisi Kunene suggest, in their very different ways, the persistence of the problematic of epic primitivism and its connection to national histories in areas coming under the control of, and resisting, the pressures of European empire. But what of the developed world itself? Is epic inevitably a dead letter here, as its origins in the pre-modern world become increasingly distant, and as the dominance of the novel becomes in turn displaced by visual media?

The example of Joyce's *Ulysses* (1922) seems to suggest a resounding affirmative answer to this question. The novelistic assimilation of epic appears complete in this novel; the narrative taken over from the *Odyssey* might imply something of an archetypal pattern, but the ironies generated by the juxtaposition of Ulysses's adventures and the petit-bourgeois world of Leopold Bloom work overwhelmingly in favour of the non-heroic virtues of Bloom and contemporary Dublin. Moreover, in strictly Bakhtinian terms, *Ulysses* is the most characteristically novelistic novel imaginable; its language is thoroughly, emphatically and blatantly dialogic, indeed represents the most complete twentieth-century example of language bathed in the proliferating heteroglossic diversity of the modern world. It is the polar opposite of epic, and the Homeric dimension of the novel only demonstrates the triumph of the modern form.

Literary history, however, is not linear; just because Joyce developed the novel form in one extreme direction does not mean that subsequent novelists are forbidden from continuing in others, any more than the publication of *Tristram Shandy* in the eighteenth century, with its proleptic parodies of all the narrative conventions of the novel, prevented the flowering of the form in the nineteenth. It is undoubtedly possible to find elsewhere in the twentieth century novelists who have exploited the generic inheritance of epic in ways that are altogether more ambivalent than the example of *Ulysses*. Novels as diverse as Neil Gunn's *Sun Circle* (1933), Halldór Laxness's *Independent People* (1934–5) and Jane Smiley's *The Greenlanders* (1988) all entail negotiations with the older form that echo the aesthetic problems of their nineteenth-century predecessors. These are necessarily *negotiations*, not epics in their own right: generic hybrids where the presence of epic tends, with more or less insistence, to overwhelm the novelistic frame which contains it.

There is, however, a thriving, though equally fraught, use of the word epic in the twentieth century in relation to a range of books stacked in another part of the bookshop from those of Jane Smiley and Halldór Laxness – on the shelves headed 'Fantasy'. The genealogy of this genre too can be traced back to the nineteenth century and the problematic of epic primitivism, for the descent of fantasy epics from William Morris is not hard to trace. This is not the Morris of *Sigurd the Volsung* so much as the writer of the prose fantasies of the end of his life, such as *The House of the Wolfings* (1889), *The Roots of the Mountains* (1890) and *The Well at the World's End* (1896). In these tales, much less self-consciously serious in Morris's own estimation than his earlier epic, though informed by just the same consciousness of the alterity of the heroic world, we can see the origins of a now hugely developed genre of fantasy epic. The mediating figure between Morris and, say, Robert Jordan's 'Eye of the World' cycle or David Eddings's 'The Maloreon' is undoubtedly J. R. R. Tolkien; the latter and his successors have widely distributed a version of epic into the popular culture of the late twentieth century.

Tolkien himself was immersed in the cultures of the North, and *The Lord of the Rings* reproduces many of the narratives of that inheritance. Their displacement onto Middle Earth is, in one sense, the condition of their continuing success in the social circumstances of modernity. This condition – that the traditions of epic can only survive in the modern world displaced into a fantasy place uncertainly related to the world we actually inhabit – seems to be one logical terminus of epic primitivism. Tolkien's successors, the Robert Jordans and the David Eddings, only repeat in larger and more elaborated gestures the fundamental incompatibility of epic and modernity.

The widespread and vivid appeal of such narratives needs some explaining in these circumstances, in ways which do not simply dismiss the phenomenon in the familiar accents of cultural snobbism. Perhaps Bakhtin was right about this also – that epic and novel are indeed continuing generic possibilities, and that fantasy epics are no more than the current manifestation of the epic genre. Or perhaps we could strengthen this hypothesis by asserting that the particular pleasures of epic, so thoroughly exorcised by the First World War from elite culture, have resurfaced in this deformed mode in popular culture. At all events, Tolkien and his successors appear to provide, albeit in the essentially private and wish-fulfilling mode of fantasy, some of the excitements, elevation and unironic heroism that characterise epic.

Perhaps here also can be detected a similar dialectic at work to that which we noticed operating in the case of Morris and *Sigurd the Volsung* – that the epic world recreated in these forms in antithesis to the modern world operates as much as an implicit critique of that modernity as an escape from it. Such a case has indeed been made with respect to *The Lord of the Rings* itself, which can convincingly be seen as bearing into the modern world some positive values from the world displaced by modernity – notably a positive valuation of nature and man's place in it.[10] Such an account of fantasy epics would naturally vary from case to case; it may well be that some of the examples of the genre are more inertly escapist than Tolkien's own story, and the uses to which the genre are put, and the purchase that they have upon the modern world, are equally variable. But the point of any such account would be to recognise that the necessary displacement of epic, in view of its fundamental incompatibility with modernity, does not mean that it simply goes away; rather, it resurfaces in these displaced locations and idioms. The potential dialectical charge generated by this displacement, the capacity of the form to react back upon the world which has expelled it, can be put to various and more or less successful uses.

EPIC AND MODERNITY

The displacements and negotiations indicated by the phenomenon of fantasy epics suggest at least two possible accounts of the place of epic in the modern world. On the one hand, the extraordinary popularity of Tolkien and his successors suggests not so much the impossibility of epic under the conditions of modernity as its displacement into a popular and fantasised form: given the history of the twentieth century, the suspicion of epic (a suspicion that has been present from the eighteenth century, as we have seen) as the product of an essentially barbaric age would appear to have been fully justified, and its banishment from the elite culture of the metropolis therefore wholly understandable. On the other hand, it may be that a profound cultural form such as the epic cannot simply be banished, and is bound to reappear, in however displaced a manner, as modern people still contain within themselves generic predispositions that they have inherited from their cultural past. Perhaps Marx was right after all, when, in seeking to answer the question why Greek epic should continue to appeal after its historic conditions had passed, he came up with the naive-sounding notion of the 'childhood of the race':

Why should not the historic childhood of humanity, its most beautiful unfolding, as a stage never to return, exercise an eternal charm? ... The Greeks were normal children. The charm of their art for us is not in contradiction to the undeveloped stage of society on which it grew. [It] is its result, rather, and is inextricably bound up, rather, with the fact that the unique social conditions under which it arose, and could alone arise, can never return.[11]

Whether such a notion can act as an aesthetic defence of *The Lord of the Rings* remains, however, a matter for discussion.

The suspicion, on the part of liberal elite culture, of the legacy of epic has excellent grounds. Russell's disgusted phrase – 'the whole foul literature of glory' – while it has not exactly echoed down the twentieth century, sums up a justifiable tradition. Consider, for example, the Nazi enthusiasm for understanding history in epic terms, and for exalting epic more generally: Goebbels declared that Fritz Lang's 1924 film, *Der Nibelung* was a 'perfect work of Nazi art'; in the last desperate stages of the war, in 1944, he authorised massive resources to be diverted from the war effort in order to make an epic film of the defence of Kolberg; and during the siege of Stalingrad, a poet was dispatched to the front line in order to prepare an epic poem about the battle.[12] The political worries suggested by artistic predilections of this kind are scarcely sweetened by talk of the 'childhood of the race'.

Yet one profoundly complicating factor is that the meanings carried by epic in the twentieth century were radically transformed by the fact that the predominant vehicle for the mode became the cinema. As I write, *The Lord of the Rings* has become a global phenomenon by virtue of a trilogy of films. Two of the epics praised by Goebbels were films. Insofar as people of the twentieth and twenty-first centuries encounter epic, it is most likely to be in the cinema; literally hundreds of epic films have been made, and they can legitimately claim the title without recourse to its popular extension of meaning which makes it roughly the film-critical equivalent to 'long'.

So here is apparently a paradox: the most characteristic art-form of modernity has proved itself the most productive home for an essentially archaic mode of art. In some respects this is because the cinema is the heir of those nineteenth-century forms which displaced epic into popular art; Cecil B. DeMille was the heir of Lytton and the other purveyors of a spectacular version of the Roman imperial past. The cinema suffers also from some of the same aesthetic problems that afflict the attempt to write literary epics: the problem of epic pastiche is especially apparent in the attempt to provide an appropriate idiom for elevated speech. Nevertheless, it is clear that cinematic epic has radically transformed the whole experience of the genre. In particular, the pleasures of visual spectacle, musical intensity and specular identification all make the nature of the experience of epic in the cinema quite different from that of reading, or for that matter of the suppositional recited performance of bardic epics. Given this, it is hard to say that epic has the same meanings now as it did in the pre-modern societies from which it emerged.

For all that, epic in the cinema does perform some of the same functions for which people in the nineteenth century sought to mobilise it, but perhaps more so when it has not sought self-consciously the role of epic. The great spectacular epics set in the classical or pre-modern or fantastic worlds – *Ben-Hur* or *El Cid* or *The Lord of the Rings* – would appear to prove the contention that there is indeed a fundamental incompatibility between epic and modernity. But insofar as Hollywood has imagined an epic American national past, it has been in the genre of the Western, and other national cinemas also have provided an epic national history in just the way that the nineteenth century imagined an epic history as doing.

David Lean's film *Lawrence of Arabia* (1962) vividly embodies some of these considerations, and its relationship to *Seven Pillars of Wisdom* is illuminating. There is no doubt that Robert Bolt's screenplay is a perhaps inevitable simplification of the texture and complexities of Lawrence's prose. Where the memoir had presented an agonised consciousness unhappily straddling two different social and historical states – the epitome of uneven development – the film makes Lawrence himself unequivocally the hero of the story. In this version, Lawrence is motivated by good faith in relation to his Arab allies and is himself betrayed both by British blimpishness and, more directly, by Allenby's duplicity. This is not to say that the film is incapable of providing a critical context for Lawrence's actions; on the contrary, it is explicit about both his creation as a media hero (he is shown unashamedly posturing for the newsreel cameras) and his descent into a kind of bloodlust in massacring Turkish soldiers. But it does suggest that the film provides a version of the *British* national story rather than the Arab one, which can at least be glimpsed in Lawrence's own version of events.

The year of production, 1962, provides a clue as to the nature of the British national story that the film tells: the early 1960s is the period of wholesale decolonisation of the empire, and more widely of the repudiation of the hidebound class and racial attitudes that visibly accompanied imperialism. So one way of seeing this film is as an epic which gives a version of heroism profoundly at odds with what it constructs as official Britain, the frock-coated bigwiggery seen attending the memorial service for Lawrence at the beginning of the film. Insofar as *Lawrence of Arabia* tells a national story in the manner of epic, therefore, it is one which is cognate with the many cultural and social renegotiations of postwar, indeed more narrowly post-Suez, Britain.

However, to seize upon this aspect of the film as indicative of its epic status would clearly be perverse. More central to such a claim must be the film's scale, its effort to place the action (in the Aristotelian sense) in as large and significant a context as possible. The technical means by which this ambition is realised are evidently as crucial as the screenplay: the cinematography, by Freddie Young, and the score, by Maurice Jarre, both insist that the events of the film are to be taken seriously and that they matter in the grandest way. By an extraordinary reversal, Matthew Arnold's 'grand style', the mode or medium by which unequivocal epic seriousness might be made available, appears to have been lost as a possibility in British poetry, only to have been found in essentially modern means of technical production.

Franco Moretti, it may be recalled, argued in *The Modern Epic* that it was epic rather than the novel which was the form best suited to provide the world texts for a modernity in which national boundaries had been surpassed by a global perspective: the effective literary space is now literally the whole world. How this argument would run with respect to national cinemas like the one that produced *Lawrence of Arabia*, or Hollywood and the dominance of the American culture industry as the cultural spearhead of globalisation, is not the province of this book – though the place of epic in such a putative history might be surprising. But we might legitimately conclude this consideration of epic and modernity by looking at a 'world text' not included by Moretti in his list: Derek Walcott's *Omeros* (1990), a poem which at once provides an epic narrative and a sustained meditation on the impossibility of epic.

The contrast between *Omeros* and a poem like Mazisi Kunene's *Emperor Shaka the Great* provides a clear starting-point. Where the latter poem is a national epic, which draws on indigenous traditions to contribute explicitly to a national liberation struggle, Walcott's poem provides a national epic for the Antilles that is based on a literary analogy to Homeric epic, and which is surrounded by further narratives concerned with American and Irish history. It is indeed a world text, in this specific sense: it is concerned with the social and cultural after-effects of empire and the impact of imperialism on indigenous communities, and the condition for its imagining this range of phenomena is Walcott's own position as a world-writer. Where the space of Kunene's epic was exclusively that of Zululand, *Omeros* inhabits the space of the Atlantic triangle, and presumes a world-readership. In these circumstances, an epic is necessarily going to be surrounded by many contextualising and mitigating counter-narratives and perspectives, which make the poem not so much an epic in itself as a negotiation with the possibility of epic.

Thus the central narrative – the triangular relationship between two fishermen, Achille and Hector, and a beautiful woman, Helen – obviously recalls Homer without demanding an explicit set of parallels. But the poem does not set up an ironic relationship between epic past and unheroic present: this is not another version of Joyce's *Ulysses*, this time in verse. On the contrary, the poem grants genuine heroic status to its protagonists, and is quite serious in the parallel it suggests between these modern Caribbean fishermen, taxi-drivers and waitresses and the

Homeric heroes and heroines they are set to recall. On the other hand, Walcott is also conscious of the alternative, heroic African history that his poetic device has effectively effaced. Achille goes on an imaginary epic journey back to Africa, where he meets his own ancestors, fishermen also, on a riverbank:

> Women paused at their work, then smiled at the warrior
> Returning from his battle with smoke, from the kingdom
> Where he had been captured, they cried and were happy.
>
> Then the fishermen sat near a large tree under whose dome
> Stones sat in a circle. His father said:
>   "Afo-la-be,"
> touching his own heart.
>   "In the place you have come from
>
> what do they call you?"
>   Time translates.
>   Tapping his chest,
> the son answers:
>   "Achille," The tribe rustles, "Achille."
> Then, like cedars at sunrise, the mutterings settle.
>
>   AFOLABE
> Achille. What does this name mean? I have forgotten the one
> That I gave you. But it was, it seems, many years ago.
> What does it mean?
>
>   ACHILLE
>   Well, I too have forgotten.
>
> Everything was forgotten. You also. I do not know.
> The deaf sea has changed around every name that you gave
> us; trees, men, we yearn for a sound that is missing.[13]

In one gesture, then, the poem grants heroic status to its fishermen by making them the heirs of Homeric heroes; in another, it recognises that this is an occlusion of an alternative heroic history, where an African past has been overtaken, and forcibly forgotten, by the intervening history of slavery. In this context, the meaning of 'Achille' is not accessible to those who bear the name, and it is a name which actively intrudes between an African past and the would-be inheritors of that past in the present. Worse still, the naming of people of African descent by classical names recalls the practice of slave-names of a similar provenance. So Walcott is acutely conscious of the ambivalence of the heroic gesture that he is making.

Nevertheless, the poem persists with its epic parallels, even to the extent of a descent into Hell for its narrator in its final book. But in one perspective entertained in its course, all such parallels are futile; after the narrator has emerged from Hell, where his guide has been a statue of Omeros, he recognises the effacing but cleansing passage – of time, of the sea, of the middle passage, of history with its ambivalent consequences – which makes the meaning of epic subordinate to other profounder rhythms:

> All the thunderous myths of that ocean were blown
> up with the spray that dragged from the lacy bulwarks
> of Cap's bracing headland. The sea had never known
>
> any of them, nor had the illiterate rocks,
> nor the circling frigates, nor even the white mesh
> that knitted the Golden Fleece. The ocean had
>
> no memory of the wanderings of Gilgamesh,
> or whose sword severed whose head in the *Iliad*.
> It was an epic whose every line was erased
>
> yet freshly written in sheets of exploding surf
> in that blind violence with which one crest replaced
> another with a trench and that heart-heaving sough
>
> begun in Guinea to fountain exhaustion here,
> however one read it, not as our defeat or
> our victory; it drenched every survivor
>
> with blessing. It never altered its metre
> to suit the age, a wide page without metaphors.
> Our last resort as much as yours, Omeros.
>
> (pp. 295–6)

This might be read as itself an epic simile, in which an extended comparison is managed between the pounding of the metrical beat with the incessant pounding of the surf. The force of this simile, however, is not the elevation sought by neoclassical epic, but in some sense its denial: in this perspective, all the narrative outcomes of all the histories, epic or otherwise, are levelled, but also, extraordinarily, 'blessed'.

Walcott's poem, then, from a number of perspectives, provides as much a meditation on the possibility of epic in the modern world as an instance of it. One reason for the difficulty that epic poses for him – as well as the opportunity – is the necessarily oblique relationship to classical European culture that a child of the Caribbean is bound to have. Many of the ambivalences of the poem can be traced back to this fundamental obliquity. One fate of epic in the modern world, it would therefore seem, is a double or ambivalent existence of this kind.

If I insist upon the poem's modernity, I do so partly to avoid a too-easy resort to the category of the postmodern, or indeed the postcolonial, both of which provide ready explanatory systems for the doublings, ambivalences and hybridities of a poem like *Omeros*. The aesthetic and ideological problem that Walcott encounters and resolves in his poem, however, are ones which have been implicit in the writing and understanding of epic since the eighteenth century, when the discovery of the antiquity of the mode coincided with the enormous expansion of the European empires and the consequent encounters with the pre-modern peoples on the margins of Europe or beyond them. More narrowly, the poem can appear modernist rather than postmodernist if only because one of its models is Pound's *Cantos*, a poem which likewise insists, extravagantly, on the equivalences between the classical and the contemporary worlds. In short, the particular resolutions of *Omeros*, and its specific regional and ideological allegiances, represent an inflection of the constantly transforming problematic which links together epic, modernity and empire.

But this is by no means the only possibility for epic in the modern world, or indeed its most characteristic mode of existence. Whether more typical or not, another response, descending also from the Enlightenment, has seized on the popular character of epic to repudiate its claims, or at least to belittle them. That is, since the eighteenth century we have been able to recognise that epic originated in peasant societies, however heroic their own pretensions, and to look askance therefore at the big language epic uses. After the grandeurs of Walcott, it may be fitting to end on an altogether smaller scale, with the astringent aesthetic of Patrick Kavanagh:

EPIC

I have lived in important places, times
When great events were decided, who owned
That half a rood of rock, a no-man's land
Surrounded by our pitchfork-armed claims.
I heard the Duffys shouting 'Damn your soul'
And old McCabe stripped to the waist, seen

Step the plot-defying blue cast-steel –
'Here is the march along these iron stones'
That was the year of the Munich bother. Which
Was more important? I inclined
To lose my faith in Ballyrush and Gortin
Till Homer's ghost came whispering to my mind
He said: I made the Iliad from such
A local row. Gods make their own importance.[14]

On second thoughts, this does not repudiate epic so much as reclaim it, with all attendant ironies, for a smaller but no less significant history. 'Gods make their own importance.' Perhaps epic can do so too.

Notes

INTRODUCTION

1 Karl Marx, *Grundrisse: Foundation of the Critique of Political Economy*, translated by Martin Nicolaus (Harmondsworth: Penguin, 1973), p. 111.

2 Marx was the heir, in particular, of Adam Ferguson, for whom epic was central to his understanding of the progress of human history through succeeding stages. See below pp. 7–8.

3 For a survey of such epics in the early nineteenth century, see A. D. Harvey, 'The English Epic in the Romantic Period', *Philological Quarterly*, 55 (1976), 241–59; and the same author's *Literature into History* (Basingstoke: Macmillan, 1988). For a critique, see G. Headley, 'The Early Nineteenth-century Epic: The Harvey Thesis Examined', *Journal of European Studies*, 21 (1991), 201–8.

4 'Interpretative circle': the phrase deliberately recalls the 'hermeneutic circle' of German Romantic philosophy, articulated above all by Schleiermacher. I have avoided the use of 'hermeneutic circle' itself because that is more strictly concerned with the movement in understanding between the whole and the part in any individual act of interpretation. However, it is worth noting that Schleiermacher articulated his general hermeneutics in part by critique of the special hermeneutics of Wolf, and that it is possible to read his hermeneutics as incorporating a moment of historical contextualisation. See Friedrich Schleiermacher, *Hermeneutics and Criticism and Other Writings*, translated and edited by Andrew Bowie (Cambridge: Cambridge University Press, 1998), and Anthony C. Thiselton, *New Horizons in Hermeneutics* (London: HarperCollins, 1992), pp. 204–36.

5 Kirsti Simonsuuri, *Homer's Original Genius: Eighteenth-century Notions of the Early Greek Epic (1688–1798)* (Cambridge: Cambridge University Press, 1979), pp. 97–8. The quotation from Vico is alternatively rendered in David Marsh's translation: 'Homer was an idea or *heroic archetype of the Greeks who recounted their history in song*', Giambattista Vico, *New Science*, translated by David Marsh (London: Penguin, 1999), p. 381. Further references to the *New Science* are to this edition and are given after quotations in the text. For other accounts of Homer and epic poetry in the eighteenth century, see Margaret Mary Rubel, *Savage and Barbarian: Historical Attitudes in the Criticism of*

Homer and Ossian in Britain, 1760–1800 (Amsterdam: North Holland Publishing Company, 1978); Donald M. Foerster, *Homer in English Criticism: The Historical Approach in the Eighteenth Century* (New Haven: Yale University Press, 1947); H. T. Swedenberg, *The Theory of Epic in England 1650–1800* (Berkeley: University of California Press, 1944); and Lois Whitney, 'English Primitivistic Theories of Epic Origins', *Modern Philology*, 21 (1923–4), 337–78.

6 Adam Ferguson, *An Essay on the History of Civil Society*, edited with an introduction by Duncan Forbes (Edinburgh: Edinburgh University Press, 1966 [1767]), p. 77. Further references are to this edition and are given after quotations in the text.

7 Thomas Gray's poem 'The Bard' (1757) is only the most famous manifestation of this interest.

8 Thomas Blackwell, *An Enquiry into the Life and Writings of Homer* (London, 1735), p. 103; p. 112. Further references are to this edition and are given after quotations in the text.

9 These terms 'parody' and 'pastiche' are not stable; I offer these brief definitions merely as ways of containing this instability for the purposes of this book. For a fuller discussion of parody and pastiche, see Simon Dentith, *Parody* (London: Routledge, 2000).

10 Jane Austen, *Northanger Abbey* (Harmondsworth: Penguin Books, 1982 [1818]), p. 202.

11 For an extended version of this argument, see Robert Mighall, *A Geography of Victorian Gothic Fiction: Mapping History's Nightmares* (Oxford: Oxford University Press, 1999).

CHAPTER I. HOMER, OSSIAN AND MODERNITY

1 F. A. Wolf, *Prolegomena to Homer 1795*, translated with introduction and notes by Anthony Grafton, Glen W. Most and E. G. Zetzel (Princeton: Princeton University Press, 1985). Further references are to this edition and are given after quotations in the text.

2 Robert Wood, *An Essay on the Original Genius and Writings of Homer: with a Comparative View of the Ancient and Present State of the Troade* (London: Payne and Elmsley, 1775), p. 247. Further references are to this edition and are given after quotations in the text.

3 For some indication of this history, which links together poetry, the conception of barbarity and the discovery of 'barbarous' societies in the New World, see Carlo Ginzburg, 'Selfhood as Otherness: Constructing English Identity in the Elizabethan Age', in *No Island Is an Island: Four Glances at English Literature in a World Perspective* (New York: Columbia University Press, 2000), pp. 25–42.

4 On this point, see Anthony Grafton, 'Introduction', *Prolegomena to Homer 1795*.

5 Richard Jenkyns, *The Victorians and Ancient Greece* (Oxford: Basil Blackwell, 1989).

6 George Grote, *A History of Greece*, 12 vols. (London: John Murray, 1846), I, xii–xiii. Further references (with one exception) are to this edition and are given after quotations in the text.

7 George Grote, *A History of Greece* (London: John Murray, 1862), I, xii.

8 William Mure, *A Critical History of the Language and Literature of Antient Greece*, 4 vols. (London: Longman, Brown, Green and Longmans, 1854), I, 236. Further references are to this edition and are given after quotations in the text.

9 W. E. Gladstone, *Studies in Homer and the Homeric Age*, 3 vols. (Oxford: Oxford University Press, 1858), III, 3; III, 12.

10 For the former claim, see Richard B. Sher, *Church and University in the Scottish Enlightenment* (Princeton: Princeton University Press, 1985), p. 254: '. . . Ossian was the product of a group effort on the part of Macpherson and a "cabal" of Edinburgh literary men'. For the alternative view, see Fiona J. Stafford, *The Sublime Savage: A Study of James Macpherson and the Poems of Ossian* (Edinburgh: Edinburgh University Press, 1988), pp. 158–9.

11 Blair's and Macpherson's dissertations are published in *The Poems of Ossian and Related Works*, edited by Howard Gaskill with an introduction by Fiona Stafford (Edinburgh: Edinburgh University Press, 1996). Subsequent references are to this edition and are given after quotations in the text.

12 For a related account of the circularity of Blair's arguments in the 'Critical Dissertation', see Susan Manning, 'Ossian, Scott, and Nineteenth-Century Scottish Literary Nationalism', *Studies in Scottish Literature*, 17 (1982), 39–54.

13 In addition to Fiona Stafford, *The Sublime Savage*, see Richard B. Sher, 'Percy, Shaw, and the Ferguson "Cheat": National Prejudice in the Ossian Wars', in Howard Gaskill, ed., *Ossian Revisited* (Edinburgh: Edinburgh University Press, 1991).

14 See above, page 8.

15 For an explanation of the plausibility of Macpherson's more sentimental view of early human society, see John Dwyer, 'The Melancholy Savage: Text and Context in *The Poems of Ossian*', in Gaskill, ed., *Ossian Revisited*, pp. 164–206.

CHAPTER 2. WALTER SCOTT AND HEROIC MINSTRELSY

1 John Sutherland, *The Life of Walter Scott: A Critical Biography* (Oxford: Blackwell, 1995), p. 47.

2 See Peter D. Garside, 'Scott and the "Philosophical" Historians', *The Journal of the History of Ideas*, 36 (July 1975), 497–512.

3 [Walter Scott], 'Report of the Highland Society upon Ossian etc.', *Edinburgh Review*, 6 (1805), 429–62. Further references are to this edition and are given after quotations in the text.

4 Walter Scott, 'Essay on Romance', in *Scott's Miscellaneous Works*, 30 vols. (Edinburgh: Adam and Charles Black, 1870), VI, 136–7. Further references are to this edition and are given after quotations in the text.

5 Walter Scott, 'Introductory Remarks on Popular Poetry', in *Minstrelsy of the Scottish Border*, edited by T. F. Henderson, 4 vols. (Edinburgh: Blackwood, 1902), I, 5–6. Further references are to this edition and are given after quotations in the text.

6 See Charles G. Zug III, 'The Ballad Editor as Antiquary: Scott and *The Minstrelsy*', *Journal of the Folklore Institute*, 13, 1 (1976), 57–73.

7 See Charles G. Zug III, 'Sir Walter Scott and the Ballad Forgery', *Studies in Scottish Literature*, 8 (1970–1), 52–64.

8 G. Malcolm Laws, Jr, *The British Literary Ballad; A Study in Poetic Imitation* (Carbondale and Edwardsville: Southern Illinois University Press, 1972).

9 Walter Scott, 'Essay on the Imitations of the Ancient Ballad', in *Minstrelsy of the Scottish Border*, 1–52. Further references are to this edition and are given after quotations in the text. Lockhart's footnote is on page 1.

10 Walter Scott, *Poetical Works* (London: Frederick Warne, n.d.), p. 4. Further references are to this edition and are given after quotations in the text.

11 The influence of the Christabel metre on nineteenth-century poetry more generally has been widely noted. See, for example, Matthew Campbell, *Rhythm and Will in Victorian Poetry* (Cambridge: Cambridge University Press, 1999), p. 56, where Campbell suggests the importance of Coleridge's verse-form for the medievalising poets from Scott and Keats through to Swinburne and Morris.

12 Nancy Moore Goslee, *Scott the Rhymer* (Lexington: University Press of Kentucky, 1988).

13 Walter Scott, *The Lady of the Lake*, in *Poetical Works*, p. 121. Further references are to this edition and are given after quotations in the text.

14 Sutherland, *The Life of Walter Scott*, p. 141.

CHAPTER 3. EPIC TRANSLATION AND THE NATIONAL
BALLAD METRE

1 William Maginn, *Homeric Ballads, with Translations and Notes* (London: Parker, 1850), p. 93. Square brackets in the original. Further references are given after quotations in the text.

2 In this context, see Richard Jenkyns's argument that Newman's translation was not so much idiosyncratic as out of date, in view of the earlier publication by Maginn of the Homeric Ballads. See Richard Jenkyns, *The Victorians and Ancient Greece*, p. 198.

3 See below, Chapter 7.

4 Lord Macaulay, *Lays of Ancient Rome, with Ivry and the Armada* (London: Longman, Green, Longman and Roberts, 1860), pp. 9–10. Further references are given after quotations in the text.

5 F. W. Newman, *The Iliad of Homer, Faithfully Translated into Unrhymed English Metre* (London: Walton and Maberly, 1856), p. iv. Further references are given after quotations in the text.

6 Lawrence Venuti, *The Translator's Invisibility: A History of Translation* (London: Routledge, 1995). The controversy between Newman and Arnold is discussed in Chapter 3, 'Nation', pp. 99–147.

7 Matthew Arnold, *On Translating Homer*, in *On the Classical Tradition*, edited by R. H. Super, *The Complete Prose Works of Matthew Arnold*, I (Ann Arbor: University of Michigan Press, 1960), 102. Further references are given after quotations in the text.

8 Venuti formulates the distinction in slightly different though cognate terms. See note 6 above.

9 Edward Earl of Derby, *The Iliad of Homer, Rendered into English Blank Verse*, 2 vols. (London: John Murray, 1864), II, 252–3.

10 F. W. Newman, *Homeric Translation in Theory and Practice: A Reply to Matthew Arnold Esq.* (London: Williams and Norgate, 1861), pp. 48–9. Further references are to this edition and are given after quotations in the text.

11 For a collection of papers on Scott's influence, see J. H. Alexander and David Hewitt, eds., *Scott and His Influence: The Papers of the Aberdeen Scott Conference, 1982* (Aberdeen: Association for Scottish Literary Studies, 1983). An excellent polemical piece on the inheritance of Scott is provided by the first paper in this collection: Richard Waswo, 'Scott and the Really Great Tradition', pp. 1–12.

12 Algernon Charles Swinburne, *Border Ballads* (London: 1909). See also *Ballads of the English Border*, edited by William A. MacInnes (London: Heinemann, 1925). Lang made the assertion that 'it is perhaps to be desired that English poets should leave Scottish ballads alone' in *Anon., Border Ballads*, with an introductory essay by Andrew Lang and twelve etchings by C. O. Murray (London: Lawrence and Bullen, 1895), p. ix.

13 Margaret Mary Rubel, *Savage and Barbarian*, Chapter 3: 'The Historicity of Homer and Ossian and the Historical Periodization'.

14 See Christopher Logue, *War Music; An Account of Books 16–19 of Homer's Iliad* (London: Faber and Faber, 1981).

CHAPTER 4. THE MATTER OF BRITAIN AND THE SEARCH
FOR A NATIONAL EPIC

1 Thomas Carlyle, *Past and Present* (London: Everyman's Library, 1978), pp. 265–6. Further references are given after quotations in the text.

2 Thomas Carlyle, 'The Nibelungen Lied', in *Critical and Miscellaneous Essays*, 2 vols. (London: Chapman and Hall, 1888), I, 221. Further references are given after quotations in the text.

3 See David Quint, *Epic and Empire: Politics and Generic Form from Virgil to Milton* (Princeton: Princeton University Press, 1993).

4 J. M. Ludlow, *Popular Epics of the Middle Ages of the Norse-German and the Carlovingian Cycles*, 2 vols. (London: Macmillan, 1865), I, viii.

5 Conybeare is quoted in Andrew Wawn, 'The Cult of "Stalwart Frith-thjof" in "Victorian Britain"', in Andrew Wawn, ed., *Northern Antiquity: The Post-Medieval Reception of Edda and Saga* (London: Hisarlik Press, 1994), p. 231.

6 Alfred, Lord Tennyson, *The Poems of Tennyson* edited by Christopher Ricks (London: Longman, 1969), pp. 1472–3.

7 William Morris, *Collected Works of William Morris*, vol. XII, *The Story of Sigurd the Volsung and the Fall of the Niblungs* (London: Routledge/Thoemmes Press, 1992, reprinted from the 1910–15 Longmans, Green and Co. edition), pp. 53–4.

8 See 'On Translations of Homer', in Tennyson, *Poems*, pp. 1153–4. On the other hand, when he came to write a version of a traditional Irish story in 'The Voyage of Maeldune', he opted for rhyming hexameters.

9 Quoted in Tennyson, *Poems*, p. 264.

10 Tennyson, *Poems*, p. 584.

11 John O. Waller, *A Circle of Friends: The Tennysons and the Lushingtons of Park House* (Columbus: Ohio State University Press, 1986). Lushington wrote to Emily Tennyson on 11 June 1859: 'almost any title that could be given wd convey a truer notion. If Alfred wishes a Greek diminutive Epylls or little epics wd answer the case better – but it will be hard if for a subject so English an English name cannot be found' (p. 202).

12 Compare Herbert Tucker's suggestion that the poem represents a complex negotiation with the epochally dominant genre of the novel, in 'Trials of Fiction. Novel and Epic in the Geraint and Enid Episodes from *Idylls of the King*', *Victorian Poetry*, 30 (1992), 441–61.

13 William Morris, *Collected Works of William Morris*, vol. VII, *Grettir the Strong; The Volsungs and Niblungs* (London: Routledge/Thoemmes Press, 1992, reprinted from the 1910–15 Longmans, Green and Co. edition), p. 286.

14 William Morris, 'How I Became a Socialist', in *News from Nowhere and Other Writings*, ed., Clive Wilmer (London: Penguin, 1993), pp. 381, 382.

15 Morris's prose romances from the last years of his life are especially marked – to the point of deformation – by the problem of pastiche. May Morris defends this diction – 'somewhat aloof from modern usage' – as one which 'rouses some note of memory within ourselves to sound again on those strings of the poet's tuning': *Collected Works of William Morris*, vol. XVII, *The Wood Beyond the World, Child Christopher and Old French Romances* (London: Routledge/Thoemmes Press, 1992, reprinted from the 1910–15 Longmans, Green and Co. edition), p. xiii.

16 William Morris, *The Story of Sigurd the Volsung and the Fall of the Niblungs*, p. 157.

17 For these identifications see *The Saga of the Volsungs*, Introduction and translation by Jesse L. Byock (Enfield Lock: Hisarlik Press, 1993), p. 12.

CHAPTER 5. 'AS FLAT AS FLEET STREET': ELIZABETH BARRETT
BROWNING, MATTHEW ARNOLD AND GEORGE ELIOT ON
EPIC AND MODERNITY

1 For other discussions of Aurora Leigh as epic, see Holly A. Laird, '*Aurora Leigh*: An Epical Ars Poetica', in Suzanne W. Jones, ed., *Writing the Woman Artist; Essays on Poetics, Politics and Portraiture* (Philadelphia: University of Pennsylvania Press, 1991), pp. 353–70; Herbert F. Tucker, '*Aurora Leigh*: Epic Solutions to Novel Ends', in Alison Booth, ed., *Famous Last Words: Changes in Gender and Narrative Closure* (Charlottesville and London: University Press of Virginia, 1993), pp. 62–85; and Sarah Anne Brown, '*Paradise Lost* and *Aurora Leigh*', *Studies in English Literature 1500–1900*, 37 (1997), 723–40.
2 Elizabeth Barrett Browning, *Aurora Leigh*, edited by Margaret Reynolds (New York: Norton, 1996), pp. 149–50; V, 210–13. All further references, which give both page and volume and line numbers, are to this edition and are given after quotations in the text.
3 Matthew Arnold, 'Preface to Poems, 1853', in *Complete Prose Works*, pp. 13–14.
4 J. A. Froude, 'Homer', in *Short Studies on Great Subjects*, 2 vols. (London: Everyman, 1924), II, 203.
5 George Eliot, *Middlemarch*, edited by David Carroll (Oxford: Oxford University Press, 1988), p. 3.
6 Matthew Arnold, 'On the Modern Element in Literature', in *Complete Prose Works*, pp. 34–5.
7 Elizabeth Barrett Browning, *Casa Guidi Windows*, in *The Works of Elizabeth Barrett Browning* (Ware: Wordsworth, 1994), p. 352.
8 Holly A. Laird, '*Aurora Leigh*: An Epical Ars Poetica', p. 365.
9 Herbert F. Tucker, '*Aurora Leigh*: Epic Solutions to Novel Ends', p. 68.
10 See above, Chapter 4, p. 65.
11 See above, Chapter 1, p. 18.

CHAPTER 6. MAPPING EPIC AND NOVEL

1 G. W. F. Hegel, *Aesthetics: Lectures on Fine Art*, translated by T. M. Knox, 2 vols. (Oxford: Clarendon Press, 1975), II, 1056. All subsequent references are to this edition and are given after quotations in the text.
2 Georg Lukács, *The Theory of the Novel*, translated by Anna Bostock (London: Merlin Press, 1971); M. M. Bakhtin, 'Epic and Novel', in *The Dialogic Imagination*, edited by Michael Holquist and translated by Caryl Emerson and Michael Holquist (Austin: University of Texas Press, 1981); Franco Moretti, *Modern Epic: The World-System from Goethe to Garcia Márquez* (London: Verso, 1996); Theodor Adorno and Max Horkheimer, *Dialectic of Enlightenment*, translated by John Cumming (London: Verso, 1979). All references are to these editions and are indicated in the body of the text.

3 Galin Tihanov, *The Master and the Slave: Lukács, Bakhtin, and the Ideas of Their Time* (Oxford: Clarendon Press, 2000). See especially Chapter 6, 'The Novel, the Epic, and Modernity'.

4 Mikhail Bakhtin, 'Discourse in the Novel', in *The Dialogic Imagination*, p. 271.

5 Benedict Anderson, *Imagined Communities: Reflections on the Origin and Spread of Nationalism* (London: Verso, 1991).

6 Franco Moretti, *Atlas of the European Novel 1800–1900* (London: Verso, 1998), p. 40.

7 Walter Scott, *Waverley* (Harmondsworth: Penguin, 1972 [1814]), p. 177. Further quotations are to this edition and are given after quotations in the text.

CHAPTER 7. EPIC AND THE IMPERIAL THEME

1 Joseph Conrad, *Victory* (London: Penguin, 1989 [1915]) p. 45; p. 193.

2 Joseph Conrad, *Selected Literary Criticism and The Shadow-Line*, edited by Allan Ingram (London: Methuen English Texts, 1986), p. 73

3 Andrew Lang, 'Realism and Romance', *Contemporary Review*, 52 (1887), 683–93, pp. 689–90.

4 Martin Green, *Dreams of Adventure, Deeds of Empire* (London: Routledge and Kegan Paul, 1983), p. 3. Further references are given after quotations in the text.

5 Patrick Brantlinger, *Rule of Darkness: British Literature and Imperialism, 1830–1914* (Ithaca and London: Cornell University Press, 1988), p. 36. Further references are given after quotations in the text.

6 Joseph Bristow, *Empire Boys: Adventures in a Man's World* (London, HarperCollins Academic, 1991).

7 See especially Robert Giddings, ed., *Literature and Imperialism* (Basingstoke: Macmillan, 1991); Robert H. MacDonald, *The Language of Empire: Myths and Metaphors of Popular Imperialism, 1860–1918* (Manchester: Manchester University Press, 1994); Cecil Degrotte Eby, *The Road to Armageddon: The Martial Spirit in English Popular Literature 1870–1914* (Durham, N.C.: Duke University Press, 1987). Further references, where appropriate, are given after quotations in the text.

8 Bertrand Russell, *The Autobiography of Bertrand Russell*, 3 vols. (London: George Allen and Unwin, 1968), I, 42–3.

9 J. A. Hobson, *The Psychology of Jingoism* (London: Grant Richards, 1901), p. 12. Further references are given after quotations in the text.

10 John M. Robertson, *Patriotism and Empire* (London: Grant Richards, 1899), pp. 30–1. Further references are given after quotations in the text.

11 C. F. G. Masterman, *In Peril of Change: Essays Written in Time of Tranquility* (London: T. Fisher Unwin, 1909), pp. 4–5.

12 Chris Brooks and Peter Faulkner, eds., *The White Man's Burden: An Anthology of the British Poetry of the Empire* (Exeter: Exeter University Press, 1996). Further references are given after quotations in the text.

13 Charles Rathbone Low, *Cressy to Tel-el-Kebîr: A Narrative Poem, Descriptive of the Deeds of the British Army* (London: W. Mitchell and Co., 1892), p. 1.

14 W. C. Bennett, *Contributions to a Ballad History of England* (London: Chatto and Windus, n.d. (1880?)). Further references are given after quotations in the text.

15 Gerald Massey, 'Havelock's March', in Brooks and Faulkner, *The White Man's Burden*, p. 196.

16 Ruth M. Robbins, 'Introduction', Charles Doughty, *The Dawn in Britain* (London: Jonathan Cape, 1943), p. 11. Further references to Doughty's poem are to this edition and are given after quotations in the text.

17 Alfred, Lord Tennyson, '*The Revenge*', in *The Poems of Tennyson*, p. 1243, ll. 50–5. Further references, to page and line numbers, are given after quotations in the text.

18 Ibid., p. 1241.

19 Lord Macaulay, *Lays of Ancient Rome*, p. 165.

20 Thomas Campbell, 'The Battle of the Baltic', in *The Complete Poetical Works of Thomas Campbell*, edited by J. Logie Robertson (London: Oxford University Press, 1907), p. 189.

21 Frederick Langbridge, *Ballads of the Brave: Poems of Chivalry, Enterprise, Courage and Constancy* (London: Methuen, 1890); William Ernest Henley, *Lyra Heroica: A Book of Verse for Boys* (London: Macmillan, 1940 [1891]). References are given after quotations in the text.

CHAPTER 8. KIPLING, BARD OF EMPIRE

1 Ann Parry, *The Poetry of Rudyard Kipling: Rousing the Nation* (Buckingham: Open University Press, 1992), passim.

2 Lafcadio Hearn, *The Life and Letters of Lafcadio Hearn* (1906), in Roger Lancelyn Green, ed., *Kipling: The Critical Heritage* (London: Routledge and Kegan Paul, 1971), p. 173.

3 J. H. Millar, (Anon.), *Blackwood's Magazine*, vol. CLXIV, pp. 470–82 (October 1898), in Roger Lancelyn Green, ed., *Kipling: The Critical Heritage* p. 201.

4 Robert Buchanan, 'The Voice of the Hooligan', The *Contemporary Review*, vol. LXVI, pp. 774–89 (December 1899), in Roger Lancelyn Green, ed., *Kipling: The Critical Heritage*, p. 236.

5 Neil Munro, 'Mr Rudyard Kipling', *Good Words*, vol. XL, pp. 261–5 (April 1899), in Roger Lancelyn Green, ed., *Kipling: The Critical Heritage*, pp. 223–4.

6 Peter Keating, *Kipling the Poet* (London: Secker and Warburg, 1994), p. 10.

7 Rudyard Kipling, *The Seven Seas* (London: Methuen, 1896), p. 162. Further references are to this edition and are given after quotation in the text.

8 David Gilmour, *The Long Recessional: The Imperial Life of Rudyard Kipling* (London: Pimlico, 2003), p. 110.

9 See Andrew Rutherford, ed., *Early Verse by Rudyard Kipling, 1879–1889* (Oxford: Clarendon Press, 1986).

10 Rudyard Kipling, *Barrack-Room Ballads and Other Verses* (London: Methuen, 1892), p. 126. Further references are to this edition and are given after quotations in the text.

11 Lionel Johnson, '*Barrack-Room Ballads and Other Verses*', *The Academy*, vol. XLI, pp. 509–10 (28 May 1892), in Roger Lancelyn Green, ed., *Kipling: The Critical Heritage*, pp. 98–9.

12 Rudyard Kipling, *The Seven Seas* (London: Methuen, 1896), p. 103.

13 See David Gilmour, *The Long Recessional*, pp. 111–13.

14 Rudyard Kipling, *Puck of Pook's Hill* (London: Macmillan, 1908 [1906]), p. 31.

15 Rudyard Kipling, *The Complete Verse*, with a foreword by M. M. Kaye (London: Kyle Cathie, 1990), p. 597.

16 David Gilmour, *The Long Recessional*, pp. 47–8.

CHAPTER 9. EPIC AND THE SUBJECT PEOPLES OF EMPIRE

1 For a sophisticated discussion of both of these poets in Bakhtinian terms (though somewhat different from that attempted here), see Colin Graham, *Ideologies of Epic: Nation, Empire and Victorian Poetry* (Manchester: Manchester University Press, 1998).

2 Samuel Ferguson, *Congal: A Poem, in Five Books* (Dublin: Edward Ponsonby, and London: Bell and Daldy, 1872), p. 109. Further references are given after quotations in the text.

3 Sir Samuel Ferguson *Lays of the Red Branch*, with an introduction by Lady Ferguson (London: T. Fisher Unwin, 1897). Further references are given after quotations in the text. This edition was published as part of the 'New Irish Library', edited by Sir Charles Gavan Duffy; it arranges the poems in the order which Ferguson would have wanted – i.e. the order of the narrative, not the chronological order of composition. The Introduction by Lady Ferguson defends the Gaelic spirit in literature in terms partly deriving from Matthew Arnold.

4 Edwin Arnold, 'Preface', *The Light of Asia; or, The Great Renunciation (Mahabhinishkramana)* (Boston: Roberts Brothers, 1880). Further references are to this edition and are given after quotation in the text.

5 Edward Tylor, *Primitive Culture: Researches into the Development of Mythology, Philosophy, Religion, Language, Art, and Custom*, 3rd edition (London: John Murray, 1891), p. 29.

6   Andrew Lang, *Homer and His Age* (London: Longmans, Green and Co.,
    1906), p. 290. Further references are to this edition and are given after
    quotation in the text.

7   H. Rider Haggard, *King Solomon's Mines* (Ware: Wordsworth's Children's
    Classics, 1993), pp. 188–9. Further references are given after quotations in the
    text.

8   H. Rider Haggard, *Cetywayo and his White Neighbours; or, Remarks on Recent
    Events in Zululand, Natal, and the Transvaal*, new edition (London: Kegan
    Paul, Trench, Trubner and Co., 1906), p. 30.

9   H. Rider Haggard, *Allan Quatermain*, edited by Dennis Butts (Oxford:
    Oxford University Press, 1998), p. 2. Further references are given after
    quotations in the text.

10 H. Rider Haggard, *Nada the Lily* (London: Longmans, Green and Co.,
    1892), p. 34. Further references are given after quotations in the text.

11 H. Rider Haggard, *Child of Storm* (London, Cassell, 1913), pp. vi–vii.

12 Joseph Conrad, *An Outcast of the Islands* (London: Everyman, 1996), p. 45.

13 Joseph Conrad, *Almayer's Folly* (Harmondsworth: Penguin, 1976), p. 37.

14 Robert Louis Stevenson, *Kidnapped* (London: Penguin, 1994), pp. 67–8.

15 Robert Louis Stevenson, *The Master of Ballantrae and Weir of Hermiston*,
    introduced by Claire Harman (London: Everyman, 1996), p. 151.

CHAPTER 10. CODA: SOME HOMERIC FUTURES

1   Adam Parry, ed., *The Making of Heroic Verse: The Collected Papers of Milman
    Parry* (Oxford: Oxford University Press, 1971), p. lxi, fn. Further references
    are to this edition and are given after quotations in the text. Adam Parry,
    Milman Parry's son and editor, is careful to point out that the minimum
    conclusion to be drawn from Milman Parry's work is that the style is oral:
    Homer himself (or a guild of Homers) might have availed themselves of
    writing to achieve the coherence and consistency of the overall poems.

2   Charles M. Doughty, *Travels in Arabia Deserta*, with an Introduction by
    T. E. Lawrence, new and definitive edition, 2 vols. (London: Jonathan Cape,
    1936).

3   Parry, *The Making of Heroic Verse*, p. 377.

4   Doughty, *Travels in Arabia Deserta*, p. 35.

5   T. E. Lawrence, *Seven Pillars of Wisdom: A Triumph* (London: Penguin
    Books, 2000 [1926]), p. 153. Further references are to this edition and are
    given after quotations in the text.

6   See Rudyard Kipling, *Puck of Pook's Hill* (London: Macmillan, 1908), p. 167.

7   A striking indication of the disjunction between the War as experienced in
    these two theatres can be gained from the fact that Robert Graves, author of
    the classic debunking memoir *Goodbye to All That*, was yet a fervent admirer
    of Lawrence and wrote an enthusiastic book about him: *Lawrence and the
    Arabs* (London: Jonathan Cape, 1927).

8 Robert Graves, *Lawrence and the Arabs*, p. 159.

9 Mazisi Kunene, *Emperor Shaka the Great; A Zulu Epic* (Oxford: Heinemann, 1979), p. 25. Further references to this edition are given after quotations in the text.

10 For an extended and largely persuasive account of Tolkien in these terms, see Patrick Curry, *Defending Middle Earth; Tolkien: Myth and Modernity* (London: HarperCollins, 1997).

11 Karl Marx, *Grundrisse*, p. 111.

12 For Goebbels's liking for Lang's *Der Nibelung*, see Stuart Klawans, *Film Follies: The Cinema Out of Order* (London: Cassell, 1999), p. 98. Klawans also gives an account of the making of Kolberg. For plans to write an epic poem about the Battle of Stalingrad see Anthony Beevor, *Stalingrad*, (London: Penguin, 1999).

13 Derek Walcott, *Omeros* (London: Faber and Faber, 1990), pp. 136–7. Further references are to this edition and are given after quotations in the text.

14 Patrick Kavanagh, *Collected Poems* (London: Martin Brian & O'Keeffe, 1972), p. 136.

Bibliography

Adorno, Theodor and Max Horkheimer, *The Dialectic of Enlightenment*, translated by John Cumming (London: Verso, 1979).

Alexander, J. H. and David Hewitt, eds., *Scott and His Influence: The Papers of the Aberdeen Scott Conference, 1982* (Aberdeen: Association for Scottish Literary Studies, 1983).

Anderson, Benedict, *Imagined Communities: Reflections on the Origin and Spread of Nationalism* (London: Verso, 1991).

Anon., *Border Ballads*, with an introductory essay by Andrew Lang and twelve etchings by C. O. Murray (London: Lawrence and Bullen, 1895).

'The English Translations of Homer', *National Review*, 2 (1860), 283–314.

Armstrong, Isobel, *Victorian Poetry: Poetry, Poetics and Politics* (London: Routledge, 1993).

Arnold, Edwin, *The Light of Asia; or, The Great Renunciation (Mahabhinishkramana)* (Boston: Roberts Brothers, 1880).

Arnold, Matthew, *The Complete Prose Works of Matthew Arnold*, edited by R. H. Super, vol. I, *On the Classical Tradition* (Ann Arbor: University of Michigan Press, 1960).

Austen, Jane, *Northanger Abbey* (Harmondsworth: Penguin, 1982 [1818]).

Bailey, R. V., *The Poet's Trade and the Prophet's Vocation: Development and Integration in the Poetry of Rudyard Kipling* (D.Phil, Oxford, 1982).

Bakhtin, M. M., *The Dialogic Imagination: Four Essays*, edited by Michael Holquist and translated by Caryl Emerson and Michael Holquist (Austin: University of Texas Press, 1981).

Barribeau, James L., 'William Morris and Saga-Translation: "The Story of King Magnus, Son of Erling"', in R. T. Farrell, ed., *The Vikings* (London: Phillimore, 1982).

Beevor, Anthony, *Stalingrad* (London: Penguin, 1999).

Bennett, W. C., *Contributions to a Ballad History of England* (London: Chatto and Windus, n.d. (1880?)).

ed., *The Lark: Songs, Ballads and Recitations for the People* (London and Birmingham: 1883).

Blackwell, Thomas, *An Enquiry into the Life and Writings of Homer* (London: 1735).

Brantlinger, Patrick, *Rule of Darkness: British Literature and Imperialism, 1830–1914* (Ithaca and London: Cornell University Press, 1988).

Bristow, Joseph, *Empire Boys: Adventures in a Man's World* (London: HarperCollins Academic, 1991).

Brooks, Chris, and Peter Faulkner, eds., *The White Man's Burden: An Anthology of the British Poetry of the Empire* (Exeter: Exeter University Press, 1996).

Brown, Sarah Ann, '*Paradise Lost* and *Aurora Leigh*', *Studies in English Literature, 1500–1900*, 37 (1997), 723–40.

Browning, Elizabeth Barrett, *Aurora Leigh*, edited by Margaret Reynolds (New York: Norton, 1996).

 '*The Book of the Poets*', *The Athenaeum*, 4 June 1842, 497–9; 11 June 1842, 520–3; 25 June 1842, 558–60; 6 August 1842, 706–8; 13 August 1842, 728–9.

 Casa Guidi Windows, in *The Works of Elizabeth Barrett Browning* (Ware: Wordsworth, 1994).

Buchan, David, *The Ballad and the Folk* (London: Routledge and Kegan Paul, 1972).

[Buchan, John], *A Lodge in the Wilderness* (Edinburgh: Blackwood, 1906)

 Prester John (London: Thomas Nelson, 1910).

Campbell, Matthew, *Rhythm and Will in Victorian Poetry* (Cambridge: Cambridge University Press, 1999).

Campbell, Thomas, 'The Battle of the Baltic', in *The Complete Poetical Works of Thomas Campbell*, edited by J. Logie Robertson (London: Oxford University Press, 1907).

Carlyle, Thomas, 'The Nibelungen Lied', in *Critical and Miscellaneous Essays*, 2 vols. (London: Chapman and Hall, 1888).

 Past and Present (London: Everyman's Library, 1978).

Conrad, Joseph, *Almayer's Folly* (Harmondsworth: Penguin, 1976).

 An Outcast of the Islands (London: Everyman, 1996).

 Selected Literary Criticism and The Shadow-Line, edited by Allan Ingram (London: Methuen English Texts, 1986).

 Victory (London: Penguin, 1989 [1915]).

Cross, Tom Peete, 'Alfred Tennyson as a Celticist', *Modern Philology*, 18 (1921), 149–56.

Curry, Patrick, *Defending Middle Earth; Tolkien: Myth and Modernity* (London: HarperCollins, 1997).

Dale, Thomas R., 'From Epic to Romance: Barbour's *Bruce* and Scott's *The Lord of the Isles*', *Studies in Scottish Literature*, 26 (1991), 515–21.

Davidson, Lola Sharon, S. N. Mukherjee and Z. Zlatar, eds., *The Epic in History* (Sydney Studies in Society and Culture, Sydney: SASSC, 1994).

Dentith, Simon, *Parody* (London: Routledge, 2000).

Derby, Edward Earl of, *The Iliad of Homer, Rendered into English Blank Verse*, 2 vols. (London: John Murray, 1864).

Doughty, Charles M., *The Dawn in Britain* (London: Jonathan Cape, 1943).

 Travels in Arabia Deserta, with an Introduction by T. E. Lawrence, new and definitive edition, 2 vols. (London: Jonathan Cape, 1936).

Eby, Cecil Degrotte, *The Road to Armageddon: The Martial Spirit in English Popular Literature 1870–1914* (Durham, N.C. : Duke University Press, 1987).

Edinburgh Review, 'Northern Homers', 95 (1995).

Eliot, George, *Middlemarch*, edited by David Carroll (Oxford: Oxford University Press, 1988).

Elley, Derek, *The Epic Film: Myth and History* (London: Routledge and Kegan Paul, 1984).

Ellis, Peter Berrisford, *H. Rider Haggard: A Voice from the Infinite* (London: Routledge and Kegan Paul, 1978).

Faulkner, Peter, ed., *William Morris: The Critical Heritage* (London: Routledge and Kegan Paul, 1973).

Ferguson, Adam, *An Essay on the History of Civil Society*, edited with an introduction by Duncan Forbes (Edinburgh: Edinburgh University Press, 1966 [1767]).

Ferguson, Samuel, *Congal: A Poem, in Five Books* (Dublin: Edward Ponsonby, and London: Bell and Daldy, 1872).

Ferguson, Sir Samuel, *Lays of the Red Branch*, with an introduction by Lady Ferguson (London: T. Fisher Unwin, 1897).

Foerster, Donald M., *Homer in English Criticism: The Historical Approach in the Eighteenth Century* (New Haven: Yale University Press, 1947).

Froude, J. A., 'Homer', in *Short Studies on Great Subjects*, 2 vols. (London: Everyman, 1924).

Garside, Peter D., 'Scott and the "Philosophical" Historians', *The Journal of the History of Ideas*, 36 (July 1975), 497–512.

Gaskill, Howard, ed., *Ossian Revisited* (Edinburgh: Edinburgh University Press, 1991).

Geary, Patrick J., *The Myth of Nations: The Medieval Origins of Europe* (Princeton: Princeton University Press, 2002).

Giddings, Robert, ed., *Literature and Imperialism* (Basingstoke: Macmillan, 1991).

Gilmour, David, *The Long Recessional: The Imperial Life of Rudyard Kipling* (London: Pimlico, 2003).

Ginzburg, Carlo, *No Island Is an Island: Four Glances at English Literature in a World Perspective* (New York: Columbia University Press, 2000).

Gladsone, W. E., *Studies on Homer and the Homeric Age*, 3 vols. (Oxford: Oxford University Press, 1858).

Goslee, Nancy Moore, *Scott the Rhymer* (Lexington: University Press of Kentucky, 1988).

Graham, Colin, *Ideologies of Epic: Nation, Empire and Victorian Poetry* (Manchester: Manchester University Press, 1998).

Graves, Robert, *Lawrence and the Arabs* (London: Jonathan Cape, 1927).

Green, Martin, *Dreams of Adventure, Deeds of Empire* (London: Routledge and Kegan Paul, 1983).

Green, Roger Lancelyn, ed., *Kipling: The Critical Heritage* (London: Routledge and Kegan Paul, 1971).

Gregory, Lady, *Gods and Fighting Men: The Story of the Tuatha de Danaan and of the Fianna of Ireland*, arranged and put into English by Lady Gregory, with a Preface by W. B.Yeats (London: John Murray, 1904).

Grote, George, *A History of Greece*, 12 vols. (London: John Murray, 1846).
A History of Greece, new edition, 8 vols. (London: John Murray, 1862).

Gunn, Neil, *Sun Circle* (Edinburgh: Canongate, 2001).

Haggard, H. Rider, 'About Fiction', *The Contemporary Review*, 58 (1887), 172–80.
Allan Quatermain, edited by Dennis Butts (Oxford: Oxford University Press, 1998).
Cetywayo and his White Neighbours; or, Remarks on Recent Events in Zululand, Natal, and the Transvaal, new edition (London: Kegan Paul, Trench, Trubner and Co., 1906).
Child of Storm (London: Cassell, 1913).
Eric Brighteyes, 3rd edition (London: Longmans, Green and Co., 1893).
King Solomon's Mines (Ware: Wordsworth's Children's Classics, 1993).
Marie (London: Cassell, 1912).
Nada the Lily (London: Longmans, Green and Co., 1892).

Haggard, H. Rider and Andrew Lang, *The World's Desire*, New Edition, (London: Longmans, Green and Co., 1894).

Hair, Donald S., *Domestic and Heroic in Tennyson's Poetry* (Toronto: University of Toronto Press, 1981).

Harvey, A. D., 'The English Epic in the Romantic Period', *Philological Quarterly*, 55 (1976), 241–59.
Literature into History (Basingstoke: Macmillan, 1988).

Headley, G., 'The Early Nineteenth-century Epic: The Harvey Thesis Examined', *Journal of European Studies*, 21 (1991), 201–8.

Hegel, G. W. F., *Aesthetics: Lectures on Fine Art*, translated by T. M. Knox, 2 vols. (Oxford: Clarendon Press, 1975).

Henley, William Ernest, *Lyra Heroica: A Book of Verse for Boys* (London: Macmillan, 1940 [1891]).

Hickey, Emily H., *Verse-Tales, Lyrics and Translations* (Liverpool: Arnold, 1889).

Hobson, J. A., *The Psychology of Jingoism* (London: Grant Richards, 1901).

Homer, *The Iliad of Homer*, done into English prose by Andrew Lang, Walter Leaf, and Ernest Myers, revised edition (London: Macmillan and Co., 1892).

[Jeffrey, Francis], 'The Giaour, A Fragment of a Turkish Tale, by Lord Byron', *The Edinburgh Review*, 21 (1813), 299–309.

Jenkyns, Richard, *The Victorians and Ancient Greece* (Oxford: Basil Blackwell, 1989).

Kavanagh, Patrick, *Collected Poems* (London: Martin Brian & O'Keeffe, 1972).

Keating, Peter, *Kipling the Poet* (London: Secker and Warburg, 1994).

Kennedy, John, 'The English Translations of *Volsunga Saga*', in Andrew Wawn, ed., *Northern Antiquity: The Post-Medieval Reception of Edda and Saga* (London: Hisarlik Press, 1994).

Ker, W. P., *Epic and Romance: Essays on Medieval Literature* (London: Macmillan, 1897).

Kiernan, Victor, 'Tennyson, King Arthur and Imperialism', in Raphael Samuel and Gareth Stedman Jones, eds., *Culture, Ideology and Politics: Essays for Eric Hobsbawm*, (London: Routledge and Kegan Paul, 1982), pp. 126–48.

Kipling, Rudyard, *Barrack-Room Ballads and Other Verses* (London: Methuen, 1892).

The Complete Verse, with a foreword by M. M. Kaye (London: Kyle Cathie, 1990).

Puck of Pook's Hill (London: Macmillan, 1908).

The Seven Seas (London: Methuen, 1896).

Klawans, Stuart, *Film Follies: The Cinema Out of Order* (London: Cassell, 1999).

Kozicki, Henry, *Tennyson and Clio: History in the Major Poems* (Baltimore and London: Johns Hopkins University Press, 1979).

Kunene, Mazisi, *Emperor Shaka the Great; A Zulu Epic* (Oxford: Heinemann, 1979).

Laird, Holly A., '*Aurora Leigh*: An Epical Ars Poetica', in Suzanne W. Jones, ed., *Writing the Woman Artist; Essays on Poetics, Politics and Portraiture* (Philadelphia: University of Pennsylvania Press, 1991), 353–70.

Lang, Andrew, *Homer and His Age* (London: Longmans, Green and Co., 1906).

Homer and the Epic (London: Longmans, Green and Co., 1893).

Myth, Ritual and Religion, 2 vols. (London: Longmans, Green and Co., 1913).

'Realism and Romance', *Contemporary Review*, 52 (1887), 683–93.

Sir Walter Scott and the Border Minstrelsy (London: Longmans, Green and Co., 1910).

Langbridge, Frederick, *Ballads of the Brave: Poems of Chivalry, Enterprise, Courage and Constancy* (London: Methuen, 1890).

Lawrence, T. E., *Seven Pillars of Wisdom: A Triumph* (London: Penguin, 2000 [1926]).

Lawry, J. S., 'Tennyson's "The Epic": A Gesture of Recovered Faith', *Modern Language Notes*, 74 (1959), 400–3.

Laws Jnr, G. Malcolm, *The British Literary Ballad; A Study in Poetic Imitation* (Carbondale and Edwardsville: Southern Illinois University Press, 1972).

Laxness, Halldór, *Independent People*, translated by J. A. Thompson (London: The Harvill Press, 2001).

Letherbrow, Emma, *Gudrun, a Story of the North Sea*, from the medieval German (Edinburgh: Edmonston and Douglas, 1863).

Linley, Margaret, 'Sexuality and Nationality in Tennyson's *Idylls of the King*', *Victorian Poetry*, 30 (1992), 365–86.

Logue, Christopher, *War Music; An Account of Books 16–19 of Homer's Iliad* (London: Faber and Faber, 1981).

Low, Charles Rathbone, *Cressy to Tel-el-Kebîr: A Narrative Poem, Descriptive of the Deeds of the British Army* (London: W. Mitchell and Co., 1892).

Ludlow, J. M., *Popular Epics of the Middle Ages of the Norse–German and the Carlovingian Cycles*, 2 vols. (London: Macmillan, 1865).

Lukács, Georg, *The Theory of the Novel,* translated by Anna Bostock (London: Merlin Press, 1971).

Macaulay, Lord, *Lays of Ancient Rome, with Ivry and the Armada* (London: Longman, Green, Longman and Roberts, 1860).

MacDonald, Robert H., *The Language of Empire: Myths and Metaphors of Popular Imperialism, 1860–1918* (Manchester: Manchester University Press, 1994).

Mackail, J. W., *The Life of William Morris,* 2 vols. (London: Longmans, 1901).

Macpherson, James, *The Poems of Ossian and Related Works,* edited by Howard Gaskill with an Introduction by Fiona Stafford (Edinburgh: Edinburgh University Press, 1996).

Maginn, William, *Homeric Ballads, with Translations and Notes* (London: Parker, 1850).

[Malory, Thomas], *The Byrth, Lyf, and Actes of Kyng Arthur,* with an Introduction and notes by Robert Southey, Esq. (London: Longman and Co., 1817).

Manning, Susan, 'Ossian, Scott, and Nineteenth-Century Scottish Literary Nationalism', *Studies in Scottish Literature,* 17 (1982), 39–54.

Marx, Karl, *Grundrisse: Foundation of the Critique of Political Economy,* translated by Martin Nicolaus (Harmondsworth: Penguin, 1973).

Massey, Gerald, *Havelock's March and Other Poems* (London: Trübner, 1861).

Masterman, C. F. G., *In Peril of Change: Essays Written in Time of Tranquility* (London: T. Fisher Unwin, 1909).

McGuinness, Arthur E., 'Lord Kames on the Ossian Poems: Anthropology and Criticism', *Texas Studies in Literature and Language,* 10 (1968), 65–75.

McGuire, Ian, 'Epistemology and Empire in *Idylls of the King*', *Victorian Poetry,* 30 (1992), 387–400.

McLuhan, H. M., 'Tennyson and the Romantic Epic', in John Killham, ed. *Critical Essays on the Poetry of Tennyson* (London: Routledge and Kegan Paul, 1960).

Mighall, Robert, *A Geography of Victorian Gothic Fiction: Mapping History's Nightmares* (Oxford: Oxford University Press, 1999).

Moretti, Franco, *Atlas of the European Novel 1800–1900* (London: Verso, 1998).
  Modern Epic: The World-System from Goethe to Garcia Márquez, translated by Quintin Hoare (London: Verso, 1996).

Mori, Masaki, *Epic Grandeur: Towards a Comparative Poetics of the Epic* (Albany: State University of New York Press, 1997).

Morris, Lewis, *The Epic of Hades* (London: Kegan Paul, Trench Trubner and Co., 1903).

Morris, May, *William Morris, Artist, Writer, Socialist,* 2 vols. (Oxford: Basil Blackwell, 1936).

Morris, William, *Collected Works of William Morris,* vol. VII, *Grettir the Strong; The Volsungs and Niblungs* (London: Routledge/Thoemmes Press, 1992, reprinted from the 1910–15 Longmans, Green and Co. edition).

Collected Works of William Morris, vol. XII, *The Story of Sigurd the Volsung and the Fall of the Niblungs* (London: Routledge/Thoemmes Press, 1992, reprinted from the 1910–15 Longmans, Green and Co. edition).

Collected Works of William Morris, vol. XVII, *The Wood Beyond the World, Child Christopher and Old French Romances* (London: Routledge/ Thoemmes Press, 1992, reprinted from the 1910–15 Longmans, Green and Co. edition).

'How I Became a Socialist', in *News from Nowhere and Other Writings*, edited by Clive Wilmer (London: Penguin, 1993).

Mure, William, *A Critical History of the Language and Literature of Antient Greece*, 4 vols. (London: Longman, Brown, Green and Longmans, 1854).

Newman, F. W., *Homeric Translation in Theory and Practice: A Reply to Matthew Arnold, Esq.* (London: Williams and Norgate, 1861).

The Iliad of Homer, Faithfully Translated into Unrhymed English Metre (London: Walton and Maberley, 1856).

Noyes, Alfred, 'Drake', in *Collected Poems*, vol. II (Edinburgh, Blackwood, 1914).

Parry, Adam, ed., *The Making of Heroic Verse: The Collected Papers of Milman Parry* (Oxford: Oxford University Press, 1971).

Parry, Ann, *The Poetry of Rudyard Kipling: Rousing the Nation* (Buckingham: Open University Press, 1992).

Percy, Thomas, *Reliques of Ancient English Poetry*, edited by Henry B. Wheatley, 3 vols. (London: Swan Sonnenschein, 1886).

Quint, David, *Epic and Empire: Politics and Generic Form from Virgil to Milton* (Princeton: Princeton University Press, 1993).

Reed, James, *The Border Ballads* (London: The Athlone Press, 1973).

Ricks, Christopher, *Tennyson* (London: Macmillan, 1972).

Robertson, John M., *Patriotism and Empire* (London: Grant Richards, 1899).

Rubel, Margaret Mary, *Savage and Barbarian: Historical Attitudes in the Criticism of Homer and Ossian in Britain, 1760–1800* (Amsterdam: North-Holland Publishing Company, 1978).

Russell, Bertrand, *The Autobiography of Bertrand Russell*, 3 vols. (London: George Allen and Unwin, 1968).

Rutherford, Andrew, ed., *Early Verse by Rudyard Kipling, 1879–1889* (Oxford: Clarendon Press, 1986).

The Saga of the Volsungs, Introduction and translation by Jesse L. Byock (Enfield Lock: Hisarlik Press, 1993).

Sandison, Alan, *The Wheel of Empire: A Study of the Imperial Idea in Some Late Nineteenth- and Early Twentieth-Century Fiction* (London: Macmillan, 1967).

Schleiermacher, Friedrich, *Hermeneutics and Criticism and Other Writings*, translated and edited by Andrew Bowie (Cambridge: Cambridge University Press, 1998).

Scott, Walter, *The Lady of the Lake*, in *The Poetical Works of Sir Walter Scott* (London: Frederick Warne, n.d.).

Scott, Walter, *Minstrelsy of the Scottish Border*, edited by T. F. Henderson, 4 vols. (Edinburgh: Blackwood, 1902).

Miscellaneous Works, 30 vols. (Edinburgh: Adam and Charles Black, 1870).

Poetical Works (London: Frederick Warne, n.d.).

Poetical Works, edited by J. Logie Robertson (Oxford: Oxford University Press, 1904).

'Report of the Highland Society upon Ossian etc.', *Edinburgh Review*, 6 (1805), 429–62.

Waverley (Harmondsworth: Penguin, 1972 [1814]).

Shaw, Marion, 'Tennyson's Dark Continent', *Victorian Poetry*, 32 (1994), 157–69.

Sher, Richard B., *Church and University in the Scottish Enlightenment* (Princeton: Princeton University Press, 1985).

Shires, Linda M., 'Patriarchy, Dead Men, and Tennyson's *Idylls of the King*', *Victorian Poetry*, 30 (1992), 401–19.

Simonsuuri, Kirsti, *Homer's Original Genius; Eighteenth-century Notions of the Early Greek Epic (1688–1798)* (Cambridge: Cambridge University Press, 1979).

Simpson, Roger, *Camelot Regained; The Arthurian Revival and Tennyson 1800–1849* (Cambridge: D. S. Brewer, 1990).

Smiley, Jane, *The Greenlanders* (New York: Fawcett Books, 1988).

Staël, Madame de, *A Treatise on Ancient and Modern Literature*, 2 vols. (London: Cauthen, 1802).

Stafford, Fiona J., *The Sublime Savage: A Study of James Macpherson and the Poems of Ossian* (Edinburgh: Edinburgh University Press, 1988).

Steiner, George, ed., *Homer in English* (London: Penguin, 1996).

Stevenson, Robert Louis, *Kidnapped* (London: Penguin, 1994).

The Master of Ballantrae and Weir of Hermiston, introduced by Claire Harman (London: Everyman, 1996).

Stone, Marjorie, *Elizabeth Barrett Browning* (Basingstoke: Macmillan, 1995).

Sutherland, John, *The Life of Walter Scott: A Critical Biography* (Oxford: Blackwell, 1995).

Swedenberg, H. T., *The Theory of Epic in England 1650–1800* (Berkeley: University of California Press, 1944).

Swinburne, Algernon Charles, *Ballads of the English Border*, edited by William A. MacInnes (London: Heinemann, 1925).

Border Ballads (London: 1909).

Tennyson, Alfred Lord, *The Poems of Tennyson*, edited by Christopher Ricks (London: Longman, 1969).

Thiselton, Anthony C., *New Horizons in Hermeneutics* (London: HarperCollins, 1992).

Tihanov, Galin, *The Master and the Slave: Lukács, Bakhtin, and the Ideas of Their Time* (Oxford: Clarendon Press, 2000).

Tillyard, E. M. W., *The Epic Strain in the English Novel* (London: Chatto and Windus, 1958).

Trumpener, Katie, *Bardic Nationalism: The Romantic Novel and the British Empire* (Princeton: Princeton University Press, 1997).

Tucker, Herbert F., '*Aurora Leigh*: Epic Solutions to Novel Ends', in Alison Booth, ed., *Famous Last Words: Changes in Gender and Narrative Closure* (Charlottesville and London: University Press of Virginia, 1993).

'Trials of Fiction: Novel and Epic in the Geraint and Enid Episodes from *Idylls of the King*', *Victorian Poetry*, 30 (1992), 441–61.

Tylor, Edward B., *Primitive Culture: Researches into the Development of Mythology, Philosophy, Religion, Language, Art, and Custom*, 3rd edition (London: John Murray, 1891).

Venuti, Lawrence, *The Translator's Invisibility: A History of Translation* (London: Routledge, 1995).

Vico, Giambattista, *New Science*, translated by David Marsh (London: Penguin, 1999).

Walcott, Derek, *Omeros* (London: Faber and Faber, 1990).

Waller, John O., *A Circle of Friends: The Tennysons and the Lushingtons of Park House* (Columbus: Ohio State University Press, 1986).

Wawn, Andrew, ed., *Northern Antiquity: The Post-Medieval Reception of Edda and Saga* (London: Hisarlik Press, 1994).

Whitney, Lois, 'English Primitivist Theories of Epic Origins', *Modern Philology*, 21 (1923–4), 337–78.

Wilde, Lady, *Ancient Legends, Myths, Charms, and Superstitions of Ireland*, 2 vols. (London: Ward and Downey, 1887).

Winckelmann, J. J., *Writings on Art*, selected and edited by David Irwin (London: Phaidon, 1972).

Wolf, F. A., *Prolegomena to Homer 1795*, translated with an Introduction and notes by Anthony Grafton, Glenn W. Most and James E. G. Zetzel (Princeton: Princeton University Press, 1985).

Wood, Harriet Harvey, 'Scott and Jamieson: The Relationship Between Two Ballad-Collectors', *Studies in Scottish Literature*, 9 (1971–2), 71–86.

Wood, Michael, *In Search of the Trojan War* (London: Penguin/BBC Books, 1996).

Wood, Robert, *An Essay on the Original Genius and Writings of Homer: with a Comparative View of the Ancient and Present State of the Troade* (London: Payne and Elmsley, 1775).

Wroe, Nicholas, 'Smiley's People', *Guardian* (London, 2 August 2003).

Zug, Charles G. III, 'The Ballad Editor as Antiquary: Scott and *The Minstrelsy*', *Journal of the Folklore Institute*, 13, 1 (1976), 52–73.

'Sir Walter Scott and the Ballad Forgery', *Studies in Scottish Literature*, 8 (1970–1), 52–64.

Index

CAMBRIDGE STUDIES IN NINETEENTH-CENTURY LITERATURE
AND CULTURE

General Editor
Gillian Beer, *University of Cambridge*

Titles Published